MW00964572

Empire Kosher® Chicken Cookbook

CLARKSON POTTER / PUBLISHERS
New York

EMPIRE KOSHER

ALL NATURAL
EMPIRE
KOSHER
U GLATT

CHICKEN COOKBOOK

225 Easy and Elegant
Recipes for Poultry and
Great Side Dishes

BY KATJA GOLDMAN AND ARTHUR BOEHM

Copyright © 1999 by Empire Kosher Poultry

All rights reserved. No part of this book may be reproduced or transmitted in any form or by any means, electronic or mechanical, including photocopying, recording, or by any information storage and retrieval system, without permission in writing from the publisher.

Published by Clarkson N. Potter/Publishers, 201 East 50th Street, New York, New York 10022. Member of the Crown Publishing Group.

Random House, Inc. New York, Toronto, London, Sydney, Auckland
www.randomhouse.com

CLARKSON N. POTTER, POTTER, and colophon are trademarks of Clarkson N. Potter, Inc.

Printed in the United States of America

Design by Julie Schroeder

Library of Congress Cataloging-in-Publication Data
Goldman, Katja.
    Empire Kosher chicken cookbook : 225 easy and elegant recipes for poultry and great side dishes / by Katja Goldman and Arthur Boehm.
        Includes index.
1. Cookery (Chicken) 2. Cookery, Jewish. I. Boehm, Arthur. II. Empire Kosher Poultry, Inc. III. Title.
TX750.5.C45G65   1999
641.6′65—DC21   98-28205
                                                                                                                   CIP

ISBN 0-517-70863-9

10   9   8   7   6   5   4   3   2   1

First Edition

For Joyce and Irving Goldman,
who put a spoon in my mouth and
a love of cooking in my heart

—KG

And, again, for
Leonore Boehm and Richard Getke
—AB

ACKNOWLEDGMENTS

Katja Goldman and Arthur Boehm wish to thank their agent, Anne Edelstein, who brought them together, and Katie Workman, their editor, whose keen eye and ongoing enthusiasm for the book made the publishing process a pleasure. Thanks also to Birgitta Wade at Empire for her support and tireless attention to so many details, large and small. To Marge Rosenthal, our deepest gratitude for her diligent recipe testing.

Many thanks to Lenard Tessler, who brought me to Empire and for his help in making this book happen. My gratitude to my collaborator, Arthur Boehm, and, again, to Marge Rosenthal for her culinary expertise and for wonderful years of cooking together. For her ongoing help with this project, endless appreciation to my sister Dorian. Thanks also to Sylvia Kier for her editorial assistance in the book's early stages and to Sheryl Lawrence for her friendship and marvelous culinary discussions. To Mercedes Abuiles and Linda Contreras, my kitchen assistants, many thanks. My appreciation, also, to all those whose discerning palates have played a role in the joy of creating this book

Lastly, my loving thanks to my husband, Michael, for years of support and encouragement, and to my children, Joya and Forest, my chief recipe testers, who, along with my nephew Jacob Israelow and his friend Richard Ma, shared and tasted at our table so many of the recipes in this book. I'm deeply grateful to my parents and grandmothers for instilling in me a love of food, cooking, and entertaining. The memories of the years of culinary pleasure passed with them have shaped and enriched my life beyond measure.

—KG

Loving appreciation to Judy Gingold and Judy Fireman, who have once again read and listened and helped in so many ways. My gratitude also to Geila Hocherman for her culinary acuity, and to Nick Malgieri for his support and friendship—*merci, mon brave*.

To Katja Goldman, my appreciation, of course.

And to Richard Getke, thanks and thanks again.

—AB

CONTENTS

Empire Kosher® Chicken Cookbook

Introduction

Today's kosher cooking is still rooted in old family favorites,
but reflects the remarkable culinary changes of the past
twenty years. Our palates have come of age. Travel and the
media have shrunk the planet, acquainting us with the
flavors of many cultures; foods of the world fill our
markets and ethnic restaurants abound.

Good riddance, therefore, to heavy kosher cooking of indifferent ingredients and indistinct tastes! Featuring chicken and other poultry, the sophisticated kosher dishes in this book celebrate the world's flavors and freshest, most vibrant ingredients. These delicious, health-conscious recipes are designed for *all* cooks while meeting kosher-keeping guidelines. They're great for family meals and entertaining, for day-in, day-out enjoyment.

As Empire's chef and food consultant, I create hundreds of innovative kosher recipes. These reflect my long involvement with the table and its joys. My mother and both grandmothers were wonderful cooks, and my father, whose family owned a grocery store in an Italian neighborhood, had his own repertoire of pasta sauces. (I think I teethed on garlic and oil!) As an executive chef for an international bank, bakery founder, and proprietor of a catering business, I've also devised easy, elegant fare.

I joined Empire at an exciting moment, when its products first enjoyed wide praise. In a number of taste tests conducted by periodicals for chefs and other food authorities, Empire chicken had come out on top. But cooks of all kinds have long believed in Empire poultry. The extra steps the company takes in breeding, raising, and processing its chickens, turkeys, and ducklings result in all-natural birds of delectable taste.

Superlative, convenient kosher poultry is an Empire tradition. Founded in 1938 by Joseph Katz, the company was the first to marry kosher law to modern production methods. Previously, if you wanted a kosher chicken, you had to go to a butcher who, under rabbinical supervision, conducted the koshering process in his own backyard. Empire's arrival made it possible for people who demand absolutely kosher poultry, and who insist on high quality and taste, to get both almost anywhere in the country.

What makes the birds so special? If you take a tour of the Empire feed mill, hatchery, and processing plant, you'll see. First, the Empire chicks roam freely within their range. Fed a scientifically devised diet without growth stimulants, antibiotics, or hormones of any kind, their meat is lean, tender, and wholesome. While most poultry producers process their chickens at six or seven weeks, the Empire birds are permitted to "grow out" to full maturity, for better taste.

The Empire birds also receive more inspections than do nonkosher poultry. While the USDA inspectors are rigorous, the Empire rabbis are more so, rejecting birds the USDA regularly passes. Other companies process their birds with hot water, for easier feather removal. Empire uses only fresh, cold water for washing their poultry, which helps retard bacterial growth. And the Empire processing takes a full three hours per bird, as opposed to an industry standard of only fifty minutes.

These extra health- and kosher-ensuring steps guarantee that every Empire bird is kosher and highest quality. But conduct your own taste test! The recipes here will help you to do so, gloriously, while expanding your poultry-cooking repertoire. From savory soups and easy-to-fix appetizers to grilling, oven, and stovetop specialties—everything is included. You'll find quick and simple meals for the family, show-stopping recipes for guests, and new and traditional holiday creations. I'm particularly proud of a chapter called "The Next Day" that shows you how to work wonders with poultry leftovers. I advise you to make extra chicken when you cook just so you can put dishes like Basil Chicken Salad on Rosemary Focaccia together in minutes. Explore also the section on great poultry go-withs like Honey-Banana Chutney, Best-Ever Tomato Sauce, and Fresh Pineapple Salsa. And because great kosher cooking begins with the best ingredients, there's a special section that introduces you to the huge range of modern kosher products now available, from balsamic vinegar to cellophane noodles.

With this cookbook in hand you'll create natural, tantalizing poultry specialties of great taste and flair. I hope this book transports you, educates you, and inspires you to new kosher culinary heights. Enjoy!

—KG

Empire maintains a customer hotline and invites you to call with cooking questions or Empire product inquiries. Tours of the plant can also be arranged; call (800) 367-4734, Mondays through Thursdays, 8 A.M. to 5 P.M. EST, or 8 A.M. to 3 P.M. on Fridays. The mailing address is R.R. 5, Box 228, River Road, Mifflintown, PA, 17059. Empire's web site is www.empirekosher.com. Send e-mail to empire@acsworld.net.

1. Know Your Ingredients

A WORD ABOUT KOSHER COOKING

The rules of kosher eating have guided the Jewish diet

since ancient times. These laws, known collectively as

Kashrus, govern the choice, preparation, and consumption

of food for Jews. A part of these rules—outlined

in the Torah and interpreted through the centuries

by rabbis—expresses reverence for human and animal life.

To keep kosher is to uphold Jewish tradition and identity,

and to preserve both, joyfully, in everyday life.

But what is kosher cooking? For many, kosher cooking is synonymous with the traditional Jewish cuisine of Central and Eastern Europe. As wonderful as that cooking can be, it is not "kosher cooking." Kosher cooking isn't a single cuisine but an approach to meal and menu making that is, within its precepts, endlessly embracing. The recipes that follow show just how versatile modern kosher cooking can be.

In recent years, many people have returned to or adopted the values of the dietary laws. Some do it to return to their roots, others to participate in a richly gratifying spiritual discipline. This revival, and a general increase in culinary sophistication, has meant a demand for the widest variety of best-quality kosher products. The result? More and better kosher-certified ingredients. Today's kosher cook can enjoy using extra-virgin olive oil, wonton skins, balsamic vinegar, phyllo dough, and much, much more. To locate and choose the best of this bounty, all you need is a little guidance.

WHERE TO FIND KOSHER FOODS

A young friend who had just begun to cook kosher asked me recently where to find superior kosher ingredients. My immediate reply was, "everywhere." I then told her that probably without knowing it, she had been "buying kosher" for years. Putting aside the thousands of prepared products that are kosher and readily available—from Heinz ketchup to Pepperidge Farm cookies—there is a wealth of "raw" kosher ingredients, including poultry, scattered throughout most supermarkets. In addition, many supermarkets have kosher food sections. Obviously, stores catering to communities with a large Jewish presence will have the widest variety of kosher products.

The greatest selection of kosher foods, including poultry, can be found, of course, in kosher markets. These markets, which have appeared with increasing frequency in recent years, will vary, depending on the Jewish communities they serve. The traditional kosher market addresses the needs of the Ashkenazic, or Central and Eastern European-rooted Jewish community. There you'll find the basics—breads and pasta, for example—as well as some ethnic ingredients such as phyllo dough. Markets that serve Iranian or Israeli Jewish communities are a sure bet for Middle Eastern products including tahini, herb mixtures like za'atar, and great olives. For Asian kosher ingredients, unfamiliar spices and such products as five-spice powder, try Asian markets and health food stores. As kosher ingredients are widely perceived as being better and safer—in short, healthier—than nonkosher products, health food and other natural foods markets are a very good source indeed for kosher foods, especially organic produce. (There are an increasing number of kosher-certified packaged organic foods.) It pays to read labels. The symbols of kosher certification appear in a lot of unexpected places—that's how I find new ingredients!

To help you locate items called for in this book that might not be readily available in your area, I've provided a reliable list of sources (see page 284).

What makes a kosher product kosher? It cannot contain nonkosher ingredients, such as pork or shellfish; its manufacturing process must conform to Jewish dietary law; it must not contain dairy ingredients if it contains meat and vice versa; it cannot contain milk or meat if it is "neutral." Generally, all processed kosher foods are certified by rabbinical authorities. To assure yourself that a product is kosher, look for a symbol of certification on the packaging. The most widely used symbol is Ⓤ, the mark of the Union of Orthodox Jewish Congregations; there are many others (check with your rabbi, if in doubt). Because the dietary laws require separation of dairy and meat products in a meal, you may see the letters *D* or *P* along with the symbol of certification on a package. *D* means that the product is a dairy food; *P* can stand for Passover or pareve (neutral), which indicates that the food may be used with meat or dairy products. In most cases, the word *pareve* appears on a package when the product is neutral.

KOSHER POULTRY AND THE ISSUE OF SALTINESS

Poultry, including chicken, duck, turkey, and goose, is kosher when processed according to the dietary laws.

Because the Torah prohibits the ingestion of blood, as much blood as possible is removed from poultry and meat by either salting or broiling (the process is called koshering). The salting process adds savory flavor to the birds; if you are sensitive to salt, however, you may want to soak kosher poultry in cold water for 10 to 20 minutes before using it. If you are on a salt-restricted diet, soak the poultry in cold water for 2 hours, changing the water every 30 minutes or so—or just enjoy the bird without its skin. Of course, all poultry should be rinsed thoroughly before cooking with it.

When I do call for salt in the poultry recipes that follow, it's usually "to taste." As a rule of thumb, and especially when preparing recipes including poultry skin, I salt minimally if at all in the cooking process, adding more salt after tasting the final dish, if necessary. (For information about the salt types I call for, see page 14.)

Many people believe that koshered poultry has a superior taste. If you have never enjoyed kosher poultry, you may be surprised by how "clean" and true-tasting its meat is.

OTHER FOOD GROUPS

EGGS To be kosher, eggs must have no blood in them. If they do, they must be discarded.

Before adding eggs to any recipe, I crack them one by one into a small bowl. If there are blood spots, I throw the egg away. This extra effort means that I avoid having to discard more than a single egg if more than one is called for by my recipe.

Eggs are pareve or neutral. Extra-large eggs were used to test the recipes in this book.

FRUITS AND VEGETABLES All are kosher and pareve.

OILS AND CONDIMENTS Many vegetable oils are kosher. Butter must not be used or served with meat. I do not find the substitution of margarine for butter acceptable when it's butter flavor I want. The recipes that follow never substitute margarine for butter (see page 8). To adapt recipes containing butter for nondairy meals, see how the butter is used. If it is added at the end of the recipe to enrich the dish, substitute margarine; otherwise, use vegetable oil.

Many condiments—mustard, hot sauces, and salsas, for example—are kosher and pareve. Check labels for the symbols of certification.

STARCHES Some bread products are made with nonkosher fats. Unpackaged bread must be bought at a kosher bakery only, or buy packaged bread, checking labels to assure yourself the bread is kosher. This is not a hardship; many good-quality baguettes are wrapped these days.

A GLOSSARY OF INGREDIENTS

Oils

CANOLA OIL AND OTHER VEGETABLE OILS Canola oil is derived from rapeseed, the source of broccoli rape (or, more usually, rabe), the delicious, slightly bitter green. I prefer canola oil to other vegetable oils because it's lower in saturated fat (about 6 percent) than any other oil. It also seems to me more delicate than many other vegetable oils. Also, canola oil contains omega-3 fatty acids, the polyunsaturated fat reputed to lower blood levels of cholesterol and triglycerides. Canola oil is bland and has a relatively high smoke point, making it good for sautéing; for frying, use a combination of canola and another light vegetable oil with a high smoke point. (Canola oil alone can sometimes break down at high temperatures.) When I don't call for canola oil, use any light, high-quality vegetable oil that does not contain saturated fats. Avoid coconut and palm oil, which do contain saturated fats.

MARGARINE People are often surprised to discover that margarine was invented in the late 1800s as a butter substitute. It has always been made primarily from vegetable oils to which milk and cream are sometimes added to provide a more butterlike taste. Examine packages carefully to avoid "hidden" dairy ingredients. Those margarines lowest in cholesterol are made with a high percentage of polyunsaturated safflower or corn oils. (Reject brands with saturated oils like palm or coconut.)

As stated previously, I never use margarine as a butter substitute, only as a cooking or baking medium, or when I need it to emulsify a sauce. In all other situations, I prefer olive oil or polyunsaturated vegetable oil.

When buying margarine, look for natural certified brands without artificial flavors or colors. Most important, in the list of ingredients, the first cited should be liquid (nonhydrogenenated) vegetable oil.

OLIVE OIL, EXTRA-VIRGIN The finest olive oil available is extra-virgin, derived from fruit that is cold pressed or extracted without heat or the use of chemicals. It also contains the lowest amount of oleic or fruit acid: 1 percent. By law, Italian and Californian olive oil producers cannot label their oils "extra-virgin" if they contain more than 1 percent oleic acid. This low degree of oleic acid makes the oil wonderfully delicate—clean tasting but with a definite fruit presence. Nonetheless, extra-virgin olive oils vary in flavor, color, and mouth feel from brand to brand and country to country. Though the production of kosher-certified extra-virgin oils is necessarily limited, excellent ones are available. Try various makes until you find the one (or ones) you like best.

Extra-virgin olive oil is best used as a dish ingredient (as opposed to a cooking medium), as a dip for bread, on salads, or sprinkled onto cooked food. Apart from the expense, it is unwise to use extra-virgin oils for frying. The oils have a low smoking point and cannot get really hot enough for most frying or sautéing without burning.

When I call for simply "olive oil" in the recipes that follow, I mean that extra-virgin olive oil is not required. You could use any "lesser" but still high-quality oil. Such oils may be labeled "pure," an official designation indicating a 4 percent fruit-acid presence. Pure olive oil is thoroughly acceptable for some sautéing and for some marinades.

SESAME OIL, DARK Made from toasted sesame seeds, dark sesame oil is thick, rich, and wonderfully nutty in taste. I specify dark sesame oil to distinguish it from lighter varieties, which may be used in the actual cooking process. Dark sesame oil, an Asian product, is for seasoning only, or is used as a delicious addition to marinades.

The oil can become rancid very quickly; store it in a cool, dry place away from the light. I like Japanese sesame oil, which seems to me more delicate than its Chinese counterpart. Buy dark sesame oil in glass bottles only; there is a greater chance of its being rancid when stored in plastic.

VEGETABLE AND OLIVE OIL SPRAYS Though lacking a glowing reputation, these cooking sprays can be wonderfully useful. I use them even on nonstick pans to prevent food from adhering to their surfaces; in many cases, they provide just enough oil presence to give a dish some richness without adding excessive calories. Check labels; some brands contain ingredients like lecithin specifically meant to prevent sticking, others do not. I like to make my own vegetable oil spray using a "spritz" bottle and light vegetable or olive oil.

Seasonings and Condiments

ALEPPO PEPPER Famous throughout the Middle East, and sometimes called Near East pepper, this dark, warmly aromatic seasoning is worth searching for. (Maras pepper, from Turkey, is similar although somewhat hotter.) Stored in the refrigerator, Aleppo pepper keeps indefinitely. You can make a credible substitute with three parts hot Hungarian paprika (or a mixture of hot and sweet, to your taste) to one part ground, flavorful, mildly hot red pepper flakes.

BALSAMIC VINEGAR This extraordinary vinegar is, in its original version, produced solely in Modena and Reggio, Italy, where it is artisan made. Unfortunately, this complex, tart-sweet condiment (for a condiment it is, used by the precious dropful) is relatively rare and always expensive. The traditional balsamic vinegar is made from the must (the unfermented juice) of the white Trebbiano grape, then aged up to a century in casks constructed from woods including oak, cherry, mulberry, and chestnut; though many believe the word *balsamic* derives from the wood used for such a cask, it actually refers to the vinegar's traditional use as a curative, or "balm." Kosher balsamic vinegars are commercially produced; the best of these, derived from a blend of wine vinegar, must, and caramel, and aged for an abbreviated period, balance sweet and tart flavors in a unified whole. Keep trying kosher brands until you find the one you like. Price is not always a guide to quality.

BROWN RICE VINEGAR Vinegars made from fermented rice have been used in Asia for over three thousand years. Brown rice vinegar, which is made solely from brown rice and well water, shares with similar Japanese vinegars a mild, light acidity and an illusion of sweetness. It is the only kosher-certified Japanese rice vinegar I know of, and is imported by Eden Foods (see "Resources," page 284). If you find other kosher brands, make sure they have been fermented; otherwise, their taste will be unpleasantly raw.

CHILI PASTE (HOT BEAN SAUCE OR PASTE) There are many varieties of this incendiary seasoning, used throughout China and Korea. Their common ingredient is soybeans, to which chili peppers and sometimes garlic, sesame oil, salt, and sugar are added. Sambal olek, an Indonesian hot sauce containing chilies but without beans, may be substituted; a kosher-certified brand is now available.

Chili paste comes in cans and bottles and, once opened, should be stored in the refrigerator. It will last for at least two months; it's hard to imagine anything spoiling it!

CHINESE RICE WINE Known more exactly as Shaoxing rice wine, this Chinese drinking and cooking staple from the Zhejiang province has been used for millennia. The amber-colored wine is aged for eighteen years or more (bottles mellowed for a century or so are much prized) and has a rich flavor resembling dry sherry, which you may substitute for it. Look for Shaoxing rice wine in Asian markets.

CORIANDER A native of the Mediterranean and Asia, coriander is available in seed and leaf form. The seeds, which are used in pickling, as well as in various cooked dishes, are mildly fragrant. The leaves, some-times referred to as cilantro or Chinese parsley, are another matter entirely. Some people—myself included—dote on the distinctly musky aroma and taste of fresh coriander; others abhor it. Store a coriander bunch with the stems ends in water and the leaves covered in a plastic bag. If the water is changed every two days, the herb will last about a week.

FENUGREEK Pleasantly bitter, fenugreek is native to Asia and south-ern Europe. The seeds, which are sold whole and ground, are used most often to flavor curries and teas, or in spice blends.

FIVE-SPICE POWDER I'm a devotee of this traditional Chinese sea-soning, made from spices including star anise, Szechuan peppercorns, fen-nel, clove, and cinnamon (or the stronger cassia). This fragrant, pungent, and slightly sweet concoction is a wonderful addition to a range of dishes. Five-spice powder is readily available and should always be used fresh. However, I like to make my own from freshly ground spices. To prepare your own blend, see the ingredients listing on page 132. For a scant $1/4$ cup, combine double the quantity of the cinnamon, allspice, nutmeg, coriander, and cloves and transfer the mixture to a small glass jar. Check periodically for freshness.

HARISSA This Moroccan seasoning paste is made from dried chilies, olive oil, garlic, and salt. It is bright red, hot, hot, hot, and used most notably to make Moroccan couscous (the dish, not the pasta). At this time, no kosher-certified brands of harissa are available. Fortunately, homemade harissa is best and easily prepared. For about $1^1/2$ cups harissa, remove the stems from $1/2$ cup jalapeño peppers. In a food processor, combine the pep-pers with the leaves from $1/2$ bunch coriander (cilantro) and 16 garlic cloves; pulse to chop. Add $1/2$ cup chili powder, $1/4$ cup paprika, 1 table-spoon cumin, 2 tablespoons cider vinegar, and season to taste with salt and freshly ground black pepper. With the machine running, gradually add $1/4$ cup olive or vegetable oil. When the mixture has emulsified, transfer it to clean, dry, wide-mouthed glass jars. The harissa will keep, refrigerated, for up to six months.

GARAM MASALA Most cooks now know that there is no such thing in Indian cookery as curry powder. The aromatics that constitute bottled or tinned versions reflect the spice combinations ground fresh by Indian cooks for specific dishes. But garam masala *is* a prepared Indian spice blend, one that varies depending on the cook. The commercial product usually contains black pepper, coriander, cumin seeds, cloves, and cinnamon. Though *garam* means "hot," garam masala never is; I use it for its wonderful aroma and intriguing taste. At least one brand of kosher-certified garam masala exists, but I like to prepare my own, fresh. For about $1/3$ cup garam masala, in a clean coffee grinder or spice grinder, combine 2 tablespoons cardamom seeds, 2 tablespoons black peppercorns, 2 tablespoons cumin seeds, two 2-inch-long crushed cinnamon sticks, 2 teaspoons whole cloves, 1 teaspoon ground mace, and 1 bay leaf. Grind as fine as possible. Transfer the mixture to an airtight container. Check unused mixture for freshness periodically.

HOISIN SAUCE This thickish, vaguely sweet Chinese ingredient is a type of bean sauce. In addition to soybean paste, it contains garlic, vinegar, sugar, spices, and other flavorings—ingredients that belie the meaning of its name, "sea freshness." Americans are most familiar with hoisin as the sauce used with Peking duck; I like to use it in marinades and sauces. The quality of hoisin sauce varies widely; look for certified brands without artificial food coloring.

HOT SAUCE With the recent popularization of spicy cooking, a raft of hot sauces, many kosher-certified, have appeared. These sauces, featuring a range of pepper types, vary in heat, texture, and in the additional ingredients (citrus juice and herbs, for example) they contain. Caribbean hot sauces are based on the fiery Scotch bonnet chili; Thai-style kinds have a tangy garlicky flavor. Experiment—carefully.

I've never heard of a hot sauce going bad; still, you might want to store opened bottles in the fridge. Besides zing, all these sauces add low-calorie interest to your cooking.

JUNIPER BERRIES When you first smell juniper berries, your reaction might well be, "Gin!" These blue-black berries are indeed the essential gin flavoring ingredient. Sold dried, usually in bottles, they are also used in marinades and sauces, and to flavor meats, in corning and pickling.

KAFFIR LIME LEAVES This is a Thai seasoning ingredient with a delightfully pungent limelike aroma. The leaves are available in small packages in Asian markets and some supermarkets. In a pinch, you can substitute $1/2$ teaspoon grated lime peel for each leaf.

LEMONGRASS One of the preeminent flavorings of Southeast Asian food, lemongrass is a wonderfully aromatic tropical plant. Gray-green in color with a citrus taste and scallionlike base, it is available in the produce section of Asian markets and, increasingly, in supermarkets. Lemongrass should be stored in moist paper toweling in the vegetable bin of your refrigerator, where it will last for up to three weeks. Remove the tough outer leaves, trim the base, and use the bottom 3 to 4 inches only.

MIRIN An essential ingredient in Japanese cooking, mirin is a sweet, syrupy rice wine. (Do not confuse it with plain rice wine vinegar, which is nonsweet.) Mirin is sometimes called sweet saki. It adds a subtle sweetness to dishes, and, traditionally, is also used to glaze grilled foods. It is sometimes sold as "sweet cooking rice wine."

MISO The main flavoring of the Japanese soup that bears its name, miso is a delicious fermented soybean paste and seasoning. There are two principal varieties: white, which contains rice and can be sweetish; and red, made with barley and deeply flavored. Try different varieties until you find the flavor and degree of mellowness you prefer. Miso, which comes in cans, jars, and plastic tubs, should be stored tightly covered under refrigeration. Kept thus, it will last for up to three months.

OREGANO Most people are familiar with the pungent herb oregano, whose name means "joy of the mountain" in Greek. What is not generally known is that various types of oregano are available and each has its own character. Mexican oregano is quite strong; Mediterranean (including Greek) oregano is milder. Fresh oregano is becoming more widely available, but any dried oregano that is fully aromatic will do.

POULTRY SEASONING This simple-to-prepare blend adds wonderful flavor to stuffings or marinades; I use it also in seasoning pastes. No commercial varieties I know of are kosher-certified, but it is easy enough to make your own. Use ground herbs and spices, or buy them whole (where possible) and crush them to a powder with a mortar and pestle, measure, then blend. Combine 2 tablespoons ground rosemary, 2 tablespoons ground oregano, 4 tablespoons plus 1 teaspoon ground sage, 3 teaspoons ground ginger, 1 teaspoon ground marjoram, $1/2$ teaspoon ground thyme, and $1/4$ teaspoon freshly ground black pepper. Stored in an airtight jar in a cool, dark place, the mixture will keep up to four months.

PRESERVED LEMONS Sometimes referred to as pickled lemons, these are an indispensable ingredient in Moroccan cooking. Their pickled taste and suave texture add greatly to tagines, stews, salads, and other dishes. As of this writing, a kosher-certified commercial version does not exist; you will have to make your own (see page 243)—it's worth it. Preserved lemons will last up to six months refrigerated.

SAFFRON The most precious and costly of all seasoning, saffron is made of the dried stamens of crocus flowers. Over 14,000 stamens are needed to make an ounce of saffron. The stamens must be hand-gathered—no wonder their price is high! Sold in thread form or powdered (the thread form is preferable), saffron is produced by a number of European countries; the best comes from Spain. Fortunately, very little is needed to impart flavor. The threads must be first infused in stock or other hot liquid to release their essence. The liquid is then used to flavor a dish. Store saffron for up to six months airtight in a cool, dark place.

SALT For many people, salt is salt. But chefs have always recognized the existence of a special kind—the coarse-grained, additive-free kosher salt, whose texture makes it ideal for koshering poultry and meats. Like many other cooks, I like to use kosher salt, and prefer it for certain recipes. Its large grain doesn't burn off foods as quickly as fine salts do, which makes it great for grilling. Measure for measure, kosher salt is less salty than other salts. To my palate, however, its flavor is particularly vibrant. I find I use less of it than I would of its fine-grain alternative.

Table salt is the fine-textured salt used commonly. It has been dissolved, purified, and recrystallized and is sometimes iodized. It dissolves more easily than kosher or other coarse salts. Many people tout the flavor of sea salt, which comes in fine and coarse grains and is sometimes used with a grinder. I like sea salt for its rich mineral-metallic savor.

In the recipes that follow, I specify kosher salt when I want to exploit its special virtues. If I call simply for salt you may use kosher salt or any finer-textured variety you prefer.

SEASONED RICE WINE VINEGAR A Japanese product, this vinegar has salt and sugar added to a rice-wine vinegar "base." Unfortunately, as of this writing, no kosher brands exist. But it is easy to make your own version, which I call for because it provides authentic taste. To do so, combine $1/2$ cup of brown rice vinegar with $1 1/2$ teaspoons sugar and $1/8$ teaspoon salt in a small saucepan. Bring to the boil, reduce the heat, and simmer until the sugar and salt are dissolved, about 2 minutes. Cool to room temperature and use. The vinegar will keep for two to four months unrefrigerated.

SHERRY WINE VINEGAR Unfortunately, this full-flavored vinegar with its hint of "sweet" sherry is not available with kosher certification. Because I like a sherry-vinegar effect in certain dishes, however, I "make" my own. It's easy to do: for 1 cup, combine 1 cup kosher dry sherry with

6 tablespoons kosher red wine vinegar in a small nonreactive saucepan. Heat over high heat to boiling, reduce the heat, and simmer gently to concentrate, about 10 minutes. Cool and transfer to a container with a lid or stopper. Store as you would other vinegars.

SOY SAUCE/LOW-SODIUM SOY SAUCE An essential ingredient in Asian cooking for over three thousand years, soy sauce is made from a mixture of soybeans, flour, and water that is naturally fermented and allowed to age. There are two main types of soy sauce—light and dark, the latter of which contains molasses. It is light soy sauce that I call for in this book. Low-sodium soy sauce, with its reduced salt level, is especially useful in kosher chicken recipes. Never buy synthetic soy sauce, made from hydrolyzed vegetable proteins, caramel, and corn syrup. It lacks the flavor depth of the naturally fermented kind and can add a fake salty sweetness to dishes.

SUMAC I'm a champion of this marvelous tart ground spice made from sumac berries and used in Middle Eastern cookery. I use it in dishes and sometimes as a final seasoning as you might use salt and pepper (try a pinch of it on salads); the flavor is deeply tangy, almost sour. It can be found in most Middle Eastern markets and should be part of your kitchen spice collection. Sumac can be stored in the freezer.

TAMARI SAUCE A type of soy sauce, tamari is unrefined yet mellow, thick, and delicious. I always assumed tamari to be a Japanese product, but it is not. True tamari is Chinese in origin. It has a special flavor that I find irresistible; sometimes I use it plain as a dipping sauce as well as in dishes. A low-sodium version is also available.

TOASTED SESAME TAHINI This paste, made from hulled white sesame seeds, is used in cooking and as a dip or condiment. Popular throughout the Middle East, it is now readily available in most supermarkets and natural foods stores.

TURKISH SPICE MIXTURE This is my name for a blend of spices similar to those found in long cellophane tubes in Istanbul markets. The spices in the tubes—cumin, turmeric, sweet paprika, oregano, black pepper, and sumac—are arranged on top of one another; when the tube is opened and emptied, the spices blend. No kosher varieties are available, but making your own mixture is easy enough, and I guarantee you you'll use every bit of it. A recipe for the blend appears on page 180.

WASABI POWDER Though assumed to be the same as horseradish, Japanese wasabi is in fact more fragrant and less sharp (though often more intense) than horseradish, to which it is not related. Wasabi powder is derived from the Japanese root, and is usually reconstituted with water to make a condiment for sushi and sashimi. I use it to create pungent dips. Wasabi powder comes in small round tins.

ZA'ATAR (ALSO SPELLED ZHA'TAR) A Middle Eastern herb blend usually containing thyme, oregano, and hyssop (a member of the mint family), za'atar is a great personal favorite. In Jordan it is used in breads or for breakfast with cheese; I use it whenever I want a pungent "green" kick. It's great sprinkled on meats before or after grilling. Look for it in herb and spice stores (see also "Resources," page 284) or substitute equal parts of the herbs named above.

Other Ingredients

BUCKWHEAT GROATS These seeds of the buckwheat plant, which is native to Russia, are the basis of the braised grout dish, kasha varnishkes (see page 95). Buckwheat grouts are not to be confused with bulgur wheat—whole wheat kernels that are steamed, dried, and then crushed to make Middle Eastern dishes such as tabbouleh. The flavor of the grouts is intensely nutlike and the texture crunchy. Available widely, the grouts are sometimes sold as "kasha," which is rather like buying eggs labeled "omelets."

COUSCOUS Couscous is the name of traditional Moroccan stewlike dish and of the semolina pasta that is its defining feature. Couscous is a kind of pasta whose bits come in various sizes, in bulk or packages. Traditional couscous preparation, lengthy and elaborate, involves various rinsings and rubbings to ensure separate grains. The couscous recipes in this book are all based on the use of quick-cooking or precooked couscous, whose quality I find excellent. As a rule of thumb, the proportion of water to couscous is one to one. Kosher precooked or quick-cooking couscous is widely available.

CELLOPHANE NOODLES Also known as bean thread or transparent noodles, these are made from ground mung beans. Their texture once prepared is delightfully slithery. Cellophane noodles are never cooked but allowed to soften in hot water for about 5 minutes. Note that cellophane noodles are never eaten as is; they are added to soups or other cooked dishes. Kosher-certified cellophane noodles, manufactured in Thailand, are available in some Asian shops or by mail order (see "Resources," page 284). Or use bi-fun, an angel-hair-like Japanese rice noodle. "Cook" bi-fun by soaking them in hot water until they soften, about 10 minutes.

CHILIES There are over 200 varieties of chili pepper, most indigenous to the New World. Among this vast assortment, used fresh and dried, I call most frequently for the following:

Poblano A dark green chili pepper with a flavor ranging from mild to pungent. Poblanos measure 4 to 5 inches long and 2 to 3 inches wide. Dried poblanos are known as ancho chilies.

Poblanos are ideal for stuffing—see Chiles Rellenos (page 266). Fresh and dried poblanos are increasingly available in supermarkets.

Jalapeño The "starter" chili pepper, this 1- to 1^1/$_2$-inch long green pepper is the best known and most widely available of all chilies. It has a full flavor and medium heat. As with most chilies, the heat in jalapeños is concentrated in the seeds and veins. Jalapeños are sold fresh and canned; the fresh are best.

Red Thai These are the small, skinny, very fiery dried chiles used to infuse oils and add instant heat to Southeast Asian dishes. Sometimes called bird peppers (it's alleged that birds like them!), they are most frequently available in bags or jars in Asian markets, gourmet shops, and some supermarkets. Use them judiciously.

Serrano These green (unripe) or red-orange to yellow (ripe) chili peppers are about 1^1/$_2$ inches long and 4 inches wide. They are savory and fairly hot, and are used typically in salsas or guacamole. They are available fresh, canned, or pickled.

DRIED SEAWEEDS These are used widely in Asian cooking for their elusive but satisfying sea-plant flavors and lovely textures. Try adding wakame, hiziki, or arame to salads or soups, or use them in stir-fries.

Nori Sometimes called laver, nori are paper-thin toasted sheets of iridescent dark green or purplish seaweed. The sheets are used principally as wrappers for maki sushi (rolled sushi), and are sold flat or folded in clear packages. The best nori have a bright sheen and a good sealike aroma. Keep nori packages tightly sealed to avoid moisture, and out of sunlight.

Wakame This seaweed, which is extremely rich in nutrients and has a pleasing slippery texture when reconstituted, is sold in 4-inch strips. Soak wakame in warm water for 5 to 20 minutes, depending on its quality, until soft.

Hiziki Black and brittle, hiziki comes in ¹/₂-inch strands and has a mildly aniselike flavor; it is high in calcium. Reconstitute it in warm water for about 20 minutes and rinse it once or twice to make certain it is free of grit.

Arame Similar to hiziki in appearance, arame is a species of kelp, with a sweet, nutty flavor. Soak it in warm water for about 15 minutes to soften it; it will double in size.

ENOKI

These delicate Japanese mushrooms have tiny caps—about ¹/₄ inch in diameter—and skinny stems, up to 5 inches long. They grow naturally on the stumps of the Chinese hackberry, which the Japanese call the enoki tree. Choose enoki that are white and crisp; if they have turned a brownish-yellow, they are past their prime. Cut away the brown section at the base and rinse the enoki briefly. The mushrooms will keep in a plastic-wrap-covered container, refrigerated, for one to two days.

KUDZU

This powdered starch, made from the kudzu vine, is a thickening agent used traditionally in Japanese cooking. Like arrowroot though lumpier in its raw state, it produces beautiful, translucent sauces. It is also used to coat foods for frying and produces a particularly crispy white crust. Look for it in 4-ounce boxes in Japanese markets and health food stores.

MATZO AND MATZO MEAL

This thin, crisp unleavened bread with its occasional brown blisters is probably the preeminent Jewish food. Created by the Israelites who, in their flight from Egypt, did not have time to let their bread rise, matzo is enjoyed year-round and is central to the Passover celebration. Matzo meal or farfel is matzo that has been ground, and is widely available.

PASTA

I refer here to Italian pasta, both dried and "fresh." Neither fresh nor dried pasta is better than the other; each has its own virtues and uses.

Fresh pasta—undried pasta made usually with eggs—is richer than factory-made dried varieties. It has a soft, tender bite and is closest to homemade. Kosher varieties are sometimes available in supermarkets enclosed in airless packages; these have been treated with nitrogen to prevent oxidation, which leads to spoilage. Quality varies.

Dried pasta, a commercial invention of the nineteenth century, should be made from durum wheat—Italian packages call it "pure semolina"; check the label. Dried pasta has a firm, chewy bite and a wonderful wheatiness all its own. Nowadays, many supermarkets carry kosher-certified imported Italian pastas. I like dried pasta for pasta "dishes"; I consider fresh pasta a noodle and use it as such, as an accompaniment or in eggy dishes like kugel. To avoid sticky or pasty results, always cook pasta in the proportion of 1 pound of pasta to 6 quarts of water (see page 83 for more pasta cooking information).

Pasta should always be cooked (or allowed to remain) al dente. The key to preparing pasta this way is simple: keep tasting as you cook, and remove the pasta from the water a little before you think it's done—it will continue to cook after draining.

RICE PAPER Associated primarily with Vietnamese cooking, rice paper is available from Thailand in round or triangular sheets that are thin, dry, and semitransparent. They are used as wrappers for spring rolls and other savory tidbits or for wrapped sandwiches. Make sure the sheets you buy are white and not brittle. Rice paper is kosher without rabbinical supervision if it is made from rice, salt, and water—pure ingredients in their simplest form. Check labels. The paper needs to be softened in water before using; see step 3 of Vietnamese Spring Rolls with Two Dipping Sauces, page 55. For rice paper suppliers, see "Resources," page 284.

SOBA (BUCKWHEAT NOODLES) A number of cultures have produced buckwheat noodles, of which the Japanese soba is probably the best known. Thin, flat, and brownish gray with a light wheaty taste, soba are sold dried in cellophane packages in Asian groceries and other markets; they are also sold fresh in vacuum-sealed packages.

UDON NOODLES A simple flour, salt, and water noodle of Japanese origin. Sold in round or flat versions, fresh or dried, udon noodles are widely available in Japanese and other Asian markets.

To prepare fresh udon noodles, bring about 4 quarts of water per pound of noodles to a rolling boil; do not salt the water. Add the udon gradually so as not to stop the boiling entirely, stir to prevent clumping, and allow the water to return to a full boil. Add $1/2$ cup cold water and allow the water to boil again. Repeat until the noodles are a bit more tender than al dente. This method ensures even cooking.

POULTRY AT A GLANCE

Chicken

Chicken welcomes so many cooking approaches, no wonder it's the most popular table bird. This great American staple—affordable, delicious, and convenient—is also deeply rooted in Jewish culinary history. What would the Jewish holidays and weekly shabbat be without it?

Kosher chicken, like other kinds, is classified by its age and weight and sold with names that are suggestive rather than prescriptive of appropriate cooking methods. Thus, young birds between seven and eight weeks old are known generally as *broilers*. Empire labels whole fresh chickens of this age young broiler chickens, and sells them at weights ranging between $2^1/_2$ and $3^1/_2$ pounds. These tender birds are best broiled, grilled, or baked. Empire also provides packaged young chickens cut into quarters or eighths, as well as chicken drumsticks, thighs, breasts, wings, and gourmettes—the "drumstick" portion of the wing of the bird.

Breasts from Empire are available in two forms primarily: unboned and unskinned half breasts, and cutlets, half breast meat. In the recipes that follow, cutlets designated "medium" weigh about $1/_3$ pound each; "large" cutlets weigh about $1/_2$ pound each.

Roasters are chickens between $2^1/_2$ and $3^1/_2$ months old. These birds, which can weigh up to 7 pounds (Empire roasters weigh between 4 and 7 pounds), are perfect candidates for the slowly penetrating heat of the oven.

Rock Cornish Chicken

Empire markets a strain of small chicken under the Rock Cornish Broiler Chicken label. These delightful birds, perfect for marinating and grilling, baking and broiling, are sold frozen at weights typically ranging between $2^1/_4$ and $2^1/_2$ pounds. I prefer the smaller birds. As with all frozen poultry, rinse the hens well after defrosting them; I recommend, also, that after washing, you soak them in cold water for about 20 minutes.

Turkey

It was Benjamin Franklin who proposed the native turkey as the official U. S. bird. First domesticated by the Aztecs, the turkey is surely one of the most important culinary gifts of the New World to the Old, and the preferred centerpiece of American holiday celebrations. The smallest Empire turkeys are typically hens weighing 8 to 10 pounds; the most common is about 13 pounds. Empire tom turkeys are sold at weights ranging from 16 to 35 pounds. Which is preferable—hens or toms? Each has its partisans. For the record, a hen turkey is considered the more moist of the two and has delicately flavorful meat. The tom has a gamier, more robust flavor.

An 8 pound turkey will serve a family of four sumptuously with leftovers (if serving a whole bird, figure about 1 pound of meat per person; if serving a breast, $3/4$ pound per person will do nicely). I always keep "the next day" in mind when it comes to turkey (see Chapter 9) and buy the birds accordingly. A 14-pound turkey is a better buy, costing less per pound and having a higher ratio of meat to bone than smaller birds.

If a turkey is frozen, it must be defrosted before cooking. You can defrost frozen turkey in the refrigerator (my preferred method, as less moisture leaches from the bird), or in a sink of cold water. Depending on how you go about it, the process can take from four hours to four days— or more. Generally, refrigerator-defrosted birds require 24 hours defrosting time for every 5 pounds of weight. In a sink of cold water, turkeys require 30 minutes per pound to defrost; leave turkeys in their wrappers and change the water every 30 minutes. I must quickly add that I always prefer fresh to frozen turkey and make every effort to find it.

You may also buy kosher turkey parts, which can be extremely convenient. Turkey breasts, thighs, or drumsticks make a royal meal for small families, usually with meat to spare. Empire markets all of these. Easily prepared, I sometimes roast a breast or thigh just to have the meat on hand for sandwiches and other next-day dishes. I also like to make dishes using a turkey "London broil"—a boned half-breast. Have your butcher halve the whole breast and then bone it, or bone a half breast yourself (see page 22). A large unboned breast (12 to 14 pounds) can be split in half and cut perpendicularly into 1-inch thick steaks. Marinated and then grilled or broiled, these make delicious eating.

Ground turkey meat, which Empire also sells, is convenient and makes delicious, low-fat dishes such as turkey burgers (see page 168). I also rely on smoked turkey breast, another Empire item, for hors d'oeuvres (page 44) or sandwiches.

Duck

Duck is fowl I make extra of, with leftovers in mind for special sandwiches and slaws (see pages 273 and 281). Like most other ducks in the marketplace, Empire's ducks are sold frozen, in weights ranging from $3^{1}/_{2}$ to

6 pounds. Because of its ample fat, duck freezes more successfully than other birds. I recommend it without hesitation.

STORING AND PREPARING POULTRY FOR COOKING

Poultry is more prone to spoilage than other meats because bacteria collect readily on its skin. If you are not cooking packaged poultry promptly, store it in the coldest spot of your refrigerator until it is cooked. Unpackaged poultry, and packaged poultry nearing its expiration date, should be unwrapped, rinsed thoroughly, rewrapped, and refrigerated immediately. Unfrozen giblets, necks, and/or livers should be removed from cavities and stored separately or frozen for future use. Use fresh poultry within two days after purchasing it, or freeze it. Observe the expiration dates on poultry packages.

Chicken parts are more perishable than whole chickens.

When ready to cook kosher poultry, wash it thoroughly under cold water. You may need to remove stray pin feathers, which is most easily done with a tweezers or strawberry huller.

Cutting Up a Whole Chicken

Buying a whole bird and butchering it yourself not only saves you money but maximizes the possibility of getting really fresh parts. For a neat, easy job, make sure your knives are very sharp. Have a pair of poultry shears on hand.

HALVING
1. Place the chicken breast side up on your work surface. With the point of your knife, make an incision over the breastbone. Turn the chicken over and do the same down the center of the backbone.
2. With a heavy chef's knife, poultry shears or cleaver, slice through breast- and backbones, dividing the chicken in half. You may trim away the backbone halves if you wish.

QUARTERING
Begin with a halved chicken. On one half, lift the leg away from the body and insert your knife between it and the body. Cut

down toward the tail, keeping the knife close to the body; you will have leg-thigh and wing-breast sections. Repeat with the remaining half.

CUTTING INTO EIGHT PIECES

1. Place a whole chicken on your work surface breast side down. Cut through the backbone. Turn the chicken over and with the heel of your hand, flatten the breastbone as much as possible.
2. On one side, pull the wing structure away from the body. With your fingers, locate the joint and cut through it, severing the wing from the body. Repeat on the other side. You may remove the wing tips, if you like; save them for making stock.
3. On one side, pull the leg away from the body. With your fingers, locate the joint that connects the thigh to the body. Cut through it, severing the thigh and drumstick from the body. Cut the thigh from the drumstick at the joint. Repeat on the other side.
4. Turn the breast over, and cut away the backbone. Save the backbone for making stock. Starting just above the cartilage, cut the breast in half. Make the cut a little off center. The bird is now cut into eighths. Collect any stray bones and save for stock making.

BONING CHICKEN BREASTS

1. Breasts are easiest to skin when cold. Starting with a whole breast, make an incision over the breast bone.
2. Working along one side of the rib cage, and as close to the body as possible, cut-scrape the flesh from the bone. Tug the meat away from the body as you cut. Repeat on the other side. To skin the breast, simply pull the skin from the meat, using the knife if necessary. The bones should be reserved for the stockpot.

Butterflying Rock Cornish Broiler Chickens and Other Birds

This method, which exposes a maximum of flesh to the heat source while keeping the bird almost intact, can also be applied to larger poultry.

1. Place the bird breast side down on your work surface. With a poultry shears or heavy knife, remove the backbone by cutting down close to it on each side.
2. Turn the bird over and press down hard at the crest of the breastbone to break the collarbones and some of the ribs; this will flat-

ten it. Using a thumb, continue to press until the lower section of the breastbone pops through the flesh on the underside; remove it.

3. Fold the wing ends behind the shoulders. Using a paring knife, make a slit in the skin at either side of the breast tip. Insert the tip of the drumsticks through each slit; this holds the legs in place.

Stuffing the Bird

It is useful to remember that stuffings can consist primarily of rice, potatoes, kasha, or barley as well as bread. The best stuffing offers a variety of textures and a play of flavors. I often use dried fruit in stuffing; it provides just the right tart and chewy contrast to the stuffing "medium." The amount of liquid you use in your stuffing also determines how porridge-like, chewy, or crunchy your stuffing will be. Stuffings should also be well seasoned to compensate for the relative blandness of the bread or other starch.

You can prepare stuffing ingredients ahead. Measure, slice, and chop as necessary, but keep the "wet" and "dry" ingredients separate until just before you intend to stuff the bird, then combine them. To avoid bacterial contamination, never allow a stuffed bird to linger before being cooked; likewise, remove stuffing from a cooked bird within two hours of roasting it.

Use day-old bread for stuffing or let fresh bread dry out slightly in the oven. Avoid stale bread; its tired taste won't do a thing for your stuffing.

When stuffing a bird under 10 pounds, figure $1/2$ cup of stuffing per pound. Over 10 pounds, estimate $3/4$ cup of stuffing per pound. Stuff any bird fairly loosely. The stuffing expands during cooking; a too-packed stuffing also cooks slowly and can remain tepid even after the bird is done. Make certain stuffing in a bird registers 160° F. When a meat thermometer is inserted in the center of the cavity; otherwise it may not be safe to eat.

To stuff poultry, first season the bird inside and out. Pack some of the stuffing into the neck cavity, than pull the neck skin over it. If the bird is large, fasten the skin to the back with a skewer. Spoon the remaining stuffing into the cavity, using skewers to close the opening or sewing it shut with heavy thread. Place extra stuffing in a greased baking dish or casserole to cook during the last 30 minutes of the bird's roasting. Periodically check the pan stuffing to make sure it isn't drying out. I like to drizzle chicken or vegetable stock over the stuffing from time to time to help maintain its moisture.

Though a large bird cries out to be stuffed—especially when it's the centerpiece of a celebratory meal—stuffing does very well cooked outside the bird. In fact, many people prefer to prepare stuffing this way, which results in a lighter, "fresher"-tasting dressing than its in-the-bird counterpart; it will also be lower in calories.

If you cook stuffing outside of the bird, estimate $1/2$ to $3/4$ pound of stuffing per person. Bake the stuffing in a covered dish until just warmed through, about 30 minutes in a 350°F. oven. Remove the cover during the last 10 minutes of cooking to allow excess moisture to escape, and to brown (or crust) the stuffing nicely.

Refrigerate leftover stuffing in a baking dish. To reheat it, place the dish in a 325°F. oven to warm, about 30 minutes. Or toss it in a nonstick skillet with a tiny bit of vegetable oil, stock, or cooking juices from the bird.

Other stuffing tips appear on page 183.

Trussing

Trussing a whole bird before it is roasted or braised ensures an attractive presentation and makes carving easier. There are a number of ways to truss poultry. Besides being simple, the following method avoids running string over the breast, which can leave an unsightly mark. When the bird is ready to be carved, one snip frees the string easily.

1. Place the bird breast side up on your work surface. To make life easiest for the carver, first remove the wishbone. To do so, turn the bird breast side up and pull back the neck skin. Locate the wishbone with your fingers and with a small, sharp paring knife, cut through the flesh along the visible contours of the bone on both sides just enough to free it. Work closely against the bone with the knife, severing the bone from the body at the joints and pulling it out.
2. Bend the wing tips back. Place the middle of a long piece of string underneath the tail. Bring the ends over the tail, crossing them and then looping them around the ends of the drumsticks.
3. Run the string snugly against the sides of the body across legs, and pull it through the base of the V made by the folded wings.
4. Turn the bird breast side down and tie the string in a knot in the back. The bird is now trussed.

CARVING A BIRD AT TABLE

The first step for successful carving is to allow the bird to rest at room temperature for 15 or 20 minutes after cooking. This allows juices to be reabsorbed by the flesh, which also firms on standing. Duck, with its tight leg and wing ligaments, requires a heavy, rigid chef's knife, or sharp, heavy poultry shears, for removing the legs and wings.

With all poultry, use a very sharp, flexible knife for carving the breast.

Directions are for a right-handed person; reverse the position if you are left-handed.

1. Place the cooked bird on a platter breast side up with the legs to your right.
2. Stick a large fork into the fleshy part of the drumstick nearest you. Pulling the leg gently toward you, cut through the skin that joins the second joint to the body. Find the connecting joint with the tip of your knife and sever the thigh-drumstick from the body. Separate the leg and the thigh.
3. With the tip of your knife, find the wing socket and detach the wing from the body. Steady the bird by placing your fork into the breast meat near the breastbone and start slicing from the front of the breast, gradually angling the knife parallel to the bone as you go (this ensures the maximum removal of meat). Carve the breast meat into thin slices. Repeat the procedure on the other side.

2. Starters and Finger Foods

Appetizers are power mouthfuls.
They get your party or dinner going, tempting
then seducing the palate; with drinks,
they can be the party itself.

The starters I like to make are full of bright, strong flavors and serve many occasions. They help friends relax, have fun, and enjoy one another.

I didn't grow up with appetizers like these. My mother and grandmother were wonderful cooks, but the world was a different place then, especially for people keeping kosher. Hors d'oeuvres in my mother's day were chopped chicken liver with crackers or meatballs in a jammy sauce—a far cry from the tempting bites I serve today.

To make appetizers work best, I've devised certain rules: Make the flavors vivid (guests won't be eating just one thing, so you can be bold with seasonings); think easy-to-handle (skewers are my friends); remember dipping sauces. Turkey Saté and Chicken Medallions with Creamy Peanut Dipping Sauce are two examples of this spirited, self-contained food. The easily made Rosemary-Lemon Chicken Wings is another, as are the Shiitake Potstickers with Ponzu Dipping Sauce. These can be used as hors d'oeuvres, imaginative starters, or part of a delectable grazing menu. And that chopped chicken liver I mentioned is reborn here as a filling for sweet-savory prune boats, enticing party morsels.

Another rule: presentation counts. This is especially important when food must hold its own among drinks and conversation. Small foods benefit from colorful garnishes. A few flowers bordering the Picadillo Empanadas, for example, not only are beautiful but also underline the food's Mexican provenance; clusters of fresh herbs enhance platters and can highlight dish flavors; red cabbage leaves run briefly under hot water to bring out their color frame appetizers like the Chicken-Stuffed Grape Leaves triumphantly. (When using flowers or other plants for dish embellishment, make certain first that they haven't been sprayed with insecticides and the like. Some varieties, such as lily of the valley and poinsettia, are poisonous if eaten and should, of course, be avoided entirely. Check plant toxicity with your florist or in books treating the subject.)

You can be equally imaginative in dealing with skewers and toothpicks. Skewers won't end up on windowsills if you pass a hollowed-out butternut squash or cucumber boat along with the skewered appetizer. Put a few skewers in the vegetable receptacle when you serve so guests get the idea.

Mix and match your own original starters with the dipping sauces and other accompaniments. Serve a simple basket of blanched asparagus with the Mustard Dill Sauce on page 228, for example, and people will rave. Try poultry or vegetable satés with the Wasabi Sauce or Fresh Coriander Chutney, pages 46 and 239. Just remember, when making your matches, to keep your starter's culinary character in mind; you wouldn't want to serve Asian potstickers with an herby Mediterranean-style vinaigrette.

The appetizers here are really versatile. One of the joys of chicken and other poultry is that they're the best possible canvas for culinary creativity. Use your imagination freely and have fun—that's what starters and finger foods are about.

Rosemary-Lemon Chicken Wings

It's always exciting when the simplest ingredients produce a dish as satisfying as this. Good olive oil, garlic, lemon, and fresh rosemary make a pungent marinade for the wings, which are baked (or grilled) and ready to eat in minutes. In summer, these tart, herby wings make a nice alternative to the usual barbecued chicken—no red sauce here.

These wings are a bit messy. Be sure to have napkins or cocktail plates handy.

16 chicken wings (about 2½ pounds)

6 garlic cloves, peeled

3 tablespoons whole fresh rosemary leaves

⅓ cup fruity olive oil

½ cup lemon juice (3 lemons)

½ teaspoon hot sauce, or to taste

4 bay leaves

1 bunch decorative greens (such as kale or chard), for garnish (optional)

1 lemon, thinly sliced, for garnish (optional)

Makes 32 pieces

1. Remove the wing tips (freeze them for stock or discard). Separate each wing into 2 pieces.

2. Chop the garlic by dropping it through the feed tube of a food processor with the machine running. Add the rosemary and pulse until chopped. Add the oil, lemon juice, and hot sauce and pulse until well blended.

3. Put the chicken wings in a jumbo plastic bag. Add the bay leaves and the marinade. Seal the bag, squeezing out as much air as possible. Refrigerate at least 4 hours or preferably overnight, turning the bag when possible.

4. Preheat the oven to 400°F. or prepare an outdoor grill. Remove the wings from marinade and pat dry. Reserve the marinade.

5. Spread the wings evenly on a baking tray. Bake, turning once or twice for even cooking, until the juices run clear when the wings are pricked with a fork, about 20 minutes. Put the wings under the broiler, with the side with the most skin facing up, and cook until golden brown, about 3 to 5 minutes. If cooking outdoors, grill the wings over medium heat about 4 inches from the heat source, turning as needed, until brown and their juices run clear, about 15 minutes. (Alternatively, precook the wings in the oven, as above, and finish browning on the grill.)

6. In a small saucepan, bring the reserved marinade to a boil and allow to boil 2 minutes.

7. Line a serving platter with the greens. Arrange the chicken wings in the center. Drizzle some of the marinade over the wings. Garnish with the lemon slices and serve.

Turkey Saté

Satés are the finger food. I use turkey tenders (the tenderloin section attached to the breast) for this soy- and honey-marinated version of the traditional Indonesian kebab, but it's also delicious made with chicken, tuna, or salmon.

Satés are simple to make, but can overcook quickly. Check them while they broil and lean toward undercooking (they'll continue to cook for a minute after taken from the heat).

I serve these with a melon ball chaser—the contrast of spicy turkey and the cool, sweet melon is sensational. Make the chaser with a melon baller and serve it in a small bowl; tell guests to spear the melon using the saté skewers. Serve the satés themselves from the melon halves you've pared of their flesh.

MARINADE

5 garlic cloves, peeled

½ cup dark sesame oil

¾ cup honey

¼ cup low-sodium soy sauce

1 teaspoon five-spice powder

1 pound turkey tenders, cut into strips about 1 inch wide by 3 inches long

1 tablespoon sesame seeds

Thirty 6-inch wooden skewers

Makes 30

1. To make the marinade, using a food processor, mince the garlic. Add the sesame oil, honey, soy sauce, and five-spice powder. Pulse to combine.

2. Place the turkey strips in a shallow glass dish. Pour the marinade over them and refrigerate at least 1 hour, preferably overnight, covered.

3. At least 1 hour in advance, soak the skewers in water to prevent their burning during cooking.

4. Remove the turkey from the marinade and thread each skewer with 1 strip of turkey. For easy eating, keep the turkey near the pointed end of the skewer, leaving one-third of the wood bare. (If you want to prepare the skewers up to 1 day ahead, first thread them with the turkey. Pour 1 to 2 inches of marinade in the bottom of a tall container and add the skewers; the marinade should just cover the turkey, to prevent its drying out. Cover and refrigerate until ready to broil.)

5. Preheat the broiler. Cover a cookie sheet with foil. Spread the skewers on the sheet and sprinkle with the sesame seeds. Drape the bare wood of the skewers with strips of foil to prevent their coloring.

6. Broil on one side until the turkey is lightly brown, 3 to 6 minutes. Turn, replace the foil, and broil on the other side. Allow to cool slightly and serve with the sesame-coated side uppermost.

Hoisin Turkey Meatballs

MEATBALLS

1 pound ground turkey

1 egg

¼ cup bread crumbs

⅓ cup hoisin sauce

2 teaspoons soy sauce

1 teaspoon dry sherry

2 scallions, white and green parts, chopped

¼ cup chopped raw cashews

SAUCE

⅔ cup hoisin sauce

1 cup apple juice

2 tablespoons dry sherry

1 tablespoon soy sauce

1 tablespoon dark sesame oil

1 teaspoon grated peeled fresh ginger

6 red cabbage leaves, for garnish (optional)

1 cup alfalfa sprouts, for garnish (optional)

3 thin orange slices cut in half, for garnish (optional)

Six-inch wooden skewers, for serving

Makes 30 to 35

These mouthfuls, crunchy with cashews and tasting of sweet-pungent hoisin sauce, redefine the meatball appetizer. Cooked and served in a gingery sauce, they're a revelation in taste and texture.

You can prepare the meatballs ahead. Form, then freeze them on cookie sheets. Once frozen, store the meatballs in resealable plastic bags in the freezer, where they'll last for months. (The sauce freezes well also.) When you're ready to prepare them, just drop the frozen meatballs into the hot sauce and cook until just cooked through and hot.

1. To make the meatballs, combine the turkey, egg, bread crumbs, hoisin sauce, soy sauce, sherry, scallions, and cashews in a medium bowl. Roll the meatballs the size of walnuts and place on a cookie sheet. Reserve.

2. To make the sauce, combine the hoisin sauce, apple juice, sherry, soy sauce, sesame oil, and ginger in a large saucepan and bring to a simmer over medium heat.

3. Add the meatballs to the sauce and simmer until just cooked through, about 15 minutes (25 minutes if previously frozen). If the meatballs don't fit in a single layer, turn them midway through the cooking.

4. To serve, arrange the cabbage leaves around the inside of a small glass bowl. With a slotted spoon remove the cooked meatballs to the bowl. Garnish with the sprouts and orange slices. Serve with skewers and put the sauce in a bowl for dipping.

Chicken Medallions with Creamy Peanut Dipping Sauce

Busy cooks need dishes that can lead more than one life. These chicken medallions do, beautifully.

To make these, chicken cutlets are rolled around a filling of chopped peanuts and scallions, braised, and then sliced into pretty medallions. Served with peanut sauce, the medallions make a perfect hors d'oeuvre; plated and drizzled with the thinned sauce, they're a great starter or luncheon dish. Serve the slices atop a mixture of steamed snow peas, orange sections, and watercress, and you've got a terrific Asian chicken salad. Versatile, no?

DIPPING SAUCE

One ½-inch piece fresh ginger, peeled

1 garlic clove, peeled

2 tablespoons toasted sesame tahini

3 tablespoons peanut butter

3 tablespoons dark sesame oil

1 tablespoon honey

¼ cup brown rice vinegar

2 tablespoons dry sherry

1 tablespoon soy sauce

¼ teaspoon five-spice powder

1 or 2 drops hot sauce

1. To make the sauce, turn on a food processor and while it is running drop the ginger and garlic through the feed tube to mince. Add the tahini, peanut butter, sesame oil, honey, rice vinegar, sherry, soy sauce, five-spice powder, and hot sauce, and blend well. Reserve.

2. Preheat the oven to 350°F. To make the medallions, place each cutlet between 2 sheets of waxed paper or freezer paper. Using a mallet, pound each cutlet to an even thickness of about ¹/₄ inch.

3. In a food processor, chop the scallions and remove to a small bowl. Add the peanuts, chop, and remove to a second bowl. Add the garlic and ginger, chop together, and place in a third bowl.

4. Sprinkle the cutlets with some of the peanuts and scallions. Starting at the wide end, roll each cutlet tightly, tucking in the edges as it is rolled. Secure with a toothpick. Place the chicken rolls seam side down in a baking pan that will hold them tightly. Sprinkle with the ginger and garlic.

5. Pour in the stock to a depth of ¹/₂ inch and cover tightly with aluminum foil. Bake until the rolls are just cooked, about 40 minutes. At 15-minute intervals, lift the foil and rotate the rolls to avoid overcooking.

MEDALLIONS

2 pounds chicken cutlets

2 scallions, trimmed

¼ cup peanuts

1 garlic clove, peeled

One ½-inch piece ginger, peeled
and chopped

⅓ cup Chicken Stock (page 61), or good
instant or low-sodium canned broth

Decorative greens, such as kale or chard,
for serving (optional)

Flat wood toothpicks

Four- or 6-inch wooden skewers,
for serving

Makes 50 pieces

6. When done, cool 10 minutes in the pan and then remove the toothpicks. Chill to facilitate slicing.

7. Bring the rolls to room temperature. To serve as an hors d'oeuvre, line a platter with the greens. Slice the rolls $1/4$ inch thick and arrange in a circular pattern on the plate, accompanied by the skewers. Pass with the sauce for dipping. As a starter, arrange the greens on 4 to 6 serving plates. Cut each roll into 6 to 8 pieces and fan atop the greens. Thin the sauce with 2 or more tablespoons of hot water. Pour a line of sauce over the medallions and serve.

Hazelnut-Crusted Chicken Bites

Appetizers need to tantalize, and these grilled or broiled hazelnut-coated tidbits do just that. Hazelnuts make a terrific, crunchy coating for these saté-like bites of chicken; served with Honey-Banana Chutney or Fresh Pineapple Salsa, they're an unusual way to kick off a party.

1 to 1¼ pounds chicken cutlets or 1 pound saved chicken tenders (chicken tenderloins), tendons removed

Juice of 1 lime

2 teaspoons walnut oil

⅛ teaspoon ground cinnamon or five-spice powder

1 egg

1 tablespoon cold water

½ cup chopped toasted hazelnuts (filberts)

2 tablespoons dry bread crumbs

Salt and freshly ground black pepper

Honey-Banana Chutney (page 238) or Fresh Pineapple Salsa (page 223), for serving

Fourteen 10-inch wooden skewers

Makes 14 pieces

1. At least 1 hour in advance, soak the skewers in water to prevent their burning during cooking. Cut the cutlets, if using, into ten ¹/₂-inch-wide strips.

2. In a medium bowl, combine the chicken with the lime juice, oil, and cinnamon. Mix well and marinate for about 30 minutes.

3. In a shallow bowl, beat the egg with the water. On a large dish with a lip, mix the hazelnuts and bread crumbs and season to taste with the salt and pepper.

4. Dip the strips or tenders in the egg and thread 1 onto each skewer. For even cooking, keep the chicken elongated rather than bunched up. Dredge the chicken in the hazelnut-bread crumb mixture.

5. Prepare a grill or preheat the broiler. Cover the bare wood of the skewers with foil strips to prevent their coloring. If grilling, place the tenders on a grilling screen or rack. Grill about 4 inches from the heat over medium heat or broil until the nuts are lightly browned and the chicken cooked through, 2 to 3 minutes per side. Serve with the salsa.

Iraqi Chicken Fritters

Recipes travel far. I got this one for crisp chicken fritters from a friend whose aunt married an Iraqi Jew from Bombay. These spicy wok-fried fritters are delicious as a starter or small meal served with rice and dal, or in pita bread with chopped lettuce and tomato, much like falafel. I like them best, though, just out of the wok accompanied by Fresh Coriander Chutney (page 239) and a squeeze of lemon juice.

1 pound chicken cutlets, ground

⅛ teaspoon turmeric

¼ teaspoon chili powder

½ teaspoon very finely minced jalapeño pepper

2 scallions, green parts and some of the white, sliced lengthwise and cut into thin half-rings

2 tablespoons all-purpose flour

Salt and freshly ground black pepper

2 eggs, beaten

Vegetable oil, for frying

Makes eighteen 2-inch fritters as a starter; or thirty-six 1-inch fritters for an hors d'oeuvre

1. In a medium bowl, combine the chicken, turmeric, chili powder, jalapeño, scallions, and flour. Season to taste with the salt and pepper and mix well. Add the eggs and combine. Cover and refrigerate at least 1 hour, or as much as a day ahead.

2. Just before you are ready to eat, pour oil to a depth of 2 inches into a wok or deep pan. Heat the oil over medium heat until it reaches a temperature of 360°F.

3. Use 2 soup spoons to make the fritters. With one, scoop out enough of the mixture to make a 1- or 2-inch ball, smaller if the fritter is to be served as an hors d'oeuvre, larger for a starter. Release it into the oil with the other spoon. Make as many balls as will fit easily across the surface of the oil. Stirring with a slotted spoon to expose all surfaces to the oil, fry until the fritters are golden brown, about 5 minutes. Adjust the heat as necessary. Remove the fritters from the pan with a slotted spoon and drain on paper towels. Continue to make all the fritters. Serve hot.

Picadillo Empanadas

Empanadas, those Latin-American turnovers filled with poultry, meat, or fish are a savory treat. This small version, which makes a perfect hors d'oeuvre, has a turkey-based picadillo filling. Fragrant with oregano, cinnamon, and clove, and touched with chocolate for depth, the filling is irresistible.

The dough can be refrigerated overnight or frozen for up to three weeks (defrost it in the refrigerator a day before rolling), and the filling prepared up to two days ahead. This recipe makes an ample quantity of empanadas, but you can freeze any you don't need immediately and use them to accompany other dishes (they're great with big bowls of soup). Or make larger empanadas, about 5 inches in diameter, and serve them as the main event for a light supper or buffet entree.

DOUGH

5 cups all-purpose flour

½ pound chilled margarine (2 sticks), cut into 16 slices

1 teaspoon salt

About ⅔ cup ice water

FILLING

2 teaspoons vegetable oil

1 small onion, finely chopped

2 garlic cloves, minced

¾ pound lean ground turkey

3 ounces tomato paste

½ teaspoon dried oregano

½ teaspoon ground cinnamon

¼ teaspoon ground cloves

⅛ teaspoon ground cumin

½ ounce unsweetened chocolate

1 bay leaf

1. To make the dough, put the flour, margarine, and salt in a food processor fitted with a metal blade. Process until mixture resembles coarse meal, 5 or 6 seconds.

2. With the machine running, slowly pour the ice water in a steady stream through the feed tube. Stop the machine as soon as the dough forms a ball. It's not necessary to use all the water.

3. Wrap the dough in plastic film and refrigerate at least 2 or up to 24 hours.

4. To prepare the filling, in a large, heavy nonstick skillet, heat the oil over moderate heat. Add the onion and garlic and sauté until the onion is golden, 3 to 5 minutes.

5. Add the turkey and cook over medium heat until it browns, about 3 minutes. As the turkey cooks, stir to break up any lumps. Pour off any fat.

6. Add the tomato paste, oregano, cinnamon, cloves, and cumin. Add the chocolate and bay leaf. Continue to cook until the meat is crumbly and the mixture is well blended, about 5 minutes.

2 tablespoons toasted pine nuts

¼ cup pitted, drained, and chopped green olives

2 tablespoons dried currants

Salt and freshly ground black pepper

2 eggs, for brushing dough

Makes one hundred 3-inch empanadas

7. Add the pine nuts, olives, and currants and season to taste with the salt and pepper. Remove the mixture from the heat and set aside to cool. Remove the bay leaf. (If the meat is still lumpy, pulse it in food processor 3 or 4 times.)

8. Remove the dough from the refrigerator and roll it on a floured board or table to a thickness of $^1/_8$ inch. Cut the dough into 3-inch rounds with a cookie or biscuit cutter. (Use a larger cutter for main course turnovers.)

9. Place 1 heaping teaspoon of filling in the lower half of each round. Brush the edges of the rounds with water. Fold the unmoistened dough over the filling and press the edges together with fork tines to seal. Filled empanadas can be kept in the refrigerator overnight or frozen up to 3 weeks.

10. Preheat the oven to 400°F. Lightly oil a cookie sheet or line it with parchment paper. Prepare an egg wash by beating the eggs with $^1/_2$ cup water.

11. Place the empanadas on the sheet and brush with the wash. Bake until golden, 12 to 20 minutes, depending on size—longer if frozen. Cool slightly and serve.

Poulets Grillés

Don't let the fancy name fool you. At heart, this is really "toast with a schmeer"—a light and delicious alternative to the usual liver-pâté hors d'oeuvre. It's made in minutes using a food processor and will become a standard in your appetizer repertoire. Try the pâté also in endive leaves for a lighter but luscious variation.

The garlic oil used in this recipe is also quickly made and great to have on hand to make bruschetta, canapés, and garlic bread. The aroma of the garlic sautéing is a great palate teaser.

¼ cup extra-virgin olive oil

6 fresh sage leaves

3 garlic cloves, chopped

4 large shallots, minced

½ pound boneless and skinless chicken thigh meat (about 4 thighs; save the bones for stock), cubed

2 tablespoons dry white wine

½ cup Italian parsley leaves

Salt and freshly ground black pepper

Juice of 1 lemon

4 tablespoons imported nonpareil capers, drained

1 loaf semolina bread (about 14 x 2 inches), cut into ¼-inch slices

2 to 3 tablespoons Garlic Oil (recipe follows)

12 pitted Kalamata olives, quartered lengthwise

Makes about 55

1. In a medium skillet, heat the olive oil over high heat. Add the sage and sauté until crisp and olive green in color. Add the garlic and shallots, lower the heat to medium, and sauté until the shallots are golden, 3 to 4 minutes.

2. Add the chicken and sauté, stirring, until cooked through, 4 to 5 minutes. Remove from the heat.

3. Using a spatula, scrape the contents of the skillet into a food processor. Return the skillet to the stove over medium heat and deglaze the pan with the wine. Scrape the pan contents into the food processor. Add the parsley to the food processor and season the ingredients to taste with the salt and pepper. Pulse-chop finely, add the lemon juice, and puree until smooth. Empty the contents into a bowl, stir in the capers, and chill.

4. Place the bread on a sheet pan and toast under the broiler until lightly golden, about 2 minutes per side. Brush 1 side of each slice of bread with the garlic oil and spread with the chicken mixture. Garnish each slice with 2 olive quarters and serve.

Garlic Oil

Cook the garlic in the oil only until it is wheat-colored to ensure a mellow result. To make garlic bread, cut baguettes in half lengthwise, brush them with the oil, wrap, and then warm them in the oven.

Stored refrigerated, this keeps for about two weeks. Use the cooked garlic with the oil.

½ cup olive oil

12 garlic cloves, pressed or finely minced

Makes about ¹/₂ cup

1. In a small, heavy skillet, heat the oil over medium-low heat. Add the garlic and cook until it just begins to turn golden, about 2 minutes.

2. Remove from the heat and cool. Use or store.

Chicken-Stuffed Grape Leaves

Stuffed grape leaves, or dolmas, *are popular in every country of the Middle East. You're probably most familiar with the rice-filled version, which is usually served at room temperature. These chicken-stuffed grape leaves, like most meat-filled dolmas in the Middle East, are served hot. They're a delicacy, and particularly good dipped in Cumin Tomato Sauce (page 239).*

The leaves can be bought preserved in brine.

1 pound ground chicken or turkey

1 cup finely chopped onion

1 tablespoon tomato paste, diluted with 2 tablespoons hot chicken broth

½ teaspoon dried mint leaves

⅛ teaspoon ground allspice

1 cup cooked short-grain brown rice

¼ cup chopped Italian parsley

Freshly ground black pepper

8 ounces grape leaves packed in brine

1½ cups chopped tomatoes, fresh or drained canned

6 garlic cloves (optional)

1 cup Chicken Stock (page 61), or good instant or low-sodium canned broth

Juice of 1 lemon

Makes 40 pieces

1. In a large mixing bowl, thoroughly combine the ground chicken, onion, diluted tomato paste, mint, allspice, rice, and parsley. Season to taste with the pepper. Reserve.

2. Rinse the grape leaves under cold running water, carefully separating each leaf. Place the leaves vein side up, a few at a time, on a flat work surface. Place 1 heaping tablespoon of filling on each grape leaf near the base. Starting at the base, fold the bottom of each leaf over its filling. Fold the sides over the filling, then roll up toward the tip.

3. Scatter half of the tomatoes in a large, heavy saucepan. Arrange the dolmas in 2 to 3 layers, scattering the garlic, if using, and the remaining tomatoes between the layers. Add a few torn grape leaves between the layers if you have any left over. Add enough stock to cover the dolmas and pour over the lemon juice evenly.

4. Weight down the dolmas using a heavy heatproof plate just large enough to fit into the saucepan. Bring the mixture to a simmer, cover the saucepan, and cook over very low heat until the leaves are tender, about 1 hour. Add additional stock to cover if needed. Serve hot.

Chicken Fingers

These simple hors d'oeuvres consist of chicken cutlet strips breaded and baked until crunchy. What makes them special is the use of challah crumbs for the breading and the fatless "frying." The fingers are crispy and naturally sweet—a delightful mouthful for many different occasions. By the way, my kids make a meal of these with applesauce or ketchup. Adults prefer them with Fresh Tomato Coulis (page 219), Honey-Banana Chutney (page 238), or Fresh Coriander Chutney (page 239).

Save leftover challah to make crumbs for these.

1½ pounds chicken cutlets

1 scant tablespoon fresh lemon juice

1 to 2 garlic cloves, pressed

2 eggs, beaten

2 tablespoons warm water

2 tablespoons canola or other vegetable oil

2 cups fresh challah crumbs

¼ teaspoon dried oregano

Salt and freshly ground black pepper

Makes 25 to 30

1. Cut the cutlets into strips that are about 3 inches long and 1 inch wide. In a medium nonreactive bowl, combine the lemon juice and garlic. Add the chicken and stir to coat. Cover the bowl and marinate, refrigerated, for 1 hour.

2. In a medium bowl, combine the eggs, water, and oil. Place the crumbs in a deep dish or shallow bowl. Add the oregano, season to taste with the salt and pepper, and mix. Line a baking sheet with foil and spray with vegetable oil cooking spray.

3. Dip the chicken strips into the egg mixture, lift to drain excess, and dredge in the crumbs. Place on the baking sheet. Refrigerate to set, 1 to 2 hours.

4. Preheat the oven to 350°F. Bake the fingers until crisp and golden, about 30 minutes. Cool slightly, and serve.

Shiitake Potstickers with Ponzu Dipping Sauce

These juicy shiitake-filled dumplings never fail to please. Their mushroom filling, the yielding wrapper, and tart-sweet dipping sauce excite compliments galore.

You can make the potstickers in advance and freeze them for up to two months. For an hors d'oeuvre, serve them with small skewers. As a starter, lay the potstickers on alfalfa sprouts, sprinkle them with sesame seeds, and surround the dumplings with steamed julienned carrots. In either case, pass the sauce separately.

FILLING

¼ cup dried shiitake mushrooms

1 garlic clove

4 scallions, trimmed

One ¼-inch piece fresh ginger, peeled

¾ pound chicken cutlets, cut into chunks

¼ teaspoon freshly ground black pepper

1 egg

1 tablespoon soy sauce

2 teaspoons dark sesame oil

PONZU DIPPING SAUCE

¼ cup tamari or soy sauce

½ cup brown rice vinegar

1 teaspoon sugar

Few drops of chili oil

1 tablespoon fresh lemon juice

1. To make the filling, reconstitute the mushrooms in enough warm water to cover them, 15 to 20 minutes. Drain and squeeze out as much water as possible.

2. Start a food processor and drop the garlic through the feed tube. Stop the processor when the garlic is chopped.

3. Add the soaked mushrooms and pulse 4 or 5 times to chop. Add the scallions and ginger and pulse until chopped. Add the chicken and pepper and pulse until chopped finely. Add the egg, soy sauce, and sesame oil, and process to puree. Reserve.

4. To make the sauce, combine the tamari, rice vinegar, sugar, chili oil, and lemon juice in a small bowl. Set aside.

5. To form the dumplings, place 1 teaspoon of filling in the center of each of 45 wrappers (reserve the rest for another use). Wet the edges and purse by gathering up the wrapper in 3 places. Pinch to seal.

6. Combine the vegetable and sesame oils. Brush the interior of a large nonstick skillet lightly with the mixture.

POTSTICKERS

1 package (50 pieces) 2½ inch round
dumpling or gyoza wrappers

¼ cup vegetable oil

2 tablespoons dark sesame oil

Makes 45

7. Heat the skillet over medium-high heat and when the oil is hot, add the potstickers in a single layer, without touching. Brown the bottoms only.

8. Partially cover the skillet, pour off the excess oil, and discard. Return the skillet to the stove, stand back (to avoid any splattering), and pour in $^1/_4$ to $^1/_3$ cup water. Cover the pan. As soon as you see steam, reduce the heat to low and cook through, 2 to 3 minutes. The wrapper will look like cooked pasta. (Frozen potstickers do not have to be defrosted before cooking. Steam in a steamer over boiling water, 2 to 3 minutes.) Serve as suggested in the headnote. Pass the dipping sauce separately.

String Bean Bundles with Smoked Turkey and Mustard Dill Sauce

This popular starter is really pretty, and very easy to prepare. You create string bean bundles enclosed in smoked turkey and arrange them in the leaves of a carved-out cabbage. Mustard Dill Sauce goes into the cabbage, and the presentation is indeed striking. The whole dish can be done ahead, covered with damp towels, and refrigerated; or you can carve out the cabbage and make the bundles and the sauce a day in advance, wrap the cabbage and bundles individually, and assemble the dish at the last minute.

1 pound string beans, trimmed at the stem ends only

1 large savoy or other green cabbage, preferably with loose outer leaves

1 pound sliced smoked turkey

½ cup Mustard Dill Sauce (page 228)

Makes 50 bundles

1. Bring a medium pot of water to a boil and have a bowl of ice water nearby. Add the string beans to the boiling water and blanch until crisp-tender, about 2 minutes. Drain well and put in the ice water to stop the cooking. Alternatively, steam the beans.

2. Remove about 8 outer leaves of the cabbage carefully. Rinse the outer leaves and dry well.

3. To carve out the cabbage, use a sharp thin-bladed knife. Cut a circle into the cabbage at its center, penetrating about 3 inches. Cut tic-tac-toe slashes back and forth through the circle to break up the inner leaves, and with your hands, remove the leaves. Trim to create a cuplike receptacle.

4. Cut each slice of turkey into thirds. Roll 2 beans in each strip to create bundles.

5. Place the cabbage on a platter. Reassemble the loose leaves around the head so the cabbage appears intact, fanning them out. Arrange the bundles decoratively on the cabbage leaves. Pour the sauce into the center of the cabbage and serve.

Chicken Liver Prune Boats

Pâté made with prunes is a traditional French delight, but too time-consuming for most home cooks to prepare. I've simplified things by turning the dish "inside out" and serving the pâté in the prunes, as an appetizer. You'll love these chewy little prune boats filled with a chopped chicken liver "pâté"; they're tempting mouthfuls for an hors d'oeuvre tray and will disappear fast.

Prepare the livers by broiling. For a sprightly garnish, use orange slices, kumquats, or grape clusters.

1 tablespoon margarine or vegetable oil

1 large onion, thinly sliced

½ pound koshered chicken livers (see headnote)

1 hard-cooked egg, peeled and quartered

2 teaspoons fresh orange juice

2 teaspoons cognac

Freshly grated nutmeg

Kosher salt and freshly ground black pepper

One 12-ounce box small pitted prunes

Makes 70

1. In a medium skillet, heat the margarine over low heat. Add the onion and sauté until lightly browned, 15 to 20 minutes.

2. Place the cooked livers in a food processor and add the sautéed onion, egg, orange juice, and cognac. Season to taste with a pinch of the nutmeg and pulse-chop the mixture to make a rough filling. Season to taste with the salt and pepper.

3. To assemble the boats, make an indentation in each prune where the pit has been removed. Stuff the prunes with a heaping $1/2$ teaspoon of the filling. Arrange on a tray, dust lightly with the nutmeg, and serve.

Chicken Nori Rolls with Wasabi Sauce

This take on traditional maki rolls is elegant, exciting, and easy to do.

Yakatori-marinated shredded chicken and rice are enclosed in a roll of nori seaweed; the rolls are then dipped in a pungent sesame-horseradish sauce (which also excels as a dunk for vegetables or as a salad dressing). Served as an hors d'oeuvre, first course, or buffet dish, these will be the hit of your party.

The maki can be prepared up to two hours ahead and stored in plastic wrap or under a damp towel. They are rolled most easily with a bamboo sushi mat available at Japanese shops, but you can use plastic-coated freezer paper.

WASABI SAUCE

¾ cup light vegetable oil

¼ cup plus 2 tablespoons dark sesame oil

3 tablespoons soy sauce

2 teaspoons wasabi powder or 1 tablespoon prepared horseradish

2 tablespoons Dijon mustard

2 scallions, trimmed, including tops

2 tablespoons fresh lemon juice

1 teaspoon sugar

1 tablespoon brown rice vinegar

1 small piece fresh ginger, peeled

YAKATORI MARINADE

⅓ cup low- or reduced-sodium soy sauce

¼ cup dry sherry

2 tablespoons light brown sugar

1 tablespoon brown rice vinegar

1 garlic clove, pressed

¼ teaspoon grated peeled fresh ginger

1. To make the wasabi sauce, combine the vegetable and sesame oils in a pitcher or measuring cup with a spout. Set aside.

2. Add the soy sauce, wasabi powder, mustard, scallions, lemon juice, sugar, vinegar, and ginger to a food processor. Process until pureed.

3. With the processor running, very slowly drizzle the oils in a thin stream through the feed tube. When the oils have been added, you will have a thick, creamy sauce. Reserve.

4. To make the marinade, combine the soy sauce, sherry, brown sugar, vinegar, garlic, and ginger in a jar with a cover. Shake the ingredients until the sugar dissolves. (The marinade can be made 3 to 4 days ahead and stored refrigerated.)

5. To prepare the rolls, place the chicken in a medium glass bowl. Pour the marinade over the chicken, cover, and allow to marinate for 30 minutes to 3 hours. For over 30 minutes, refrigerate.

ROLLS

1½ pounds chicken cutlets, pounded to
¼-inch thickness and cut into thin strips
(about ¹⁄₁₆ inch wide)

1 teaspoon vegetable oil or
vegetable spray

4 nori sheets (8 x 7 inches)

3 cups Sushi Rice (page 211)

5 scallions, white and light green parts
only, cut into 2-inch lengths and julienned

Makes 8 rolls (48 pieces)

6. In a large nonstick skillet, heat the vegetable oil over high heat. Drain the chicken and stir-fry in batches until just done, about 2 minutes.

7. Have a small bowl of room-temperature water ready to facilitate filling the maki. If not using a bamboo mat for rolling, cut plastic-coated freezer paper 1 inch larger on all sides than the nori. Cut the nori sheets in half lengthwise and place a half sheet dull side up on the paper or a bamboo rolling mat with a short side nearest you. Dip your fingers in the water to prevent sticking and take a handful of the rice (about $^1/_3$ cup). Wetting your fingers as necessary, make a flat bar of rice (about 1 inch wide) on the sheet end nearest you, almost at its edge. Lay chicken pieces atop the rice, slightly overlapping. Place a row of scallion pieces over the chicken.

8. To roll the maki, hold the ingredients firmly in place with your fingertips and begin to roll, enclosing the filling. Continue to roll until the nori ends meet. The ends should just meet, overlapping slightly; the mat acts to form and compress the maki evenly, gliding over it as you roll. Gently but firmly press the mat or paper around the roll to round and tighten it. If not serving immediately, wrap the completed roll in plastic wrap. Repeat with the remaining ingredients to make 8 rolls.

9. When ready to serve, remove the plastic wrap, if necessary, and place the rolls seam side down on a cutting surface. Using a sharp thin-bladed knife, slice each roll crosswise into 6 equal pieces. If serving as a first course, drizzle the wasabi sauce on top; otherwise, serve the wasabi sauce as a dip.

Sesame Minted Meatballs

These delicious meatballs, made with ground turkey, mint, and sweet spices, are coated before baking with black and white sesame seeds. Served with Minted Apricot Sauce (page 220) or Tahini Sauce (page 230), they make a visually stunning and completely satisfying hors d'oeuvre. The sesame seeds ensure crispy meatballs without frying.

½ teaspoon olive oil

½ cup minced onion

1 teaspoon minced garlic

1 teaspoon dried mint, crumbled

½ teaspoon salt

¼ teaspoon ground allspice

Large pinch of ground cinnamon

1 pound ground turkey

1 cup fine fresh bread crumbs

1 large egg, lightly beaten,
plus 1 egg white

2 tablespoons finely chopped dried
apricots (about 6 halves)

Freshly ground black pepper

¼ cup black sesame seeds

¼ cup white sesame seeds

8-inch wooden skewers, for serving

Makes about 36

1. In a small nonstick skillet, heat the oil over low heat. Add the onion and garlic and cook, stirring, until softened, about 3 minutes.

2. Transfer the mixture to a medium bowl and stir in the mint, salt, allspice, and cinnamon. Add the turkey, bread crumbs, whole egg, and apricots. Combine well. Season to taste with the pepper.

3. Form the mixture into meatballs that are approximately 1 inch in diameter and place on a tray. Pour the black and white sesame seeds into small bowls, one for each. In another small bowl, beat the egg white until lightened. Dip each meatball in the egg white and coat half the meatballs with the black seeds, half with the white. Place on a cookie sheet. (You can prepare the meatballs up to this point 1 day in advance. Store them loosely covered in the refrigerator.)

4. Preheat the oven to 450°F. Bake the meatballs in the upper third of the oven until just cooked through, 8 to 10 minutes. Pass with a dip (see the headnote), and the skewers for serving.

Curried Chicken Kebabs

A curry-flavored mouthful is always welcome, as these zippy kebabs unfailingly prove. Each kebab consists of a single cube of chicken that has absorbed the flavors of curry, ginger, lemon, and mustard. The kebabs are broiled in a flash and make a perfect tidbit served with sweet, cool Honey-Banana Chutney (page 238) for dipping. You could also serve several of them per plate as a starter for an informal dinner.

Curry powders vary in flavor and spiciness. Shop around to find a blend you like.

MARINADE

1 tablespoon canola or olive oil

6 garlic cloves

One 1-inch piece fresh ginger, peeled

Juice of 2 lemons (about 6 tablespoons)

3 tablespoons Dijon mustard

2 teaspoons turmeric

1 teaspoon ground cumin

1 teaspoon curry powder

1½ pounds chicken cutlets, cut into 1½-inch cubes

Thirty-six 8-inch wooden skewers

Makes about 36

1. Add the canola oil, garlic, ginger, lemon juice, mustard, turmeric, cumin, and curry powder to a food processor and process to blend well. The mixture will be pastelike.

2. Place the chicken cubes in a medium bowl and spoon over the marinade. Turn to coat the chicken completely. Cover and refrigerate 2 to 3 hours.

3. Thirty minutes before cooking, soak the skewers in warm water to prevent their burning when the kebabs are broiled.

4. Make the kebabs, placing a single cube of chicken at one end of each skewer. Place in a long dish or pan.

5. Preheat the broiler. Arrange the kebabs in rows on a broiling tray with all the skewers facing in a single direction. To prevent its coloring during cooking, cover the wood with strips of aluminum foil.

6. Broil the kebabs about 4 minutes, turn, brush with the marinade, and broil until the chicken is just cooked through, 3 to 5 minutes. Serve immediately.

Bisteeya Triangles

Moroccan bisteeya is one of the world's great dishes. It consists of phyllo dough surrounding a mixture of shredded poultry, ground almonds, and spices. The "pie" is baked until golden, then sprinkled with cinnamon and confectioners' sugar, an unexpected ingredient that enhances the sweet spice and almond flavors. The result is spectacular.

This irresistible hors d'oeuvre version is easy to make once you get the hang of the phyllo folding. You can prepare these ahead and freeze them in plastic or foil containers with sheets of parchment or waxed paper between the layers. People think these are just another phyllo morsel until they taste them. Then they're amazed.

1 cup Chicken Stock (page 61), or good instant or low-sodium canned broth

¼ teaspoon turmeric

One ¾-inch piece fresh ginger, peeled and finely chopped

Small pinch or saffron threads or saffron powder

One 1½-inch cinnamon stick

1½ sprigs fresh coriander, plus ¼ cup chopped coriander leaves

¼ pound chicken from a cutlet, or the equivalent uncooked dark meat, cut into 1-inch pieces

2 eggs, well beaten

4 tablespoons coarsely ground toasted almonds

1 teaspoon confectioners' sugar, plus additional for dusting the triangles

1 teaspoon ground cinnamon

Salt and freshly ground black pepper

½ pound phyllo dough; defrosted (see note)

4 tablespoons canola or other light vegetable oil, warmed

Makes 60 triangles

1. In a small saucepan, combine the stock, turmeric, ginger, saffron, cinnamon stick, and coriander sprigs. Bring the liquid to the simmer and cook for 30 minutes. Add the chicken and poach gently until just done, 3 to 5 minutes. Discard the cinnamon stick and coriander sprigs. Remove the chicken with a slotted spoon and keep it warm.

2. Return the liquid to a simmer. Slowly pour in the eggs, stirring constantly, and cook until the eggs have congealed into a soft, curdlike mass, about 5 minutes (they will absorb the liquid). Do not let the eggs cook to dryness. Pour off any liquid that is not absorbed by the eggs.

3. In a food processor, chop the chicken until roughly minced. Allow it to cool.

4. In a small bowl, combine the nuts, sugar, and cinnamon. Add the chicken, the eggs, and the chopped coriander. Season to taste with the salt and pepper and mix well.

5. To make the triangles, using a ruler, slice the half-roll of phyllo through the plastic to make three 2-inch widths. Unroll one 2-inch roll and lay the strips flat on your work surface. Cover the strips with waxed paper to prevent drying.

6. One at a time, brush the bottom half of each of the strips lightly with the oil. Fold the uncoated half of the strip over the coated. Place about 1 teaspoon of the chicken filling in the bottom left corner of the strip. Fold the bottom left corner over the filling to meet the right edge of the strip, creating a triangle. Continue folding corner to corner along sides of the triangle (the action is like folding a flag) and place the completed triangle flap side down on your work surface. Repeat with the remaining strips. (The triangles can be frozen at this point; do not defrost them before baking.)

7. Preheat the oven to 400°F. Place the triangles on a baking sheet and brush lightly with the oil. Bake until golden, about 10 minutes. Cool slightly and dust lightly with the additional sugar.

Note: Phyllo dough is available in 1-pound boxes. For this recipe, cut the dough in half through the plastic and wrap and refrigerate or freeze one half for future use.

Lahma Bi Ajeen

Pizza doesn't belong entirely to Italy. The delicious Arabic-Sephardic pies known as lahma bi ajeen, *made traditionally with lamb, are a different take on the ever-popular snack. (Actually, pizza is believed to have evolved from Egyptian flat bread.)*

This lighter version is prepared with a ground turkey, tomato, and red pepper topping. It makes a perfect hors d'oeuvre or starter, depending on the size, or a great rolled "sandwich" with chopped lettuce. You can prebake the pies, undercooking them slightly, then finish them just before serving. When I'm in a hurry I use frozen mini-pizza dough (small untopped pizza shells) in place of the homemade dough.

DOUGH

1 package active dry yeast

Pinch of sugar

1½ cups warm water

3½ to 3¾ cups all-purpose flour, or more as needed

1 teaspoon salt

2 tablespoons olive oil, plus more for oiling the bowl

1. To prepare the dough, dissolve the yeast and sugar in ½ cup warm water. Place in a warm place until foamy, 5 to 10 minutes.

2. Flour a work surface. In a large mixing bowl, combine 3½ cups flour and the salt. Make a well in the center of the mixture and stir in 1 cup of warm water, the yeast mixture, and oil. Work the mixture in the bowl to form a rough ball and transfer it to the floured surface. Using your palm, push the dough away from you, gathering it and pushing it away again until it is smooth and elastic, about 8 minutes of kneading. Add more flour as needed to get the dough just past the sticky point.

3. Oil a bowl lightly, add the dough, and turn to coat all sides. Cover with a damp cloth and allow to rise until double in bulk, about 2 hours.

4. Meanwhile, prepare the topping. Add the oil to a large, heavy skillet and heat over medium heat until hot but not smoking. Add the turkey and cook, stirring, until it begins to brown, about 3 minutes. Break up any clumps as you work.

5. Add the onions, garlic, red pepper, tomato puree, tomatoes, sugar, allspice, lemon juice, salt, pepper, and red pepper flakes. Reduce the heat to low, and cook until all liquid has evaporated, about 10 minutes. Taste and adjust the seasonings.

2 tablespoons olive oil

1¼ pounds ground turkey

2 large onions, finely chopped

2 garlic cloves, minced

1 large red bell pepper, cored, seeded, and minced

3 tablespoons tomato puree

3 to 4 tomatoes, preferably peeled, seeded, and minced, or one 16-ounce can diced tomatoes, drained

1 teaspoon sugar

¾ teaspoon ground allspice

1 tablespoon fresh lemon juice

1 teaspoon salt

1 teaspoon cracked black peppercorns

½ teaspoon red pepper flakes

2 teaspoons cornmeal, for the pans

¼ cup chopped Italian parsley

½ cup toasted pine nuts

Makes eight 6- to 7-inch appetizers or thirty-six 1½- to 2-inch hors d'oeuvres

6. Lightly flour a work surface. Turn the dough out on to it, punch it down, and divide it into either 8 or 36 pieces. Roll each piece into a ball, cover, and let rest to rise again, 20 to 30 minutes. Preheat the oven to 400°F.

7. Using a lightly floured rolling pin, roll each ball into a circle 6 to 7 inches or $1\frac{1}{2}$ to 2 inches in diameter and $\frac{1}{16}$ inch thick. Press the edges to make a rim and spoon 1 to 2 tablespoons of the filling on each of the small circles, or $\frac{1}{8}$ of the topping on each of the large.

8. Sprinkle 2 large baking sheets with the cornmeal. Place the pies on the sheets and bake until just cooked through, 7 to 10 minutes. The pies should still be soft and light colored, almost white. Sprinkle with the parsley and pine nuts and serve.

Persian Brochettes with Apricots

Brochettes appear in almost every culture. It's easy to imagine their beginnings in available meat, a pointy stick, and fire. This Persian variation is considerably more evolved, and contrasts apricots and chicken delightfully.

The brochettes can be served as a starter or main dish. If cooking the brochettes for a meal, accompany them with basmati rice.

1 large onion, cut into chunks

½ cup fresh lemon juice

1 tablespoon paprika

4 garlic cloves, peeled

½ cup olive oil

3 tablespoons dried oregano

12 chicken thighs, boned and the meat of each cut into 3 chunks

36 small dried apricots

Salt and freshly ground black pepper

Eighteen 6-inch or four 12-inch wooden skewers

Makes 18 pieces as an appetizer, 4 pieces as a main dish

1. In a food processor, combine the onion, lemon juice, paprika, garlic, olive oil, and oregano. Process until pureed.

2. Transfer the mixture to a nonreactive medium bowl. Add the chicken and apricots and toss to coat well. Cover and refrigerate at least 6 hours or overnight.

3. At least 1 hour in advance, soak the skewers in water to prevent their burning during cooking.

4. Bring the chicken mixture to room temperature. Prepare a grill or preheat the broiler.

5. If making the brochettes for an appetizer, skewer the chicken and apricots on the skewers in this order: apricot, chicken, apricot, chicken. If serving as a main dish, continue to alternate apricots and chicken, filling the 4 skewers almost completely. If making appetizers, use strips of foil to cover the bare wood. This will prevent their coloring during cooking.

6. Season the brochettes to taste with the salt and pepper. Grill the brochettes over medium heat about 4 inches form the heat source or broil until the chicken is just cooked through, turning once, 6 to 8 minutes per side. Serve warm.

Vietnamese Spring Rolls with Two Dipping Sauces

Spring rolls—the delicate, rice paper-wrapped appetizers of Asian cooking—make fabulous hors d'oeuvres cut into bite-size pieces. They're elegant and don't fill you up.

This version has a filling made with shredded chicken (freshly prepared or leftover), romaine lettuce, herbs, and roasted peanuts; it's served with two dipping sauces: a tart-sweet Ponzu Sauce and a Vietnamese Dipping Sauce.

Note that the rolls can't be prepared more than three hours ahead or the rice paper will dry out, nor can they be refrigerated.

1 cup Chicken Stock (page 61), or good instant or low-sodium canned broth

2 tablespoons dry sherry

1 small chicken cutlet, or ½ cup leftover thinly shredded chicken

1 cup shredded romaine lettuce

⅓ cup fresh basil leaves, cut into thin strips

⅓ cup fresh mint leaves

1 medium cucumber, peeled, seeded, and cut into fine julienne

2 tablespoons chopped roasted peanuts

1 teaspoon brown rice vinegar

⅛ teaspoon chili powder

Four 12-inch sheets rice paper

Ponzu Dipping Sauce (page 42)

Vietnamese Dipping Sauce (page 234)

Makes 32 rolls

1. If using a chicken cutlet, in a small saucepan, combine the stock and sherry. Bring to a simmer over medium heat and add the chicken. Cook gently until just done, about 4 minutes. Remove the breast, cool, and shred very finely. Reserve.

2. Place the lettuce, basil, mint, cucumber, and peanuts in small separate bowls and arrange these on your work surface. In a small bowl, toss together the chicken, vinegar, and chili powder and place with the other bowls. Fill a wide, shallow bowl or baking dish large enough for soaking the rice paper with warm water. Place it nearby.

3. Moisten a clean linen kitchen towel with water and spread it on your work surface. Soak a sheet of the rice paper in the water until pliable, about 20 seconds, then place it on the towel. Place one-quarter of the lettuce evenly along the near edge of the rice paper. Top with ¼ of the basil, mint, cucumber, chicken, and peanuts, in that order. Roll the paper gently but firmly, tucking in the sides as you work, to make a roll about 1½ inches in diameter. Work quickly to keep the paper from drying out. Repeat with the remaining rice paper and fillings. Cover the completed rolls with plastic wrap or a damp paper towel until ready to serve.

4. To serve the rolls, cut each into 8 pieces. Pass with the sauces for dipping.

Baked Turkey Kibbe

Call them what you will—kibbe, kibbah, kubba, or kofte (their Israeli, Lebanese, Palestinian, and Turkish names, respectively)—these mouthfuls are one of the delights of Middle Eastern cooking. Traditionally about three inches long and football-shaped, kibbe are made from a paste of meat and bulgur and formed using dexterous hand movements. Stuffed sometimes with fragrant fillings, they're fried, baked, or steamed—the variations are almost endless.

The objective when making kibbe is to produce moist, tender yet firm tidbits. This baked version is lighter than the more traditional fried variation and easier to prepare. (You can make patties with the kibbe mixture, if you like, and cook them in a grill pan.) The kibbe can also be prepared ahead, frozen, and baked without defrosting, in which case add 2 minutes to the cooking time.

½ cup very fine bulgur wheat

2 pounds ground turkey meat, combined light and dark (ask your butcher to do this)

2 tablespoons Turkish Spice (see page 180)

½ teaspoon ground allspice

½ cup finely minced onion

3 tablespoons olive oil

⅛ teaspoon Aleppo pepper (optional)

2 tablespoons flour

1 teaspoon salt

½ cup packed fresh mint leaves

Grilled Red Pepper Sauce (page 231)

Makes about 55 pieces or 8 patties

1. Place the bulgur in a fine sieve and wash under running water. Set aside to drain.

2. Place the turkey in a food processor and process to make a paste. Add the bulgur, Turkish spice, allspice, onion, olive oil, pepper (if using), flour, salt, and mint. Pulse to break up the turkey mass, stopping to scrape down the sides of the work bowl as necessary, then process to create a very smooth paste, about 3 minutes. Scrape the paste into a bowl, cover, and chill at least 2 hours (the mixture must be cold to shape easily).

3. Preheat the oven to 450°F. Oil a 9 x 13 x 2-inch baking dish.

4. Moisten your fingers with cold water and shape bits of the chilled mixture into 1½-inch football-like ovals. Alternatively, make 8 patties no more than ⅔ inch thick. Place each kibbe in the baking dish as you make them or freeze, covered, on a tray.

5. Bake the kibbe about 5 minutes, turn, and bake 5 minutes more. Run the kibbe under the broiler to brown the tops, 3 to 4 minutes. To cook the patties, lightly coat a grill pan with 1 tablespoon of oil (or spray with vegetable spray), heat to hot, and grill the patties 5 minutes per side, or bake 3 to 5 minutes per side and broil to brown. Serve with the Grilled Red Pepper Sauce.

Citrus Saté with Spicy Papaya Mustard Sauce

Satés are so easy to do, and deliver so much flavor, that no cook should be without a repertoire of many kinds. Here's a special version featuring a tart citrus marinade made with grated lime peel. As you'll be using the peel, do try to get unsprayed limes, grown without any chemicals.

If you grill these satés outdoors, try adding fruitwood chips, like those of applewood, to the embers. The Spicy Papaya Mustard Sauce, an all-around condiment, is a perfect match for the tart, smoky satés.

1 to 1¼ pounds chicken cutlets or
1 pound saved chicken tenders
(chicken tenderloins), tendons removed

2 garlic cloves, pressed

¼ cup fresh grapefruit juice

¼ cup fresh orange juice

1 tablespoon extra-virgin olive oil

Pinch of kosher salt

Coarsely ground black pepper

Finely grated peel of ½ lime

Spicy Papaya Mustard Sauce (page 227)

16 wooden skewers

Makes 16 pieces

1. Cut the cutlets, if using, into ten ¹/₂-inch wide strips.

2. In a medium bowl, combine the garlic, grapefruit and orange juices, olive oil, and salt. Season to taste with the pepper and whisk together. Stir in the lime peel, add the chicken, and toss. Cover and marinate, refrigerated, for 1 to 3 hours.

3. At least an hour in advance, soak the skewers in water to prevent their burning during cooking.

4. Prepare a grill or preheat the broiler.

5. Thread 1 strip or tender onto each skewer. For even cooking, keep the chicken elongated. Cover the bare wood of the skewers with foil strips to prevent their coloring. If grilling, place the chicken on a grilling screen or rack and grill over medium heat about 4 inches from the heat source or broil, turning once, until just cooked through, 2 to 3 minutes per side. Serve with the sauce.

Yakatori

This savory skewered chicken began, of all places, in Milan. Besides being a fashion center, Milan is a great dining city. Visiting a new Japanese restaurant there, I discovered the model for these fabulous, mustardy yakatori, which are baby-simple to prepare.

For this version, scallion pieces are skewered with the chicken and make a fine, slightly sweet accompaniment to the grilled meat. These are really irresistible.

2 tablespoons grainy mustard

1 teaspoon dark sesame oil

1 teaspoon soy sauce

1 teaspoon honey or sugar

1 pound chicken cutlets, cut into 1-inch cubes

12 scallions, root ends trimmed and cut to leave only 1 inch of the green parts

1 teaspoon light vegetable oil

Sixteen 8-inch wooden skewers

Makes 16 pieces

1. A least 1 hour in advance, soak the skewers in water to prevent their burning during cooking.

2. In a nonreactive medium bowl, combine the mustard, sesame oil, soy sauce, honey, and chicken. Mix well, cover, and allow to marinate refrigerated, about 30 minutes.

3. Cut the scallions into 2-inch pieces. In a medium bowl, combine the scallions and the vegetable oil and toss. Thread 3 scallion pieces and 2 chicken pieces per skewer, starting and ending with scallion.

4. Prepare a grill or preheat the broiler. Using strips of foil, cover the bare wood of the skewers to prevent their coloring during cooking.

5. Grill the yakatori over medium heat about 4 inches from the heat source or broil, turning once, until the chicken is cooked through and the scallions lightly charred, about 3 minutes per side. Serve warm.

3. Soups–
Light and
Substantial

What is it about chicken soup—
about soup itself—
that makes it so important?

Soup is a basic, deeply comforting food, and chicken soup is the most fundamental of all soups in most cultures. Every cook needs a great chicken soup in his or her repertoire—see page 63—but this beloved staple is only the beginning. There are rich whole-meal soups and delicate small-cup broths, suave purees and soups that stimulate the appetite for coming food. There are soups for every season. Once you think of soups as year-round basics, you expand your menu making horizons.

In spring, for example, when the world awakens, I make Asparagus-Corn Soup. It's an elegant broth that celebrates the season's first tender asparagus, and a great company dish or simple lunch. When the days are warmer but the nights still cool, Indonesian Basil Coconut Soup is a light but bracing starter. Once the heat is on, Chilled Yellow Pepper Soup makes a lovely first-course delicacy, the perfect prelude to simple grilled food. Curried Squash and Mushroom Soup is an ideal fall soup and a great opening to the season's first roast chicken. And come winter, whole-meal soups like Chicken Goulash Soup, a sturdy brew brimming with chicken, warm heart and soul. All a soup like this needs to satisfy the heartiest appetites is some crusty bread and a crisp salad.

Whatever the soup, its foundation is almost always good chicken stock. I encourage you to make your own. Gather ingredients "as you go," saving vegetable and poultry trimmings you might otherwise discard. Store chicken parts, necks, giblets, and bones in the freezer; keep leek tops or carrot peelings, parsley, dill, or other herbs in plastic bags and freeze them, too. A pantry like this will make the creation of a richly flavored stock a breeze, using either the traditional method or the super-efficient slow cooker (see page 62). And think soup before scrapping poultry leftovers, no matter how humble. That Thanksgiving turkey carcass plus lentils or split peas can yield a delicious, full-flavored soup; leftover diced roast chicken combined with spinach, white beans, and stock can also produce great soup. You get the idea. (See "The Next Day," page 262, for delicious soups made with cooked and stored poultry.)

Soups fits into busy lives in other ways. Most soups freeze well and can be prepared ahead. Defrost frozen soups beforehand and you've got a great meal in minutes; just add embellishments. I enjoy serving the Tomato Rice Chowder (page 261), for example, with corn bread and a small arugula salad. The Velvet Carrot Soup is perfect served with stored herb bread. It's also one of those soups that work equally well hot or a little below room temperature. (I don't think any soup should be served refrigerator-icy.)

And bring soup with you—there's nothing better than a thermos of tart, chilled soup as part of a picnic meal, or a hot hearty soup served in mugs at a sports event or other cold-weather outing. Indoors, serve soups from a large tureen or an attractive soup pot. Steaming soup served into plates passed hand to hand on Friday nights in winter or on other occasions nourishes us and brings us closer. It cheers and comforts us as no other food can.

Chicken Stock

A good stock makes a world of difference to your cooking. By good *I mean stock that is light but fully flavored, not too sweet, and has a nice amber color. Like this one.*

Stock is simple to make. It cooks while you go about your business and freezes perfectly. I use different size containers for freezing this stock—1 cup, 4 cup, and so on—so defrosting and cooking with it is really convenient. You can add herbs such as thyme, chives, or rosemary to the cooking stock, but use a light hand and keep in mind the dishes the stock will flavor—the seasonings of the stock shouldn't compete with them. By the way, you'll notice that I don't add salt to the stock. That increases its versatility.

10 pounds chicken parts and/or bones, necks, wings, reserved trimmings

4 large onions, unpeeled and quartered

6 large carrots, scrubbed and cut into 2-inch pieces

5 celery stalks with tops

4 leek tops, or 2 whole leeks, well washed and cut into 2-inch lengths

1 bunch Italian parsley

1 tablespoon black peppercorns

1 to 2 sprigs fresh thyme, or ½ teaspoon dried

2 bay leaves

2 to 3 garlic cloves (optional)

1 bunch dill (optional)

Makes about 6 quarts

1. Rinse the chicken parts under cold running water. Remove excess fat.

2. Place the chicken parts in a large pot. Add cold water to cover and bring to a boil. Reduce the heat to a simmer and using a skimmer, remove surface scum as it forms.

3. Simmer for 1 hour. Add the onions, carrots, celery, leeks, parsley, peppercorns, thyme, bay leaves, garlic, and dill. Simmer, uncovered, until the stock is richly flavored, about 1 hour more. (For an even richer stock, boil it gently until it's reduced by half.)

4. Allow the stock to cool. Strain the stock and discard the solids. For a very clear stock, first line the strainer with cheesecloth. Chill the stock and, using a large spoon, remove the solidified fat. If using the stock immediately, skim off the fat with a spoon or blot it with paper towels. Use the stock within 2 days or freeze.

No-Work Chicken Stock

A slow cooker makes wonderful, very full-flavored stock. It's incredibly efficient: you put all those chicken trimmings, vegetable stems, tops, and scrapings you've wisely saved into it, add water, and turn on the pot. (You could use poultry and vegetables bought to make the stock, but the point of this method is to utilize the scraps that accumulate as you cook.) About twelve hours later, without any supervision on your part, you've got great stock. Following this method, there's minimal liquid loss due to evaporation—just rich flavor.

Feel free to add whatever vegetable combinations you like (suggestions are below), with the exception of strong-flavored types like cabbage and broccoli. Carrots add sweetness—they should be present, but not in excess. Celery is great. Use as many or as few poultry trimmings as you have (taking into account that water must cover the ingredients by 1/4 inch), including frozen "scraps." You'll end up with a delicious stock with the absolute minimum of work.

Poultry parts and/or bones, wing tips, necks, reserved trimmings

Vegetable trimmings including leek tops, zucchini ends, onion and tomato skins, mushroom stems, celery ends and leaves, parsnip ends, scallion tops, celeriac peel, herb stems

Parsley and/or dill

10 black peppercorns

Makes about 3 quarts

1. Fill a 4-quart slow cooker with the poultry and vegetables. Add the parsley and peppercorns.

2. Add 3 quarts water. The water should come to within 1/4 inch of the pot rim, and cover all of the ingredients. Cover, set the pot on low, and cook for 10 to 12 hours.

3. Turn off the pot and allow to cool. Strain the stock and discard the solids. Use or freeze the stock in containers.

Golden Chicken Soup

This is the last chicken soup recipe you'll ever need. Deeply chickeny and flavored with leeks, root vegetables, parsley, and dill, it's glorious as is or as the basis for other soups (see Tante Genia's Chicken Kneidlach Soup, page 68, for example). Used in place of stock, it adds incredible richness and flavor to your cooking.

This soup is liquid gold in your kitchen, so make plenty. I keep quarts of it in plastic containers in my freezer and add more fresh dill and parsley when heating it to freshen its flavor. For Friday nights, I dress the soup up with matzo balls; I also add egg noodles, kreplach, kasha varnishkes, or wontons on other occasions. Sometimes I make the soup with a bouquet garni of fresh herbs—rosemary, thyme, tarragon, or coriander. However you fix it, it's always welcome, always delicious.

5 pounds chicken, whole parts cut into eighths, backs, wings, necks, with or without skin

3 leeks, trimmed, white parts only, halved (save the greens for stock)

1 large or 2 small parsnips, scrubbed

1 bunch fresh dill, well washed

1 bunch Italian parsley

8 black peppercorns

6 medium carrots, scrubbed, plus 4 small, scrubbed and cut into julienne (about 1 cup)

4 celery stalks with tops

One 2-inch chunk of celery root, scrubbed (optional)

Salt

Makes about 3 quarts, 6 to 8 servings

1. Rinse the chicken in cold water. Remove excess fat.

2. Place the chicken in a large soup pot and add water to cover (about 20 cups). Bring to a boil and reduce the heat to a simmer. Use a skimmer to remove surface scum as it forms. Cook until well flavored, about 30 minutes.

3. Add the leeks, parsnip, dill, parsley, peppercorns, whole carrots, celery, and celery root, if using. Simmer until the chicken has begun to fall from the bones and the vegetables are very soft, about 1 hour.

4. Using a slotted spoon, remove the chicken and reserve for other uses. Strain the soup to remove the herbs and vegetables and discard. For a very clear soup, first line the strainer with cheesecloth. Set aside to cool.

5. When the soup has cooled, remove the surface fat. To do this easily, chill the soup and remove the congealed fat with a tablespoon. Heat the soup gently. Add the julienned carrots and simmer until crisp-tender, 5 to 7 minutes. Adjust the seasonings and serve.

Moroccan Chicken and Lentil Soup

This is my lightened version of the Moroccan soup called harira, *served to end Ramadan. Traditional harira is peppery and lemon-flavored, rich with lentils and lamb. I've kept the lentils and lemon—a marriage made in heaven—but substituted chicken for the lamb to make the dish delicate. I've also included chickpeas for their subtle texture.*

Don't be put off by the lengthy list of ingredients—everything goes together fast.

1 tablespoon plus 1 teaspoon canola or light olive oil

3 garlic cloves, minced

¾ cup finely chopped onion

1 cup finely chopped celery, including leaves

½ cup parsley leaves, finely chopped

2 teaspoons turmeric

2 teaspoons ground cinnamon

¾ teaspoon ground ginger

1½ teaspoons freshly ground black pepper

½ teaspoon saffron threads

3½ cups peeled, seeded, and fine chopped tomatoes or diced canned tomatoes, drained

¾ cup lentils

2 quarts Chicken Stock (page 61), or good instant or low-sodium canned broth

½ teaspoon salt

1 pound chicken cutlets, cut into ½-inch cubes

Juice of 2 lemons

1. In a large soup pot, heat 1 tablespoon of the oil over medium heat. Add the garlic, onion, and celery and sauté until softened, about 5 minutes. Add the parsley, stir, and add the turmeric, cinnamon, ginger, pepper, and saffron. Sauté 2 minutes more. Add the tomatoes, stir, and cook until soft, about 15 minutes.

2. Rinse the lentils well under cold running water and add them to the pot. Add the stock and bring to a boil. Add the salt, lower the heat, and simmer about $1^{1}/_{2}$ hours.

3. Meanwhile, in a nonstick skillet, heat the remaining teaspoon of oil over medium-high heat. Sauté the chicken until it loses its raw look, about 3 minutes. Add half the lemon juice to the pan, scraping up the browned bits from the skillet.

4. Add the pearl onions and chickpeas and simmer 30 minutes longer.

5. Meanwhile, in a separate pot of boiling water, cook the noodles until al dente. Drain and set aside.

16 small pearl onions, peeled

One 16-ounce can chickpeas, rinsed and
drained

½ pound thin egg noodles

½ lemon, cut into 8 slices

**Makes about 4 quarts,
8 servings**

6. Add the remaining lemon juice to the soup. Taste and correct the seasonings. To serve, spoon some noodles into each soup dish, ladle the soup over, and garnish each portion with a lemon slice.

Chicken Goulash Soup

This stewlike soup was inspired by my Hungarian grandmother's wonderful goulash and chicken paprikash. Rich with chicken and vegetables, and touched with caraway, it's almost a meal in itself. Just add a salad and some good crusty bread for a perfect dinner.

The chicken is sautéed, then added to the soup to finish cooking. Be sure not to overcook it at either step.

2 tablespoons plus 1 teaspoon canola or other light vegetable oil

6 garlic cloves, minced

3 medium onions, chopped

½ cup chopped celery

1½ cups green bell peppers cut into ½-inch cubes

½ cup chopped fresh dill

1 teaspoon hot paprika or 2 teaspoons sweet

½ teaspoon crushed caraway seeds

¼ teaspoon cayenne pepper

1½ cups chopped fresh tomatoes or canned diced tomatoes, drained

2 cups Chicken Stock (page 61), or good instant or low-sodium canned broth

Salt and freshly ground black pepper

1 pound potatoes, washed and cut into ½-inch cubes

1 pound chicken cutlets, cut into ½-inch cubes

Juice of ½ lemon

Makes about 3 quarts, 6 servings

1. In a soup pot, heat the 2 tablespoons of oil over medium heat. Add the garlic, onions, celery, green peppers, and dill. Cook until the vegetables have softened, about 3 minutes. Stir in the paprika, caraway seeds, and cayenne.

2. Add the tomatoes and stock and season to taste with salt and pepper. Bring to a boil, reduce the heat to low, cover, and cook about 1 hour. Add the potatoes and simmer until almost cooked through, about 10 minutes.

3. In a large nonstick skillet, heat the teaspoon of oil over medium-high heat. Add the chicken pieces and stir-fry just to brown, about 4 minutes. Do not let the chicken cook through.

4. Add the lemon juice to the pan, scraping up the browned bits. Scrape the contents of the pan into the soup pot. Cook until the chicken is just done, about 5 more minutes, and serve.

Asparagus-Corn Chicken Soup

I'm always on the lookout for light, elegant soups with well-defined flavors. This one, which celebrates the tastes of fresh corn and asparagus, fills the bill perfectly. It also features a special technique—grating frozen chicken breasts to produce a delicate, delicious soup addition.

Hot or at room temperature, this makes a fabulous first course or luncheon soup.

6 ounces chicken cutlets, pounded to ¼-inch thickness

1 tablespoon olive oil

3 large leeks, white parts only, well washed and chopped, tops washed and reserved

4 medium ears fresh corn, kernels removed, cobs reserved

1 pound asparagus, trimmed and sliced diagonally into ¼-inch pieces (about 2 cups), trimmings reserved

1 bay leaf

Small bunch fresh coriander, stems reserved, leaves chopped

10 cups Chicken Stock (page 61), or good instant or low-sodium canned broth

3 egg whites

Salt and freshly ground black pepper

Makes about 4 quarts, 6 to 8 servings

1. One to 2 hours before serving (or as much as a day ahead), roll the chicken cutlets into a log or 2 logs, each ½ inch in diameter (or a diameter your food processor feed tube will accommodate). Wrap the log(s) in plastic film or foil and freeze.

2. In a large skillet, heat the olive oil over medium heat. Add the chopped leeks and sauté until soft and translucent, about 4 minutes. Remove from the heat and set aside.

3. In a large stockpot, combine the leek tops, corn cobs, asparagus trimmings, bay leaf, coriander stems, and stock. Bring to a boil, reduce the heat, and simmer over low heat 30 minutes. Cool, strain, and return the stock to the pot. Add the sautéed leeks and the corn kernels. Return to the simmer and cook gently 5 minutes.

4. Meanwhile, grate the chicken using a food processor with a grating disc. Push the log(s) through the feed tube. Spoon and scrape the grated chicken into the soup. Work quickly to ensure that the chicken does not defrost before adding it or it will clump. Stir to combine and distribute the noodlelike chicken pieces. Add the asparagus and simmer until just done, about 5 minutes.

5. In a small bowl, whisk the egg whites with 4 tablespoons of water. Drizzle the mixture into the simmering soup, stirring continuously. Cook just until the egg whites are opaque, about 3 minutes. Add the chopped coriander, season to taste with the salt and pepper, and serve.

Tante Genia's
Chicken Kneidlach Soup

My friend Sylvia's Tante (aunt) Genia is a terrific Eastern European cook. Her chicken kneidlach soup—chicken soup with chicken matzo balls—is unique. The kneidlach are prepared mostly with ground chicken, which makes them more like French quenelles, tasty and light. Crisp green snow peas and fresh spinach add delicate vegetable taste and texture. The soup is still the deeply satisfying dish we all love—perfect for Friday nights—but now it's modern and elegant.

Use a large pot for preparing the kneidlach—they expand as they cook. For an ideal dinner, serve the soup with freshly baked challah.

KNEIDLACH

2 pounds ground chicken

4 egg whites and 2 yolks (save the remaining yolks for another use)

¼ cup matzo meal

1 tablespoon cold water

1 tablespoon sugar

Salt and white pepper

SOUP

1 large onion, peeled and quartered

3 medium carrots, peeled and cut into 2-inch pieces

1 bunch parsley, washed and tied with kitchen twine

12 ounces dried or fresh udon noodles, or other dried or fresh flat noodles or pasta, like linguine (see Note)

3 quarts Golden Chicken Soup (page 63) or other rich chicken soup, or Chicken Stock (page 61)

1. To make the kneidlach, in a large bowl, combine the ground chicken, egg whites and yolks, matzo meal, cold water, and 1 teaspoon of the sugar. Season to taste with salt and pepper. Chill, covered, for 15 minutes.

2. Fill a large pot with 8 quarts of water. Add the onion, carrots, parsley, and the remaining 2 teaspoons sugar and bring to a boil.

3. Wet your hands with water. Form the kneidlach mixture into thirty-six $1^1/_2$-inch balls and drop into the boiling water. Half-cover the pot and simmer until tender-firm, about 45 minutes. Turn off the heat.

4. With a slotted spoon, remove the kneidlach to a dish, cover, and keep warm. Remove the onion, parsley, and carrots from the water and discard. Return the liquid to the boil. Add the noodles and cook according to packaged directions until al dente. Drain and set aside, covered to keep warm.

1 medium carrot, scrubbed and julienned

1 parsnip, scrubbed and julienned

1 celery stalk, julienned

⅓ pound snow peas, trimmed

½ cup sliced scallions, green and white parts

4 cups washed and torn spinach leaves

2 tablespoons chopped dill

Salt and freshly ground black pepper

Makes about 4 quarts, 6 servings

5. Put the chicken soup in a pot. Bring to a simmer and add the julienned carrot, parsnip, and celery. Cook 3 minutes and add the snow peas. Cook 2 minutes and add the scallions, spinach, and dill. Stir and turn off the heat.

6. Put the kneidlach, soup, and noodles in a large tureen. Season to taste with salt and pepper. Divide the noodles, kneidlach, vegetables, and soup among 6 very large soup bowls and serve.

Note: If using fresh udon, see page 19.

Mediterranean Lemon Soup

A relative of the tantalizing Greek lemon soup called avgolemono, *this refreshing soup is tangy with lemon and features fresh mint. It is said that in Salonika, the ancient Sephardic city (now Thessalonika), this soup was served to break the Yom Kippur fast. In Egypt, it was served preceding the fast! In any case, it was and is a popular Sephardic specialty.*

It's also made in minutes. Serve it cold with a garnish of freshly snipped chives or hot with orzo or rice added to it. The addition of wispy egg white strands gives the soup a velvety texture and delicate body.

1 teaspoon vegetable or olive oil

2 medium onions, finely chopped
(about 1 cup)

Freshly ground black pepper

¼ cup fresh lemon juice

3 cups Golden Chicken Soup (page 63) or
other rich chicken soup, or Chicken Stock
(page 61)

1 large carrot, peeled and finely chopped

3 egg whites, lightly beaten,
at room temperature

1 tablespoon chopped fresh dill or mint

½ cup finely chopped Italian parsley

Salt

1 cup cooked orzo (optional)

1 tablespoon snipped fresh chives

**Makes about 1½ quarts,
4 servings**

1. In a medium saucepan, heat the oil over medium-low heat. Add the onions and sauté until soft and translucent, about 5 minutes. Season to taste with the pepper. Add the lemon juice, soup, and carrot. Bring to a gentle boil.

2. Drizzle the egg whites slowly into the soup, stirring continuously. The whites will ribbon and become noodlelike. Add the dill and parsley and remove immediately from the heat. Season to taste with the salt.

3. If serving the soup warm, add the cooked orzo to soup plates and ladle the soup over. If serving cold, allow the soup to cool to room temperature and chill. Snip chives on top of each portion and serve.

Chinese Mushroom Soup

If you're looking for a light, foolproof, and unusual starter that will please everyone, choose this soup. It combines the smoky flavor of black mushrooms with milder white mushrooms, ginger, and garlic. I sometimes serve this following Shiitake Potstickers with Ponzu Dipping Sauce (page 42).

1 ounce dried black mushrooms

2 shallots, peeled

6 scallions, trimmed, white parts reserved, green parts minced for garnish

One 1-inch piece fresh ginger, peeled

1 garlic clove

2 teaspoons peanut or canola oil

½ pound white mushrooms, thinly sliced

2 teaspoons cornstarch or kudzu

1 to 2 tablespoons plus 1 cup Chicken Stock (page 61), or good instant or low-sodium canned broth

2 tablespoons tamari or soy sauce

¼ cup dry sherry

1 teaspoon sugar

2 tablespoons brown rice vinegar

Freshly ground black pepper

Dark sesame oil

Makes about 1½ quarts, 4 servings

1. Bring 3 cups of water to a boil. Meanwhile, rinse the dried mushrooms and place them in a medium bowl. Add the boiling water and soak until mushrooms are soft, about 30 minutes.

2. Remove the mushrooms and set aside, squeezing all the liquid into the bowl. Strain the soaking liquid through cheesecloth and save. Rinse the mushrooms thoroughly, squeeze again, and save any liquid, adding it to the soaking liquid.

3. Remove and discard the mushroom stems. Slice the caps thinly and set aside.

4. Using a food processor, chop together the shallots, scallion whites, ginger, and garlic.

5. Heat the oil in a large, nonstick saucepan or deep skillet over medium-high heat. Add the chopped mixture and sauté quickly until slightly softened, about 3 minutes. Add the fresh white mushrooms and sauté until slightly softened, about 2 minutes. Meanwhile, in a small bowl, combine the cornstarch or kudzu with the 1 to 2 tablespoons stock and stir to dissolve. (If using kudzu, crush any lumps with the back of a spoon before adding the stock.) Add the starch mixture, tamari sauce, sherry, remaining 1 cup stock, sugar, vinegar, soaked black mushrooms, and the reserved soaking liquid to the white mushrooms. Season to taste with the pepper. Cover and simmer until the flavors are blended, about 15 minutes.

6. Pour the soup into a tureen or individual plates. Garnish with the scallion greens and a drizzle of sesame oil.

Chicken, Corn, and Potato Chowder

This great recipe is from my cooking friend Levana Kirshenbaum. It celebrates the simple but profound pleasures of corn, potatoes, and leeks. As you may have noticed, leeks—once called the asparagus of the poor, are among my favorite vegetables in the onion family. As a base for this simple, hearty chowder, they add earthy, piquant goodness.

This elegant, easily made dish happily accommodates leftover chicken or corn.

2 tablespoons olive oil

1 medium onion, finely chopped

3 leeks, white parts only, well washed and sliced ¼ inch thick

2 tablespoons flour

6 cups Chicken Stock (page 61), or good instant or low-sodium broth

½ cup dry white wine

2 medium potatoes, peeled and cut into ¼-inch dice

2 cups cooked chicken, cut into ½-inch cubes

2 pinches of saffron threads

Salt and freshly ground black pepper

1 cup fresh or frozen corn kernels, defrosted

Pinch of ground nutmeg

Makes about 3 quarts, 6 servings

1. In a large saucepan, heat the olive oil over medium-high heat. Add the onion and leeks and sauté until translucent, about 4 minutes.

2. Turn the heat to low. Add the flour and cook, stirring, to make a light roux, about 2 minutes. Do not allow the flour to color.

3. Slowly add the stock. Increase the heat to high and cook, stirring, until the stock is thickened. It should have a lightly creamy consistency. If it is too thick, add more stock; if too thin, cook down gently.

4. Add the wine, potatoes, chicken, and saffron. Season to taste with the salt and pepper. Reduce the heat to medium and cook until the potatoes are tender, 15 to 20 minutes. Add the frozen defrosted or fresh corn, and cook to heat through, 2 to 3 minutes. Thin the soup with stock if it seems too thick.

5. Add the nutmeg, adjust the seasonings, and serve.

Velvet Carrot Soup

Carrots have a seductively sweet flavor. Most people consider them a flavoring ingredient primarily, but allowed to take center stage, they really shine. They're at their best in this velvety soup, which salutes their sweet, golden goodness. This is elegant enough for your fanciest party, or serve it for Sunday supper, with a green salad and crusty bread.

3 large onions, peeled and quartered

5 medium carrots, peeled

3 tablespoons canola or other vegetable oil

1 teaspoon dried thyme

10 cups Chicken Stock (page 61), or good instant or low-sodium canned broth

¾ cup white rice

½ bunch Italian parsley, stems removed

Juice of ½ lemon (optional)

Salt and freshly ground black pepper

Makes about 3 quarts, 8 servings

1. Using a food processor, chop the onions finely. Remove and set aside. Coarsely chop the carrots.

2. In a large, heavy-bottomed skillet or Dutch oven, heat the oil over medium heat. Add the onions and sauté until golden, about 20 minutes. Add the carrots and the thyme, reduce the heat, and sauté until the carrots are soft, about 15 minutes.

3. Add the stock and rice and allow to simmer slowly until the rice is very tender, about 40 minutes. Remove the pan from the heat.

4. In a blender or food processor, puree the stock-vegetable mixture in batches. Before pureeing the last batch, add the parsley. Puree and add the lemon juice, if using. Season to taste with the salt and pepper. Heat gently before serving.

Canton Dumpling and Snow Pea Soup

Light-as-air chicken and turkey dumplings, snow peas, and cellophane noodles make this soup a joy of contrasting textures. It could be offered as a tempting first course, but you could also serve it as a family-style main dish.

The dumplings are easily made—the food processor does most of the work. They cook quickly in the soup, as do the snow peas and noodles. Everything happens in one pot so not a drop of flavor is lost.

DUMPLINGS

One 1¼-inch piece fresh ginger, peeled

2 medium scallions, trimmed and cut into 1-inch pieces

5½ ounces smoked turkey breast, cut into 1-inch cubes

1 pound chicken cutlets, cut into 1-inch cubes

2 tablespoons margarine, chilled

1 egg white, lightly beaten

2 tablespoons Chinese rice wine or dry sherry

1 teaspoon dark sesame oil

2 tablespoons cornstarch

¼ teaspoon freshly ground white pepper

1. To make the dumplings, drop the ginger through the feed tube of a food processor with the motor running. Process until finely chopped, about 10 seconds. Reserve.

2. Process the scallions until finely chopped, about 5 seconds. Reserve. Pulse the turkey until finely chopped, about 15 seconds and reserve. Process the chicken cutlets until pureed, about $1^1/_2$ minutes. Do not remove.

3. Add the turkey and margarine to the chicken and pulse 8 times to combine. Add the egg white, rice wine, sesame oil, reserved ginger, 2 teaspoons of the reserved scallions, and the cornstarch. Add the white pepper and pulse 6 to 8 times to combine. Transfer the mixture to a large bowl, cover, and chill until firm, 30 to 45 minutes.

4. Make the dumplings using about 1 tablespoon of the mixture for each. Form into 1-inch balls.

5. To make the soup, in a large soup pot, bring the chicken soup and rice wine to a boil and season to taste with the salt. Add the chicken dumplings gradually and simmer until the dumplings come to the surface, 5 to 7 minutes.

SOUP

6 cups Golden Chicken Soup (page 63), strained, or other rich strained chicken soup, or Chicken Stock (page 61)

¼ cup Chinese rice wine or dry sherry

Salt

1 teaspoon cornstarch mixed with ¼ cup water

6 ounces fresh snow peas, trimmed and strings removed

2 ounces cellophane noodles, or Japanese bi-fun noodles, softened in hot water for 10 minutes and drained

1 teaspoon dark sesame oil

Makes about 3 quarts, 4 to 6 servings

6. Stir in the cornstarch mixture and allow the soup to thicken lightly. Add the snow peas, noodles, and sesame oil and cook until the snow peas are tender-crisp, about 10 seconds. Remove from the heat.

7. Divide the dumplings and soup among 6 bowls, garnish with the remaining scallions, and serve.

Thai Anise Soup with Rice Noodles

Salty, sweet, sour, hot, and spicy—these are the "flavors" of Thai cookery. This marvelous soup, based on a traditional recipe, contains just about every one. Replete with rice noodles and featuring the flavor of star anise, it's appropriately tongue-tingling; it's also easy to make. Mint or basil adds an unexpected note of freshness, as does the lime wedge accompaniment. You must try this one.

One 2-inch piece fresh ginger

5 cups strained Golden Chicken Soup (page 63) or other rich strained chicken soup, or Chicken Stock (page 61)

4 star anise

One 2-inch cinnamon stick

2 medium onions, chopped

4 tablespoons cider vinegar

2 tablespoons peanut or canola oil

8 shallots, sliced thinly

1 pound chicken cutlets, cut into ⅛-inch slices

1 pound fresh rice noodles or ½ pound dried

2 scallions, green and white parts, very thinly sliced

4 small fresh Thai red chilies (about 1 inch long each) or 2 jalapeños, seeded and finely sliced

4 tablespoons fresh coriander leaves (cilantro)

40 mint leaves or 20 small basil leaves

2 limes, quartered lengthwise

Makes about 2 quarts, 4 servings

1. Peel the ginger and julienne it finely.

2. In a large saucepan, combine the soup with the ginger, star anise, cinnamon, onions, and vinegar. Bring to a boil, reduce the heat, and simmer, covered, 10 minutes. Strain and discard the solids.

3. Meanwhile, in a small skillet over high heat, heat the peanut oil. Add the shallots and sauté, stirring, until crispy-brown, about 10 minutes. Drain on paper toweling. Reserve.

4. Return the stock to the saucepan and bring to a simmer. Add the chicken and simmer until just cooked, about 5 minutes. Meanwhile, bring about 1 quart of water to a boil. Place the fresh noodles in a heatproof bowl and cover with the water. Let stand until cooked, about 5 minutes. Alternatively, add dried noodles to boiling water, turn off the heat, and allow the noodles to soak until just soft, about 10 minutes.

5. Drain the noodles. Place in 4 soup bowls. Fill with the soup, sprinkle with the scallions, chilies, coriander, and basil or mint. Top with the reserved shallots. Serve with the lime.

Indonesian Basil Coconut Soup

This delicious specialty is a version of a classic Indonesian soup that features chicken as well as the traditional pairing of coconut and basil. This interpretation of the soup is great served as a first course or as a light meal itself.

Store the coconut pulp left from making the milk in the refrigerator or freezer; it's great added to cookies or quick bread.

4 cups unsweetened coconut milk (see Note)

1 cup Chicken Stock (page 61), or good instant or low-sodium canned

½ teaspoon turmeric

1 lemongrass stalk, trimmed, white part only, cut into 1-inch-long pieces, or ½ teaspoon dried lemongrass

6 kaffir lime leaves, or 2 bay leaves

Four ¼-inch slices fresh ginger

2 to 4 small green chilies, to taste

Salt

1 pound chicken cutlets, cut into very thin strips

Two 15-ounce cans straw mushrooms, drained

2 tablespoons light soy sauce

1 cup sliced scallions, green and white parts

20 fresh basil leaves, torn if large

2 tablespoons torn fresh coriander leaves (cilantro)

2 to 4 tablespoons lime juice, to taste

Makes about 2 quarts, 4 to 6 servings

1. In a medium saucepan, combine the coconut milk, stock, turmeric, lemongrass, kaffir leaves, ginger, and chilies. Bring to a boil, lower the heat, and simmer 20 minutes. Season to taste with the salt.

2. Add the chicken, mushrooms, and soy sauce. Simmer just until the chicken becomes white and opaque, about 3 minutes. Do not let the soup boil. Using a slotted spoon, remove the kaffir leaves, ginger, chilies, and lemongrass.

3. Sprinkle in the scallions, basil, and coriander. Allow the leaves to come to vivid color, about 1 minute, stir in the lime juice, and serve.

Note: Canned unsweetened coconut milk is available at Asian and specialty stores and many supermarkets. Be sure to buy the unsweetened version, not the sweetened coconut cream used in drinks and desserts. To prepare 4 cups of homemade coconut milk, combine in a medium bowl 2 cups dried unsweetened coconut and 4 cups boiling water. Allow the coconut to soak for 30 minutes. Squeeze the coconut to extract as much milk as possible. Drain the solids and reserve for other uses (see the headnote).

Turkey Vegetable Gumbo

A final addition of sautéed vegetables, including cauliflower, and fresh dill makes this hearty gumbo lively. Use dried wild Polish mushroom pieces (available in many supermarkets) for this dish; their quality is good and they're economical.

¼ cup dried wild Polish mushroom pieces, or dried Italian porcini

1 turkey leg and thigh (about 2 pounds)

½ cup pearl barley, rinsed

1 cup dried great northern beans, picked over, rinsed, and soaked overnight in 8 cups of water

1 cup dried yellow or green split peas

3 garlic cloves, scored with a paring knife

2 bay leaves

½ teaspoon freshly ground black pepper

1 tablespoon canola or other vegetable oil

4 shallots, minced

3 medium onions, finely chopped

2 large carrots, scrubbed and finely chopped

1 parsnip, scrubbed and finely chopped

2 to 3 celery stalks, finely chopped

2 cups small cauliflower florets

2 cups sliced small fresh mushrooms

½ cup chopped fresh dill

½ teaspoon kosher salt, or to taste

Makes about 4 quarts, 8 servings

1. Place the dried mushrooms in a small bowl and pour 1 cup of boiling water over them. Let soften for 10 minutes, drain, then strain the liquid and reserve.

2. Remove the skin and any visible fat from the turkey. Place it in the bottom of a heavy soup pot (or a slow cooker).

3. Add the barley, beans, peas, dried mushrooms and their soaking liquid, garlic, bay leaves, pepper, and 11 cups of water. Place the pot on the stove and bring the liquid to a boil. Reduce the heat to as low as possible, cover, and cook, stirring occasionally, $2^1/_2$ to 3 hours. (If using a slow cooker, cook 5 hours on automatic or 8 hours on low.)

4. Meanwhile, heat the oil in a large skillet over medium heat. Add the shallots and onions and sauté until softened, about 5 minutes. Add the carrots, parsnip, and celery and sauté until softened, about 5 minutes. Add the cauliflower and sauté 2 to 3 minutes, stirring. Stir in the fresh mushrooms and sauté until they begin to soften, about 2 minutes. Remove the mixture from the heat and stir in the dill. Place in a bowl, cool, cover with foil, and reserve.

5. When the turkey-barley mixture is ready, remove from the heat. Extract the bone and remove any gristle. Most of the meat will have come off the bone; remove any that remains on it and return all the meat to the pot. Remove the bay leaves. Stir in the salt and the sautéed vegetables. Reheat the soup, adjust the seasonings, and serve.

Chilled Yellow Pepper Soup

Maybe it's the bright yellow color of this subtly refreshing soup, but whenever I eat it, I'm cheered. Served with crumbled blue tortilla chips and a flurry of fresh coriander leaves, this chilled soup enlivens tables in any but the coldest months. Follow the soup with the Grilled Chicken Niçoise Salad (page 254) and you're really in business.

You can keep the soup for four days refrigerated. Take it out of the fridge about fifteen minutes before you want to serve it so it isn't absolutely chilled and re-emulsify it by whisking.

2 tablespoons olive oil

2 large onions, finely chopped

5 garlic cloves, minced

4 celery stalks, chopped

6 brightly colored yellow peppers (or orange or red peppers), seeded and cut into ¼-inch julienne

2 tablespoons flour

6 to 8 cups Chicken Stock (page 61), or good instant or low-sodium canned broth, completely defatted

Salt and freshly ground black pepper

2 to 3 shakes of hot sauce

3 tablespoons fresh coriander leaves (cilantro), chopped

Blue corn chips, crumbled

Makes about 3 quarts, 8 servings

1. In a large, deep, heavy skillet or Dutch oven, heat the oil over medium-low heat. Add the onions and garlic and sauté until the onions are translucent, 5 to 7 minutes. Do not allow the onions to brown.

2. Add the celery and peppers, partially cover, and cook without browning until soft, about 15 minutes. Stir in the flour and cook 5 minutes. Add 4 cups of the stock, bring to a boil, lower the heat, and simmer, stirring occasionally, until the soup thickens, about 10 minutes.

3. Transfer the mixture to a food processor or blender and process until smooth. Remove to a large bowl and whisk in the remaining stock until the soup reaches a lightly creamy consistency. Season with the salt, pepper, and hot sauce and chill, covered. Garnish with the coriander and chips and serve, or pass the chips, allowing diners to add them.

Curried Squash and Mushroom Soup

Squash soup can be disappointingly bland or too sweet-spice-ish. The flavors in this one are perfectly balanced. It's got a nice curry presence plus mushrooms and chopped almonds. The optional ground ginger called for adds punch.

The soup goes together quickly and would be lovely as a starter for a meal featuring Grandma Regina's Roast Chicken (page 112). Or serve it by itself—it's especially nice for lunch when the weather turns cool.

2 small butternut or medium acorn squash (about 2 pounds each)

3 cups Chicken Stock (page 61), or good instant or low-sodium canned broth

1 cup fresh orange juice

2 tablespoons canola or other vegetable oil

¾ cup chopped onion

1 garlic clove, pressed

¾ teaspoon ground cumin

½ teaspoon ground coriander

¾ teaspoon ground cinnamon

¼ teaspoon mustard powder

½ teaspoon ground ginger (optional)

½ pound fresh mushrooms, thinly sliced

Salt

2 tablespoons fresh lemon juice

2 tablespoons chopped roasted almonds

Makes about 2 quarts, 6 servings

1. Preheat the oven to 375°F. Cut the squash in half and scoop out the seeds. Oil a baking sheet and place the squash face down on the sheet. Bake until soft, about 30 minutes.

2. Allow the squash to cool, then scoop out the flesh; you should have about 4 cups. Put the flesh into a food processor or blender. Add the stock and orange juice and process until smooth.

3. Meanwhile, in a heavy soup pot or Dutch oven, heat the oil over low heat. Add the onion, garlic, cumin, coriander, cinnamon, mustard, and ginger, if using. Sauté, stirring, until the onion is soft, about 5 minutes. Add the mushrooms, cover, and cook 10 minutes.

4. Add the puree, heat gently, and season to taste with the salt. Correct the seasonings. Add the lemon juice and stir. Ladle into bowls and sprinkle with the almonds.

Roast Fennel and Sweet Onion Soup

Fresh fennel, with its delicate, licoricelike flavor, is becoming increasingly popular nowadays, and I couldn't be more pleased. Its subtle taste adds distinction to numerous dishes, including this lovely soup. With only four ingredients (salt and pepper aside), the soup's a breeze to make—so easy, in fact, and so good that it will become a household favorite. Roasting the fennel first enriches its special flavor while sending wonderful aromas through the house.

Serve this with bruschetta as a prelude to a meal of Chicken with Garlic and Tomato Essence (page 86) or Chicken Scarpariello (page 103).

2 to 3 medium fennel bulbs (about 2 pounds total), fronds trimmed and reserved

2 tablespoons olive oil

2 large onions, thinly sliced

7 cups Chicken Stock (page 61), or good instant or low-sodium canned broth

Salt and freshly ground black pepper

Makes about 3 quarts, 5 or 6 servings

1. Preheat the oven to 500°F.

2. Quarter, core, and slice the fennel into $1/4$-inch slices. In a large bowl, toss the fennel with 1 tablespoon of the olive oil and spread in a single layer on a baking sheet with sides. Roast the fennel until it is sizzling, softened, and beginning to brown, about 20 minutes. Stir once or twice to allow for even roasting.

3. In a Dutch oven or heavy soup pot, heat the remaining tablespoon of oil over medium heat. When hot, reduce the heat to low, add the onions, and sauté until soft and browned, about 25 minutes.

4. Meanwhile, chop some of the reserved fronds to make 1 cup. Stir the roasted fennel into the onions. Stir in half of the chopped fronds and half of the stock. Simmer over low heat for about 10 minutes.

5. Remove the mixture to a food processor or blender and puree. Return the puree to the pot and thin with the remaining stock. Warm, season to taste with the salt and pepper, and pour into bowls. Garnish with the remaining fronds and serve.

4. On the Range

*Roasting, broiling, and bread making
are truly gratifying kitchen activities.
But the real cooking action happens on the range.
Stovetop techniques like stewing, sautéing,
braising, or stir-frying excite a special,
intimate relationship with food and its
preparation—and produce great dishes.*

Take stewing, the covered-pot simmering of food that is barely immersed in liquid. For many of us, growing up, a stew meant chicken fricassee. Though I've enjoyed the world's fricassees since then, the defining dish is still my mother's—a homey but peerless creation that includes browned onions, tomato-enriched rice, and delicate turkey meatballs, a traditional family addition (see page 85). Stewing and its culinary cousin braising also invite kitchen invention. The Chicken Fricassee with Pappardelle and Sun-Dried Tomatoes takes the traditional fricassee to the Mediterranean; French-African Chicken Stew and Chicken Couscous with Butternut Squash are other original stews-of-the-world.

A braise involves the moist-heat stewing of food that's been browned first. When browning chicken for a braise (or a sauté), make sure to dry it well before cooking or steam will inhibit its coloring. For the same reason, don't crowd the pan when you add the chicken. Like other dishes in this chapter, Chicken with Garlic and Tomato Essence, a true brown braise, can be made with skinless chicken for less fat and fewer calories. And it can be prepared ahead or in stages. Stews and braises are better made in advance; they'll keep for three to four days refrigerated, and need only to be brought to room temperature then reheated gently.

Sautéing and stir-frying involve pan-cooking in just enough fat to brown food. Stir-frying is actually closer to French sautéing, in which the pan is shaken over fairly high heat to brown food evenly (the French verb *sauter* means "to jump"). Chicken Scarpariello, my sweet, moist version of the lemon-flavored Italian dish, and Stir-Fried Chicken with String Beans are examples of these "small-oil" techniques. People often ask me if they can sauté or stir-fry in nonstick pans without oil. Sorry, but a bit of oil is always needed to ensure surface searing.

PERFECT PASTA

Pasta is undoubtedly the fastest, easiest, and most versatile stovetop dish. Pasta preparation, however, requires care. Every pasta dish has its own preferred pasta shape, which depends on the relative thickness of the sauce and its ingredients.

Before preparing pasta, think about its sauce or accompaniment. As a general rule, chunkier sauces require sturdy or specially shaped pastas that can trap bits of meat or vegetables—tubes or shells, for example. Light sauces require long or ribbonlike pastas, such as linguine or fettuccine. Radiatore with Chicken and Shiitake Mushrooms, featuring pasta "radiators," and Cavatelli with Saffron and Turkey Tomato Sauce, with small ridged shells, both make use of some the many kosher-certified pastas now available. Every shape has its own distinct personality and mouth feel.

For most of the pasta dishes I prepare, I choose imported dried eggless pasta made with hard-wheat durum flour. It has the rich wheaty flavor and chewy, toothsome cooked texture that gives your pasta dishes real character.

Use plenty of boiling water for cooking pasta—4 to 6 quarts per pound of pasta. Make sure the water comes to a rapid boil before you add the pasta, then add salt. You could add the salt before the water boils, but I wait to ensure that the salt dissolves instantly; and by fixing a set time for the salt's inclusion, I never wonder if I've added it or not.

It is not necessary to add oil to the water to keep the pasta from sticking together. If you cook pasta in enough water, sticking isn't an issue. (If, however, you find that there's too much pasta in the pot in relation to the water, do add a little oil.) Coat cooked pasta lightly with oil when you have to hold it, or when using it for a pasta salad.

All pasta should be cooked al dente—tender-firm to the bite. In the following recipes I've suggested cooking times for pasta, but, really, you must keep tasting the pasta as you cook it to gauge its doneness. A little before the pasta is done (it will continue to cook off the stove), remove the pasta from the heat and drain it immediately. And here's a trick for warming the pasta serving platter: rather than heating it in the oven (which can damage your china), set it half-covering the pot as the pasta cooks. Dry it while the pasta drains and there's your warm platter. Or put the platter beneath the colander as you drain the pasta. Dry the heated platter and you're in business. Toss your pasta with sauce, pass the steaming platter, and dig in!

Joyce's Chicken Fricassee with Turkey Meatballs

¼ cup canola or other light vegetable oil

2½ cups coarsely chopped onions

1 teaspoon minced garlic

One 3½- to 4-pound chicken, cut into eighths, skin removed, trimmed of all visible fat, gizzard reserved

1½ teaspoons sweet Hungarian paprika

2 cups Chicken Stock (page 61), or good instant or low-sodium broth, brought to a boil

2 to 3 cups tomato juice

1 to 2 teaspoons salt, or to taste

¼ teaspoon freshly ground black pepper

MEATBALLS

1½ pounds ground turkey

2 tablespoons quick-cooking oats

2 tablespoons minced onion

1 egg white

Salt

¼ teaspoon freshly ground black pepper

1 cup long-grain white rice

Serves 6 to 8

This stellar dish, passed down from Hungarian kitchens past to my grandmother, and perfected by my mother, Joyce, departs from traditional versions in two ways. The typical meatball accompaniment is prepared from ground turkey and not beef (a change of my own), making the dish lighter. And the rice, usually served with the dish, is cooked in it, absorbing the delicious flavors. I've made another alteration—a skinless bird. This creates a leaner dish, one everybody applauds.

1. In a large, heavy pot or Dutch oven, heat the oil over medium-high heat. Add the onions, garlic, and gizzard and sauté until all are golden, about 5 minutes. Using a slotted spoon, remove the vegetables and gizzard. In the remaining oil, brown the chicken on all sides, about 10 minutes.

2. Return the vegetables and gizzard to the pot and sprinkle all the ingredients with the paprika. Add the boiling stock, 2 cups of the tomato juice, the salt, and pepper. Cover and simmer over very low heat for $1^1/4$ hours.

3. Meanwhile, make the meatballs. In a large bowl, combine the ground turkey, oats, onion, egg white, salt, and pepper. Stir to combine fully. Form into $1^1/2$-inch balls, place on a plate, and reserve.

4. Uncover the fricassee, push the chicken pieces aside, and add the meatballs. Shake the pot to distribute the meatballs and coat them with the liquid.

5. Add the rice and additional tomato juice, if you prefer a saucier dish. Stir gently. Cover and cook until the rice is done, about 20 minutes. Adjust the seasonings and serve.

Chicken with Garlic and Tomato Essence

This is one the great all-time dishes. A stovetop stew, it features whole garlic that is cooked down to mellow sweetness and pureed to season a savory, tomato-based sauce. The sauce, made with tomatoes that cook with the chicken, is robust but sophisticated, and full of warm flavors. The chicken is served over polenta—the perfect accompaniment to the bird and its sauce. Sautéed broccoli rabe is ideal to complete the meal.

16 garlic cloves (12 unpeeled and 4 minced)

3 tablespoons canola or other light vegetable oil

One 4-pound chicken, all visible fat removed, cut into eighths and skin removed, if desired

Freshly ground black pepper

⅓ cup mild red wine vinegar

⅓ cup dry white wine

½ teaspoon ground cumin

1½ tablespoons fresh rosemary, chopped, or 1 teaspoon dried

1 bay leaf

5 canned Italian tomatoes, chopped

1¼ cups Chicken Stock (page 61), or good instant or low-sodium canned, approximately

Polenta, for serving (page 193)

½ cup Italian parsley

Serves 3 to 4

1. Bring a small saucepan of water to a boil. Add the whole garlic cloves and boil for 3 minutes. Remove, drain well, and reserve.

2. In a large skillet, heat the oil over medium-high heat. Add the boiled whole garlic and stir. Season the chicken pieces with the pepper and add them to the skillet. Brown on all sides, about 8 minutes. Remove the chicken and reserve. Reduce the heat to medium-low. Add the minced garlic to the skillet and allow to cook until golden, stirring, about 3 minutes. Add the vinegar and wine to deglaze the pan. Add the cumin, rosemary, bay leaf, and tomatoes.

3. Bring the ingredients to a simmer and add the chicken. Reduce the heat to medium-low, cover, and cook for 15 minutes, turning the chicken pieces once.

4. Remove the chicken and the whole garlic cloves. Add ³/₄ cup stock and stir to combine. Skim the fat from the pan sauce. Pour the hot polenta onto a large platter, top with the chicken pieces, and keep warm. Squeeze the soft pulp from the garlic cloves directly into a blender or food processor (discard the garlic husks). Add the parsley and pan contents and puree. Add the remaining chicken stock gradually, blending, until the mixture is saucelike. Pour the sauce over the chicken and polenta and serve.

Perciatelli with Turkey and Broccoli Sauce

Spaghetti aglio e olio, *or pasta with garlic and oil, is a great Roman dish. Here it's recast with perciatelli—the thickish spaghetti-like pasta that's hollow in the center—ground turkey, and fresh broccoli florets. (Linguine work equally well.) Fennel seeds are also added, which gives the dish a warm aniselike note. The result is a lovely pasta meal that's simplicity itself to make.*

3 cups Chicken Stock (page 61), or good instant or low-sodium canned broth

4 tablespoons olive oil

15 garlic cloves, minced

1 teaspoon whole fennel seeds, crushed with a mortar and pestle

2 fresh sage leaves, or ½ teaspoon dried leaves, crumbled

1 pound ground turkey

4 cups broccoli florets (1 small bunch)

1 pound perciatelli or linguine

Salt

¼ teaspoon red pepper flakes

¼ cup chopped parsley leaves

Serves 4 to 6

1. In a small saucepan over high heat, reduce the stock by half. Reserve.

2. In a large skillet, heat 2 tablespoon of the oil over medium heat. Add half of the garlic and sauté until it just begins to turn golden, about 5 minutes. Make sure the garlic does not brown or it will be bitter. Add the fennel seeds and sage, turn the heat to medium-high, and slowly add the turkey, breaking it up with your fingers. Sauté until the turkey is no longer pink, 5 to 8 minutes, stirring intermittently to break up clumps. Remove from the heat and spoon the skillet contents into a bowl. Reserve.

3. Return the skillet to heat, add the remaining 2 tablespoons oil and the remaining garlic and sauté until just beginning to turn color. Add the broccoli and sauté, stirring and tossing until the broccoli is bright green, 3 to 5 minutes. Add the reduced stock, lower the heat, and cover. Pan-steam the broccoli until crisp-tender, about 3 minutes. Turn off the heat and reserve the broccoli and the stock in the skillet.

4. In a large pot, bring about 6 quarts of water to a boil. Salt the water, add the perciatelle, and cook until very al dente, 5 to 7 minutes (it will cook more later). Drain and return to the pot. Add the sautéed turkey and broccoli mixtures, turn the heat to medium-high, and stir the contents to combine well. Cook, stirring, until the liquid is absorbed, 2 to 3 minutes. Transfer to a large platter and season with the salt. Sprinkle with the red pepper flakes and parsley and serve.

Radiatore with Chicken and Shiitake Mushrooms

I first discovered radiatore—radiator-shaped pasta—in an Italian market years ago. I was immediately delighted with this fanciful shape, which like all pasta types has a culinary reason for being. The little crannies of the radiatore catch and hold sauce beautifully, while their compact shape provides a satisfying "bite." This delicious dish features radiatore, chicken strips, and an herby "sauce" with mushrooms and sun-dried tomatoes. Light and not too saucy, it's great for supper or lunch. It can also be prepared a day ahead and served at room temperature as a pasta salad.

Radiatore are increasingly easy to find, but if you can't locate any, use lumache—small shells—or fusilli. If you can't get shiitake mushrooms, just increase the quantity of the domestic mushrooms by one-half pound. The dish will still be delicious.

½ cup fruity olive oil

6 shallots, minced (about 1 cup)

½ cup white wine vinegar

2 tablespoons sherry wine vinegar (see page 14)

½ cup Chicken Stock (page 61), or good instant or low-sodium canned broth

¾ teaspoon dried oregano

½ cup Italian parsley leaves

⅛ teaspoon dried thyme

3 garlic cloves, pressed

½ pound shiitake mushrooms, sliced in half

1 pound domestic mushrooms, quartered

1. In a large skillet, heat half the olive oil over medium heat. Add the shallots and sauté until soft and beginning to brown, 4 to 5 minutes. Stir in the vinegars and simmer for 2 minutes. Remove from the heat and allow to cool. When cool enough to handle, scrape the shallots into a blender or food processor and blend until smooth. Add the chicken stock, oregano, parsley, and thyme. Blend in and set aside.

2. In a small bowl, combine the remaining ¼ cup olive oil with the pressed garlic. In a large bowl, toss all the mushrooms with 2 tablespoons of the garlic-oil mixture. Spread the mushrooms on a cookie sheet at least 1 inch deep. Season to taste with the salt and pepper and reserve. Brush the chicken lightly with the remaining garlic-oil mixture and reserve. Drain the sun-dried tomatoes, discard the liquid, and cut the tomatoes into tiny slivers. Preheat the broiler.

Salt and freshly ground black pepper

1½ pounds chicken cutlets,
cut into ¼-inch strips

16 dry-packed sun-dried tomatoes,
soaked in 1 cup boiling water for
30 minutes to soften

1 pound radiatore, lumache, or fusilli

½ cup fresh peas, blanched,
or frozen and defrosted

½ cup fresh basil leaves (about 20)

Serves 6

3. In a large pot, bring about 8 quarts of water to a boil. Salt the water, and cook the radiatore until al dente, drain, and place in large serving bowl or platter. Toss with the blended sauce. Add the sun-dried tomatoes and peas and toss.

4. Meanwhile, broil the mushrooms until brown and sizzling, turning once, 2 to 5 minutes per side. Reserve.

5. Line a pan with foil. Place the chicken strips in the pan and broil until just tender, 2 to 3 minutes per side.

6. Place the mushrooms and chicken strips on top of the pasta. Tear the basil leaves and scatter over the top. Toss everything together just before serving onto plates.

Chicken Fricassee with Pappardelle and Sun-Dried Tomatoes

This Mediterranean-influenced fricassee is fragrant, robust, and a cinch to prepare. Its rich pan sauce is served with pappardelle, the square pasta so popular in Tuscany and Bologna. Often accompanied in northern Italy by a hare stew, pappardelle welcome any meaty sauce; here they receive the bonus of winey braised chicken pieces.

¼ cup olive oil

Two 2½- to 3-pound chickens, each cut into eighths and skinned, wings removed and reserved for another use

2 large onions, finely chopped

6 garlic cloves, pressed

2 cups dry white wine

4 cups canned crushed tomatoes

¼ cup shredded fresh basil leaves, or 2 teaspoons dried

2 tablespoons dried oregano

3 tablespoons drained capers

½ cup black oil-cured olives, pitted and slivered

1 cup dry-packed sun-dried tomatoes, soaked in hot water for 15 minutes to soften, squeezed dry, and cut into slivers

2 cups Chicken Stock (page 61), or good instant or low-sodium canned broth

Salt and freshly ground black pepper

1½ pounds pappardelle or other wide flat pasta

½ cup chopped Italian parsley leaves

Serves 6

The fricassee's sauce is so good I have no difficulty serving any remaining the next day without the chicken, over pasta alone. If I'm serving this dish for kids, I omit the olives and capers.

1. In a large, heavy pot or Dutch oven, heat the oil over medium heat. Add the chicken and brown on all sides. Remove the chicken and reserve.

2. Add the onions to the oil and sauté over medium heat until soft, 8 to 10 minutes. Add the garlic and cook 3 minutes.

3. Return the chicken to the pot and add the wine, tomatoes, basil, oregano, capers, olives, sun-dried tomatoes, and chicken stock. Season to taste with salt and pepper. Cook, covered, over medium heat until the chicken is done (a fork will pierce it easily), turning occasionally, and the sauce is thickened, about 1 hour.

4. Meanwhile, bring about 6 quarts of water to a boil and warm a large serving platter. Salt the water, add the pappardelle, and cook until al dente. Drain the pasta and toss with about $^1/_2$ cup of the sauce. Place the pasta on the platter and arrange the chicken on top. Spoon about 1 cup of the sauce over the chicken, sprinkle with the parsley, and serve. Pass additional sauce separately.

Chicken Ragù with Tagliatelle

The famous Bolognese ragù, clinging to toothsome pasta, is one of the great eating experiences. I've done little to alter the recipe for this traditional sauce, substituting only ground chicken for beef and adding stock in the meat braise. These changes make the finished dish lighter and even more enjoyable than its delicious precursor.

The use of tagliatelle with the sauce is time-honored, but it can also be served successfully with ziti, rotelle, conchiglie, or rigatoni. When preparing the sauce, you must sauté the chicken barely long enough to lose its raw color, simmer it in stock to make it sweeter, then allow the sauce to simmer very long and very slowly. These hints reflect the ragù techniques of Marcella Hazan, with whom I studied years ago in Venice. This ragù is a variation of her wonderful version.

3 tablespoons olive oil

½ cup chopped onion

¼ cup chopped celery

½ cup chopped peeled carrots

1½ pounds ground chicken or turkey

Salt

1 cup dry white wine

1 cup Chicken Stock (page 61), or good instant or low-sodium canned broth

¼ teaspoon grated nutmeg

5 cups canned Italian tomatoes (two 28-ounce cans), roughly chopped, with their liquid

2 pounds tagliatelle, preferably fresh

Serves 8 to 10

1. In a large, deep, heavy pot, heat the oil over medium heat. Add the onion and sauté until translucent, about 4 minutes. Add the celery and carrots and cook gently for 2 minutes.

2. Add the ground chicken, breaking it up with a fork. Season lightly with the salt. Cook the chicken just until it loses its raw color, about 3 minutes. Add the wine, increase the heat to medium-high, and cook until all the wine has evaporated, 5 to 7 minutes.

3. Reduce the heat to medium and add the stock and nutmeg. Cook until the stock has evaporated, about 15 minutes. Add the tomatoes and stir thoroughly. When the tomatoes begin to bubble, reduce the heat so the sauce barely simmers and cook for 1¼ hours. Check periodically to make sure the sauce isn't burning, or use a heat-diffusing mat.

4. Heat a serving platter. Bring 6 to 8 quarts of water to a boil. Salt the water and add the tagliatelle. Cook until al dente, only 5 to 10 seconds after the water returns to a boil if the pasta is fresh, 6 to 8 minutes if dried. Drain. Spoon some of the hot sauce into the bottom of the platter, add the noodles, and pour the rest of the sauce over. Toss gently and serve immediately.

Duck Ragout with Rigatoni

This hearty, deeply flavored duck stew is based on a classic Tuscan ragout. It's served over rigatoni, the large tubular pasta that traps food bits so delightfully. The combination of the duck, its garlicky, tomato-based sauce, and the pasta is mouthwatering. Don't let the large quantity of garlic called for put you off; it cooks down to sweet mellowness.

This dish gets even better with time. Prepare it in advance and chill it (this also allows easy removal of the fat released during cooking). You can bone the duck before serving it, in which case I would substitute pappardelle for the rigatoni. I've found, however, that people enjoy gnawing on the bones as they eat the pasta and the delicious sauce.

2 tablespoons canola or other light vegetable oil

Two 5-pound ducks, all visible fat removed, each cut into eighths, wing tips removed and reserved for another use

Garlic cloves of 3 medium heads, peeled

5 sprigs fresh rosemary, leaves only, or 2 tablespoons dried

1 teaspoon freshly ground black pepper

Juice of 6 lemons

One 1½-inch piece peeled fresh ginger

4 cups cleaned chopped leeks, white parts only, or onions

8 medium carrots, peeled and chopped

1 bottle Cabernet Sauvignon or other dry, full-bodied red wine

1. In a large, heavy pot or Dutch oven, heat 1 tablespoon of the oil over medium-high heat. Add the duck a few pieces at a time and brown on all sides. Transfer the pieces to a colander to drain the fat. Pour out fat, if any, from the pan. Do not wipe out the pan.

2. Add the garlic, rosemary, pepper, lemon juice, and ginger to a food processor. Process to make a paste. Reserve.

3. Add the remaining 1 tablespoon oil to the pan and heat over medium-high heat. Add the leeks and sauté until soft, about 3 minutes. Add the reserved paste, stir, and cook to combine, 3 to 4 minutes. Stir in the carrots.

4. Place the duck on top of the vegetables. Add the wine, stock, tomatoes with their liquid, and bay leaves. Cover and simmer until the duck is done, about 2 hours. Remove the duck and bone it if desired. Reserve.

5. Add the sherry to the pot and cook over medium-high heat to reduce the sauce until thickened, about 45 minutes. Remove the bay leaves. Return the duck pieces to the pot, remove from the stove, and allow to cool. When cool, transfer to a relatively narrow container (for easier removal of surface fat) and chill. Using a tablespoon, remove any accumulated solid fat from the surface of the stew. Alternatively, before you add the duck to the sauce, eliminate the accumulated fat with a large spoon or paper towels.

2 cups Chicken Stock (page 61), or good instant or low-sodium canned

One 16-ounce can peeled tomatoes, chopped, with liquid

4 bay leaves

1 cup dry sherry

2 pounds rigatoni

1 bunch Italian parsley, leaves only, chopped (⅔ cup)

Serves 6 to 8

6. Bring the stew to room temperature and heat (it can also be warmed in a 325°F. oven for 40 minutes). Meanwhile, bring a large pot of water to the boil. Salt the water, add the rigatoni, and cook until al dente, 10 to 12 minutes.

7. Drain the pasta and toss it with $1/4$ cup of the sauce. Place the rigatoni on a large, deep serving platter.

8. Stir the parsley into the stew. Place the duck on top of the pasta, spoon some of the sauce over, and serve. Pass the remaining sauce separately.

Cavatelli with Saffron and Turkey Tomato Sauce

This great pasta dish features a savory sauce of ground turkey, fennel, and tomatoes. The sauce is lightly flavored with saffron, which imparts a delicious taste and a pretty yellow color. I like cavatelli—longish ridged pasta shells—for this, but you could use conchiglie or similar shapes. The sauce keeps perfectly for three or four days refrigerated and freezes well for up to four months. Having a sauce like this on hand is really a pleasure; all you need to do is boil some water and throw in the pasta.

2½ cups drained canned peeled tomatoes in puree, puree reserved (about 1 cup)

2 tablespoons extra-virgin olive oil

2 large red onions, finely chopped

½ teaspoon crushed fennel seeds

1 pound ground turkey

One 8-ounce can tomato sauce

Pinch of saffron threads, or ⅛ teaspoon saffron powder

Salt and freshly ground black pepper

2 tablespoons chopped Italian parsley leaves

1 pound cavatelli or conchiglie

Serves 4 to 6

1. Chop the tomatoes coarsely, combine with the puree, and reserve.

2. In a large, heavy skillet, heat the oil over moderate heat. Add the onions and cook until soft, about 10 minutes. Add the fennel seeds and cook to bring out their flavor, about 2 minutes. Add the turkey, stirring to break up, and cook 8 minutes. Add the tomatoes with their puree and the tomato sauce.

3. Heat a small skillet over medium heat. Add the saffron threads or powder and toast lightly until aromatic, about 2 minutes. Watch to make sure the saffron doesn't burn. Add the saffron to the sauce, crushing the threads first, if using, between your fingers.

4. Reduce the heat and simmer the sauce until thick, 20 to 30 minutes. Season to taste with the salt and pepper and stir in the parsley.

5. Meanwhile, bring about 6 quarts of water to the boil and warm a serving plate. Salt the water, add the cavatelli, and cook until al dente, about 10 minutes. Drain and toss with some of the sauce. Place the pasta on the serving plate and spoon the remaining sauce over. Serve.

Poached Chicken Breasts

Every cook needs to know how to poach chicken breasts, a simple process that yields delicate meat with no added calories.

The uses for the poached breasts are endless. I poach breasts for pasta dishes and main-course salads, or use them in sandwiches. I sometimes substitute white wine or orange juice for some of the poaching water, which flavors the breasts delicately. For Asian poached chicken breasts, I add scallions, ginger, and a splash of soy sauce or sherry to the liquid—you get the idea. Note that two chicken cutlets, cut into 1-inch cubes, will yield about 1 cup of poached meat.

The recipe below will poach six half-breasts with skin and bones (about 4 pounds), or 6 medium cutlets (about 2 pounds).

2 celery stalks, cut into 2-inch pieces

2 small carrots, peeled

1 medium onion, sliced

Few sprigs of parsley

2 to 3 black peppercorns

1 bay leaf

About 1 cup additional fresh herbs, such as dill, thyme, or tarragon (optional)

6 unboned, unskinned chicken breast halves, or 6 cutlets

Makes 6 half-breasts or cutlets

1. In a skillet just large enough to hold the breasts in one layer, combine the celery, carrots, onion, parsley, peppercorns, bay leaf, and fresh herbs, if using. Add water to cover the vegetables well, 3 to 6 cups.

2. Bring to a boil, reduce the heat, and simmer 10 minutes. Add the breasts, shifting the vegetables to make sure the breasts are well submerged; add more water, if necessary. Cover and simmer gently until the breasts are just done, 12 to 15 minutes for breast halves, 5 to 7 minutes for cutlets. The chicken should be lightly springy to the touch. Never allow the chicken to boil.

3. Remove the chicken and cool. Bone and skin, if necessary. Use as is or cut into cubes or neat pieces. Save the cooking liquid for stock or soup, refrigerated, up to 2 days.

Poached Chicken Breasts with Green Sauce

I'd revise the classic phrase, "a chicken in every pot," to "a chicken breast in every pot." Make that a poached chicken breast. Enormously versatile, poached chicken breasts are the perfect beginning to a host of easy dishes, like this one. Here, julienned poached breasts sit atop fresh baby greens; the breasts are dressed with Green Sauce, an herby-spicy mixture that would make just about anything taste good. Try this for lunch or a light supper.

8 cups baby greens, spinach, or arugula

2 tablespoons olive oil

1 tablespoon fresh lemon juice

6 poached chicken cutlets (see page 95), cut into ½-inch julienne

Green Sauce (page 235)

2 cups cubed ripe tomatoes

Serves 4 to 6

1. In a medium bowl, combine the greens, oil, and lemon juice. Toss well.

2. Line 4 to 6 plates with the greens and top attractively with a portion of the julienned breasts. Pour half of the sauce over the chicken and top with the tomatoes. Serve with the remaining sauce passed separately.

Chicken Couscous with Butternut Squash

Couscous, the Moroccan dish that combines the grain-like semolina pasta called couscous with a stew of vegetables and meat, is one of the world's great eating experiences. This delicious version features butternut squash as well as chicken, zucchini, tomatoes, and the customary chickpeas (best bought dried and reconstituted, if you have the time to do it).

The traditional method of preparing couscous involves multiple washings, dryings, and steamings. I use quick-cooking (or precooked) couscous, which saves time and produces fine results. This is a marvelous dish for entertaining; accompany it with harissa and Apple Tomato Chutney.

1½ pounds medium onions (about 6), peeled and quartered

½ cup dried chickpeas, soaked overnight, or one 10-ounce can cooked chickpeas, drained and rinsed

Pinch of saffron threads

1 cinnamon stick

½ teaspoon turmeric

½ teaspoon freshly ground black pepper

Salt

One 3-pound chicken, cut into eighths, wings removed and reserved for another use

1 small butternut squash, peeled, seeded, and cut into 2-inch chunks

1 medium zucchini or yellow squash, cut into ¼-inch slices

1 large, ripe tomato, roughly chopped

1¼ cups Chicken Stock (page 61), completely defatted, or good instant or low-sodium canned broth

1¼ cups quick-cooking couscous

2 tablespoons canola or other light vegetable oil

¼ cup dried currants (optional)

2 tablespoons chopped Italian parsley leaves or coriander leaves (cilantro)

Harissa (page 11), for serving

Apple Tomato Chutney (page 240), for serving

Serves 4

1. Place the onions, chickpeas, if soaked, saffron, cinnamon stick, turmeric, and pepper in a heavy pot. Add 3 cups of water and bring to the boil. Reduce the heat to medium and cook, covered, 1 hour. Season to taste with the salt.

2. Add the chicken and simmer, covered, for 45 minutes. Add the butternut squash and cook, uncovered, for 20 minutes. Add the zucchini, tomato, and canned chickpeas, if using, and cook, uncovered, until the butternut squash is soft and the other vegetables are tender-crisp, about 10 minutes. The pot liquid will be brothlike.

3. Meanwhile, prepare the couscous. In a small saucepan, bring the stock to a boil. In a medium bowl, mix the couscous with the oil and hot stock. Season with the salt and pepper and add the currants, if using. Mix quickly with 2 forks, breaking up lumps. Cover immediately very tightly with aluminum foil and let rest for 15 minutes to absorb the stock. Remove the foil and fluff with the forks, breaking up any lumps. Cover again tightly with the foil and let rest another 15 minutes.

4. To serve, arrange the couscous on a big serving platter. With a slotted spoon, transfer the stew to the top of the couscous. Pour some of the broth on top—only as much as the couscous will absorb; the dish should look moist, but not soupy. Sprinkle with the parsley. Serve any remaining broth on the side accompanied by the harissa and the chutney.

Japanese Steamed Chicken and Vegetables

The Italians have their bollito misto, *or mixed boil, and we American have our New England boiled dinner. Many cuisines offer dishes in which one or more component parts are boiled or poached. This Japanese-influenced dish is the result of experimentation on that theme, and it's really delicious. Steamed chicken pieces are combined with vegetables that are steamed or left uncooked, and served with a scallion-brush garnish and Wasabi Sauce, for dipping. The vegetables are left whole or sliced decoratively.*

Besides being delectable, the dish is low in fat. You could serve it as a kind of crudité platter, but it really shines as a simple, elegant dinner after, say, a concert or play.

1 to 2 tablespoons sake or sherry

1½ pounds chicken cutlets, cut into 1-inch strips

3 scallions, root ends trimmed, for garnish

1 medium carrot, peeled and thinly sliced lengthwise

2 cups additional vegetables, such as asparagus, daikon, jicama, radishes, snow peas, and zucchini, decoratively sliced or left whole (see Note)

8 strands (about 4 by ¼ inch each) wakame (Japanese dried seaweed), soaked in warm water 30 minutes to soften, cut into bite-size pieces, or soaked hiziki seaweed (both optional)

1 medium cucumber, peeled and thinly sliced lengthwise

1 tablespoon sesame seeds, toasted

1 cup Wasabi Sauce (page 46)

Serves 3 to 4

1. Prepare water for steaming and add the sake. Using a steamer basket or improvising one, steam the chicken until just cooked, 7 to 8 minutes. Set aside to cool.

2. Make scallion brushes for garnishing: Using a small, thin-bladed knife, cut a 5-inch segment from the white portion of each scallion including some green. Cut 2-inch-long slits all around both ends of each scallion piece, leaving an uncut middle section of about 1 inch. Immerse the sliced scallions in ice water; the shredded ends will curl. Set aside until needed or cover and place in refrigerator (the brushes will keep for 4 days).

3. Steam the carrot and, if using, asparagus, snow peas, and zucchini until tender-crisp, 1 to 5 minutes. Run the vegetables under cold water to stop cooking and drain well. Do not steam daikon, jicama, radishes, or wakame, if using.

4. Arrange the chicken pieces, cucumber, and vegetables decoratively on a platter, keeping each vegetable type together. Sprinkle with the sesame seeds. Garnish with the scallion brushes and serve with the wasabi sauce.

Note: Treat the vegetables as follows:

Asparagus: cut diagonally into 1 1/2-inch pieces
Daikon: cut into matchsticks
Jicama: peel, cut into matchsticks
Radishes: cut into thin slices, matchsticks, or roses
Snow peas: remove stem ends and leave whole
Zucchini: cut diagonally into 1/4-inch rounds

Warm Vanessa Salad

Vanessa was a wonderful restaurant in Manhattan's Greenwich Village. It was the place where I first experienced warm chicken salad and the excitement of walnut oil. This salad, my version of the Vanessa specialty, combines chicken with walnuts, mushrooms, and fresh tarragon. Served over slightly wilted greens, it's a flavorful dish that makes a great simple meal, and one that can be prepared in minutes.

2/3 cup walnut oil

1 1/2 pounds chicken cutlets, cut lengthwise into 1/2-inch-wide strips

9 cups mixed salad greens, such as Boston, red leaf, romaine, watercress, and/or baby spinach leaves

1 tablespoon finely minced shallots

1 cup thinly sliced fresh mushrooms

3/4 cup walnut halves

1/2 cup minced roasted pepper (see steps 1 and 2, Grilled Red Pepper Sauce, page 231) or pimiento

Salt and freshly ground black pepper

1/3 cup sherry wine vinegar (see page 14)

1 teaspoon fresh tarragon leaves, or 1/4 teaspoon dried and crumbled

Serves 6

1. In a skillet large enough to accommodate the chicken in one layer, heat the oil over medium-high heat. Add the chicken and brown quickly on both sides, about 4 minutes. Do not allow the chicken to cook through.

2. Distribute the greens evenly on a large platter. Remove the chicken from the skillet and reserve. To the skillet add the shallots, mushrooms, walnut halves, and roasted pepper. Season to taste with the salt and pepper and sauté, stirring, about 1 minute. Add the chicken, sauté 1 minute more, and add the vinegar and tarragon. Toss the ingredients together and remove from the heat.

3. Spoon the chicken mixture over the greens in a circular pattern and serve.

Chicken Agen

Agen, a region in southwest France, is known for the sweetness and fine flavor of its prunes. This dish is my variation of an old Agen recipe that pairs prunes with chicken, a delightful coupling. This version is mildly flavored with curry, sweet spices, and mustard. The finished dish is intriguing with its touch of fruit sweetness, and one that children just love. Serve it with Basmati Rice (page 210) and Moghlai Spinach (page 205) for a perfect meal.

¼ cup canola or light olive oil

3 medium onions, finely chopped

1 teaspoon curry powder

½ teaspoon ground coriander

½ teaspoon ground ginger

½ teaspoon ground cinnamon

2 tablespoons fresh lemon juice

2 tablespoons cider vinegar

2 tablespoons coarse-grain mustard

¼ cup fresh orange juice

3 medium carrots, peeled and chopped

12 ounces moist pitted prunes

Salt and freshly ground black pepper

One 3½-pound chicken, cut into eighths and skin removed

Serves 4

1. In a large nonstick skillet, heat the oil over medium heat. Add the onions and sauté, stirring, until the onions are translucent, about 10 minutes.

2. Stir in the curry powder, coriander, ginger, cinnamon, lemon juice, cider vinegar, mustard, orange juice, carrots, and prunes. Season to taste with the salt and pepper.

3. Add the chicken, meaty side down. Cover the pan, reduce the heat, and simmer 45 minutes. Turn the chicken pieces and simmer, covered, until almost done, 30 minutes. Uncover the pan and cook 15 minutes more to reduce pan juices slightly. Warm a serving platter.

4. Transfer the chicken and prunes to the platter. Pour the pan juices into a small bowl, allow the fat to rise to the surface, and spoon it off. Pour some of the juices over the chicken and serve. Pass the remaining juices separately.

Chicken Chili

4 tablespoons olive oil

10 garlic cloves, minced

4 medium onions, minced

5 celery stalks with tops, finely chopped

3 red, yellow, or green bell peppers, cored, seeded, and diced

4 tablespoons tomato paste

2½ pounds ground chicken, or combination of ground chicken and ground turkey

½ cup Dijon mustard

¼ cup chopped fresh basil, or 1 tablespoon dried

3 tablespoons ground cumin

1 tablespoon dried oregano

5 tablespoons chili powder

2 to 3 bay leaves

2 cups dry red wine

⅛ to ¼ teaspoon cayenne pepper, to taste

1 tablespoon molasses

One 16-ounce can pinto beans, drained and rinsed

One 16-ounce can navy beans, drained and rinsed

One 16-ounce can kidney beans, drained and rinsed

6 cups (two 28-ounce cans) canned crushed tomatoes

1 cup chopped fresh tomato

2 cups beer, approximately, preferably dark

Salt and freshly ground black pepper

½ to ¾ cup chopped Italian parsley leaves and/or coriander leaves (cilantro)

Serves 10 to 12

Everyone loves chili, but not the heaviness of traditional beef-based versions. This chili variation uses chicken, but it's just as satisfying and spicy-hearty as the dish made with beef. In fact, it's better. Three "secret" ingredients create a superior bowl of red: molasses for just a hint of sweetness, mustard, and beer (which is, by the way, a great flavor-enhancing liquid to cook beans in).

The ingredient list for this chili is rather long, but everything goes together quickly. The dish also freezes and reheats well; it's even better the next day. Serve the chili with bowls of chopped scallions, chopped fresh tomatoes, crushed tortilla chips, and one or two chopped fresh jalapeños mixed with two chopped red or yellow bell peppers —extra heat!

1. In a large, heavy-bottomed pot, heat the oil over medium heat. Add the garlic and sauté until golden, about 4 minutes. Add the onions, celery, and peppers and cook until the vegetables are soft, about 5 minutes.

2. Add the tomato paste, stir to combine, and cook 2 minutes. Add the chicken or chicken-turkey mixture and sauté, stirring to keep the meat from clumping, until cooked through, about 7 minutes. Stir in the mustard, basil, cumin, oregano, chili powder, bay leaves, wine, and cayenne. Add the molasses, beans, and tomatoes. Stir in 1 cup of the beer, reduce the heat, and simmer 1 hour, stirring occasionally.

4. Season the chili to taste with the salt and pepper. Add the remaining beer if necessary to thin. Add the parsley, stir thoroughly, and cook 5 minutes. Remove the bay leaves and serve with the suggested garnishes (see Headnote).

Turkey Milanese with Chopped Salad

Food prepared à la Milanese is usually dipped in egg and bread crumbs, then pan-fried. As delicious as such dishes may be, they're bound to be high in calories and rather heavy. By substituting egg whites for whole eggs, and using a nonstick pan with just a small amount of olive oil, the calorie and fat counts go down. Great taste is ensured by the use of savory turkey tenders (the tenderloin section attached to the breast) and the addition of a sprightly chopped salad.

If one tender per diner seems too much to you, halve the tenders before breading them. This easy dish would be perfect for an informal dinner party or middle-of-the-week family meal.

4 turkey tenders (about 1¾ pounds total)

Salt and freshly ground black pepper

½ cup flour, approximately

2 egg whites, whisked lightly with 2 tablespoons water

½ cup dry bread crumbs, approximately

¼ teaspoon paprika

12 fresh basil leaves, julienned, or 1 teaspoon dried

1 cup ¼-inch diced seeded cucumber

1 cup ½-inch diced tomato

3 tablespoons finely chopped red onion

1 teaspoon extra-virgin olive oil

1½ lemons, 1 quartered, ½ for juice

2 tablespoons olive oil

1 bunch arugula, washed and dried

Serves 4

1. Place each tender between 2 pieces of plastic wrap and pound to a ¼-inch thickness. Season the tenders with the salt and pepper.

2. In 3 separate shallow bowls, place the flour, egg whites, and bread crumbs. Mix the paprika into the flour.

3. Dip each tender into the flour, shake off the excess, then into the egg whites, then into the bread crumbs. Place the tenders on waxed paper.

4. In a small bowl, toss the basil, cucumber, tomato, onion, extra-virgin olive oil, and the juice of the ½ lemon. Season with the salt and pepper. Set aside.

5. Heat the olive oil in a large nonstick frying pan over high heat. Add the tenders and sauté until golden brown and cooked through, about 1 minute per side. Drain on paper towels.

6. Divide the arugula among 4 plates, or line 1 medium serving platter with it. Place a tender over the arugula on each plate, or arrange them on the platter. Spoon the chopped salad on top of each tender, garnish with lemon wedges, and serve.

Chicken Scarpariello

My family and I comb Italian restaurants in pursuit of the ultimate pollo alla scarpariello, *or shoemaker's chicken. This longtime favorite, featuring chicken, garlic, and fresh lemon, can be marvelous or very pedestrian. After years of tasting, comparing, and debating, I devised this version with chicken pieces. It's much sweeter, moister, and more flavorful, with the zip of fresh lemon and a touch of vinegar.*

½ cup olive oil

One 3½-pound chicken, trimmed of all visible fat and cut into 16 pieces

6 garlic cloves, chopped

Salt and freshly ground black pepper

2 tablespoons red wine vinegar

Juice of ½ lemon

1 tablespoon chopped fresh rosemary, or 1 teaspoon dried and crumbled

2 tablespoons Chicken Stock (page 61), or good instant or low-sodium canned

1 tablespoon chopped Italian parsley

Serves 4

1. In a large skillet, heat the olive oil over medium-high heat. Add the chicken, skin side down.

2. Cook, turning until golden brown, about 10 minutes. Add the garlic and season to taste with the salt and pepper. Cook until the garlic is golden brown, about 3 minutes.

3. Drain off as much oil as possible. Add the vinegar, lemon juice, rosemary, and stock. Sauté the chicken, turning to coat with the pan sauce. Cook until the chicken is done, 3 to 5 minutes, sprinkle with the parsley, and serve.

Basque Chicken with Peas

At some point this simple and delicious dish was declared "Basque," as it includes toma-toes, sweet peppers, and garlic—ingredients associated with the Basque cooking of north-ern Spain and southwestern France. Here peas are added, which provide a sweet vegetable accompaniment to the sautéed chicken and its savory pan sauce.

A great Friday night favorite, you can make the dish even more colorful by using a com-bination of red, yellow, and green peppers instead of the green alone.

3 tablespoons olive oil

One 3½-pound chicken, cut into eighths, trimmed of all visible fat, wing tips removed and reserved for another use

Freshly ground black pepper

3 large bell peppers, preferably 1 each red, green, and yellow, cored, seeded, and sliced into ¼-inch pieces

2 large onions, finely chopped

2 leeks, white and pale green parts only, clean and sliced

¼ cup coarsely chopped Italian parsley

4 garlic cloves, minced

½ cup dry vermouth

½ cup Chicken Stock (page 61), or good quality instant or low-sodium canned

2 pounds fresh peas, shelled, or 16 ounces frozen

Salt

Serves 4

1. In a large skillet, heat the olive oil over medium-high heat. Add the chicken and brown on all sides, 5 to 7 minutes. Season generously to taste with the pepper.

2. Remove the chicken and reserve. Reduce the heat to medium and add the peppers, onions, leeks, parsley, and garlic. Cook, stir-ring continuously, until the garlic and onion become translucent, about 5 minutes.

3. Return the chicken to the pan and add the vermouth and stock. Cover and cook over medium-low heat, stirring occasionally, until the chicken is nearly cooked, about 30 minutes. Warm a serving platter.

4. Add the peas, stir gently, cover, and cook until crisp-tender for fresh, 2 to 3 minutes, or heated through for frozen, 3 to 5 min-utes. Check the chicken to make sure it's cooked; if not, continue to cook briefly. Transfer the chicken and vegetables to a warm serving platter, pour the cooking juices over, and serve.

Barbara's "Wild" Balsamic Chicken

My first cousin Barbara gave this wonderful dish of sautéed chicken cutlets its name because of the wild mushrooms it contains. I've made this dish with shiitake, oyster, and cremini mushrooms, alone or in combination, and the results are fantastic. You can also make it with domestic mushrooms, and it turns out beautifully. Balsamic vinegar lends its sweet-tart woodiness to the dish, which is ready in about a half-hour.

For a vivacious spring dinner, serve the chicken on wilted arugula with steamed asparagus.

4 medium chicken cutlets (about 1½ pounds total), pounded to a ¼-inch thickness

2 tablespoons flour

1 tablespoon olive oil

6 to 8 garlic cloves, peeled and very lightly crushed

1 pound shiitake, oyster, or cremini mushrooms, or a combination, left whole if small, otherwise cut into bite-size pieces, or domestic mushrooms, sliced ¼ inch thick

¼ cup balsamic vinegar

¾ cup Chicken Stock (page 61), or good quality instant or low-sodium canned

1 bay leaf

3 sprigs fresh thyme, or ¼ teaspoon dried leaves

1 tablespoon unsalted margarine, chilled, cut into 3 pieces

Serves 4

1. Dust the cutlets lightly with the flour.

2. In a large nonstick skillet, heat the oil over medium-high heat. Add the garlic and sauté until brown, 3 to 4 minutes. Remove with a slotted spoon and reserve.

3. Add the chicken to the skillet and brown on one side, about 3 minutes. Turn the chicken, place the reserved garlic and the mushrooms on top, and cook 3 minutes. Add the vinegar, stock, bay leaf, and thyme. Cover the skillet, reduce the heat to low, and cook until the chicken is done, about 10 minutes, shifting the pieces occasionally for even cooking.

4. Remove the chicken. Increase the heat to medium-high and cook the pan liquids, uncovered, until reduced and thickened, and the mushrooms are cooked, about 7 minutes. Remove the bay leaf. Remove the pan from the heat and add the margarine one piece at a time, stirring, to emulsify the sauce. Place the cutlets and mushrooms on 4 serving plates, divide the sauce evenly over them, and serve.

French-African Chicken Stew

Imagine a French chicken stew that also includes African, Turkish, and Chinese ingredients. This dish does just that to create a delightful mélange of flavor. The optional sumac, the tangy Turkish spice, makes a great flavor addition.

This stew does particularly well prepared a day or two ahead. Or stagger the preparation, completing the vegetables beforehand (see Note).

¼ cup loosely packed coriander leaves (cilantro)

¼ cup loosely packed Italian parsley leaves

3 tablespoons dry-roasted unsalted peanuts

1 tablespoon olive oil

4 pounds chicken cutlets, cut into 1½-inch cubes

3 medium onions, finely chopped

4 garlic cloves, minced

One 1¼-inch piece of fresh ginger, peeled and finely chopped

5 leeks, trimmed of all but 1 inch of green above white portion, cleaned and finely chopped

4 red, green, or yellow bell peppers, or a combination, seeded, cored, and very thinly sliced

2 lemons, thinly sliced and seeds removed

3 to 4 cups Chicken Stock (page 61), or good instant or low-sodium canned broth

Juice of 1 lemon

1 teaspoon sumac (optional; see Headnote)

Salt and freshly ground black pepper

Serves 8

1. Chop the coriander, parsley, and peanuts together and reserve for final inclusion.

2. In a large, heavy nonstick pot, heat the oil over high heat. Add the chicken in batches and sauté until browned, about 4 minutes. Remove with a slotted spoon and set aside.

3. In the same pot, sauté the onions, garlic, ginger, and leeks until limp, about 3 minutes. Add the peppers and sauté 4 minutes more. Add the lemon slices, and 3 cups of the stock, and simmer, covered, until the vegetables have softened, about 30 minutes. One-quarter to ¹/₂ inch of stock should be maintained in the pot to cook the vegetables; add more stock if necessary (see Note).

4. Uncover and add the chicken. Simmer until the chicken is just done, 10 to 15 minutes.

5. Stir in the lemon juice, sumac, if using, and chopped coriander, parsley, and peanuts. Season to taste with the salt and pepper and serve.

Note: If preparing the dish partially ahead, do not sauté the chicken (step 2). Sauté the vegetables in the oil and simmer in the stock with the lemon slices, step 3. Cool and refrigerate the vegetables. When ready to complete the dish, bring the vegetables to room temperature and sauté the chicken as in step 2. Combine the chicken and vegetables, step 4, and proceed.

Stir-Fried Chicken
with String Beans

There is a wonderful rhythm to stir-frying, the quick flip-flops, the sweeps and turns. The results are equally satisfying—appealing, quickly cooked food with all its taste and texture intact. This dish of stir-fried chicken features crisp string beans and the Chinese flavors of soy, ginger, and garlic. It's very beautiful, too—the whiteness of the chicken together with the vivid green of the beans makes a striking presentation. This easy dish is fabulous for a party or makes a satisfying weekday dinner. For a nice luncheon, try it served at room temperature over a bed of watercress, with rice.

2 pounds chicken cutlets, lightly pounded and cut into ¼-inch-wide strips as long as the halved string beans (see below)

1 teaspoon salt

3 egg whites

2 tablespoons cornstarch

1½ pounds fresh string beans, trimmed and halved diagonally

1 garlic clove, crushed

⅓ cup canola or other light vegetable oil

6 thin slices peeled fresh ginger

1 red bell pepper, cored, seeded, and cut in strips the size of the beans

½ cup, approximately, Chicken Stock (page 61), or good instant or low-sodium canned

5 tablespoons dry sherry

4 teaspoons sugar

½ cup light soy sauce

Serves 6 to 8

1. Rub the chicken with the salt. Place the egg whites and cornstarch in 2 separate small bowls. Immerse the chicken in batches in the egg white, drain, and dredge it with the cornstarch. (The strips will look sticky and clump together; they will separate in the cooking process.)

2. Bring a pot of water to a boil. Drop in the beans and blanch, for 2 minutes only. Drain the beans and run under cold water to stop the cooking.

3. Rub a large nonstick wok or large skillet with the garlic. Add 2 tablespoons of the oil and heat it over medium-high heat.

4. Add the ginger and pepper and stir-fry 1 minute. Add the chicken, spreading the chicken strips evenly over the bottom of the wok, and stir-fry until the chicken is done, about 2 minutes. Remove the chicken and pepper and reserve. Do not crowd the pan; you may need to do this in 2 batches.

5. Add the remaining oil and turn the heat to high. Toss in the string beans and stir-fry until crisp-tender, 1 minute. Pour in the stock, sherry, sugar, and soy sauce. Cook, stirring, for 2 minutes. Return the chicken and pepper to the pan and stir-fry for an additional minute. Serve at once.

Fanny's Chicken Cutlets

My grandmother Fanny was a great cook and these golden sautéed chicken cutlets, crisp and juicy, were one of her specialties. She produced mountains of them for family gatherings. Fanny served them with the Best-Ever Tomato Sauce (page 232), but you could pass them with lemon wedges for spritzing.

You can also prepare these ahead. Don't sauté them to completion; spread the partially prepared cutlets on a baking sheet and finish the cooking in a 300°F. oven. By the way, these make great sandwiches (see Fanny's Finale, page 283).

During Passover, substitute matzo meal for the bread crumb coating.

6 large chicken cutlets
(about 3 pounds total)

1¼ cups bread crumbs or matzo meal

Salt and freshly ground black pepper

2 eggs, beaten

3 to 4 garlic cloves, pressed

⅔ cup canola or other light vegetable oil

Serves 4 to 6

1. Remove the tenders (the partially attached striplike pieces) from the cutlets. Reserve.

2. Place the cutlets between waxed, parchment, or freezer paper. Pound the cutlets lightly to a uniform thickness.

3. Pour the crumbs onto a shallow dish, and season with the salt and pepper. Mix and distribute the crumbs evenly. Pour the eggs onto a second shallow dish. Add the garlic and beat with a fork to incorporate.

4. Cover a platter with waxed paper. Dip the tenders into the egg and then into the crumbs. Turn to coat well, shake to remove excess crumbs, and place on the waxed paper. Repeat the procedure with the cutlets.

5. In a large, heavy skillet, add the oil to a depth of ¹/₄ inch. Heat the oil over medium-high heat until hot. Add the cutlets and sauté until golden and firm to the touch, turning once, 5 to 10 minutes per side. Remove from the pan and drain or brown paper or paper toweling. Add the tenders and sauté 2 to 3 minutes per side. Serve.

Cozy Turkish Chicken

The cooking of Turkish Jews is vegetable based. This delicious Turkish-influenced dish features string beans stewed with skinless chicken, turmeric, and tomatoes. Don't let the long cooking of the beans put you off—they're meant to stew thoroughly until soft and flavorful. The finished dish, brightened with lemon juice, is perfect family eating.

The pan you use should accommodate the chicken with enough room to allow the cooking liquid to reduce somewhat and intensify in flavor as everything simmers. This goes beautifully with rice, couscous, or polenta.

2 tablespoons olive oil, or canola or other light vegetable oil

3 pounds chicken parts, excluding wings, skin removed

1 medium onion, chopped

3 garlic cloves, pressed

3 ripe plum tomatoes, seeded and chopped, or 1 cup canned crushed tomatoes or canned diced tomatoes

2 large pinches of saffron threads

2 teaspoons turmeric

2½ cups tomato juice

1 bay leaf

1 cup Chicken Stock (page 61), approximately, or good instant or low-sodium canned broth

1 pound string beans, trimmed

Juice of ½ lemon

1 tablespoon chopped fresh chervil or Italian parsley leaves

Serves 4

1. In a large, deep nonstick skillet, heat 1 tablespoon of the oil over medium-high heat. Add the chicken in batches and sear-brown on all sides, about 3 minutes per side.

2. Remove the chicken and reserve. Add the remaining tablespoon of oil to the skillet, allow to heat, and add the onion. Sauté the onion until soft, about 5 minutes. Add the garlic and cook for 3 minutes. Add the tomatoes and cook for 10 minutes. Add the saffron and turmeric.

3. Return the chicken to the pan and add the tomato juice and bay leaf. Bring to a boil, reduce the heat, and simmer, covered, for 40 minutes. Check the chicken while cooking, adding the chicken stock as needed to maintain a pourable sauce.

4. Add the string beans and cook, covered, until very tender, about 30 minutes. Add the lemon juice and cook, uncovered, 10 minutes more. Remove the bay leaf. Stir the chervil into the sauce and serve.

5. In the Oven

Is there any dish better than roast chicken?

Nothing pleases people more than a tender,

crisp-skinned bird, trailing curls of fragrant steam.

Everyone loves its golden skin and succulent meat,

moist with sweet juices.

In roasting, high, dry heat caramelizes food surfaces and intensifies flavors to ensure deeply delicious eating. But that same heat can also rob meat of its succulence. Successful poultry roasting or baking (the difference is one of cooking temperature) depends on guarding against moisture loss.

To shore up moisture, I add humidifying liquid to the roasting pan (which should always be the size of the roast and sturdy enough to support it). An overcooked bird has lost its moisture forever. To avoid overcooking, test smaller roasts frequently toward their completion by pricking a joint; if the juices run clear, the roast is done. When roasting large poultry and poultry parts (such as a turkey breast), use a meat thermometer inserted into the thickest part of the meat. When it registers 155° to 160° F., the bird is done. (This range may seem low to you, but remember that the roast continues to cook even as it cools.) Finally, be sure not to serve the bird immediately after it comes out of the oven. Wait 15 or 20 minutes for the reabsorption of moisture drawn to the roast's exterior by the heat.

Some people think of roasting as a big deal, but it can be easy on the cook. Though dishes like the sensational Roast Turkey with Fennel-

Cornbread Stuffing require time, many oven-cooked birds are simply done, or can be prepared ahead. Over time, I've devised an approach that guarantees delicious poultry roasts with less work for the cook: marinate the bird and/or use a seasoning paste to create flavor, then roast with vegetables or fruits, which become an accompaniment. You can make an easy sauce using the roast's natural juices—no gloppy gravies!

For example, the Roast Cranberry Chicken with Shallots begins with a seasoning paste of mustard, maple syrup, herbs, and spices. The bird is roasted and served with plumped dried cranberries and shallots. The finished dish is spicy, sweet, and tangy all at once. Roast Chicken in Cinnamon-Scented Plum Sauce and Sylvia's Autumn Chicken, a curry-perfumed bird with sweet potatoes and red lentils, are other examples of this fast, flavor-building approach.

Take advantage also of clay pot cookery. Chicken in a Clay Pot, an herby no-fuss bird, introduces you to the virtues of meal-in-one cooking in a sealed enclosure. It's the perfect technique for weekdays when you want great food but haven't much time. Turkey Meatloaf is another great everyday "roast." Savory and comforting, the turkey loaf is lighter and healthier than the traditional dish. (Using the same basic loaf mixture, make simmered Turkey Meatballs, a second-night dish your kids will love.)

Oven cooking also excels for relaxed entertaining. Five-Spice Roast Turkey Breast with Pear-Garlic Sauce is the perfect dish for a buffet or elegant dinner, as is Chili-Rubbed Chicken and Corn Ragout, a fresh take on the sunny tastes of the Southwest. I prize the oven also for Friday night or holiday meals. Grandma Regina's Roast Chicken, the best roast chicken ever, is a superb cook's master dish—and really easy to do. Pungent Shabbat Chicken with Dried Fruit, redolent of tangy fresh orange, is *the* perfect Friday night treat and Rosh Hashanah specialty.

People sometimes think that duck is a big production and unsuitable for occasions when the host is also the cook, but duck can be prepared ahead. Though you'll probably want to serve Slow-Roast Crispy Duck right from the oven, all of the duck recipes in this chapter can be made in advance. Rich duck meat is naturally moist and reheats beautifully. Or save the meat to use in Rice Paper Rolls (page 281), for a duck salad, or reheated with Every-Way Cherry Sauce (page 244). And whenever you roast duck, make an extra for the next day. That way, you'll have delicious roast duck on hand for all to enjoy.

Grandma Regina's Roast Chicken

The smell of this chicken cooking takes me back to my grandmother Regina's home. Its scent of paprika, garlic, celery, and herbs sizzling together will always mean comfort, open arms, love, and East 29th Street in Brooklyn, where Grandma lived. Hungarian by birth, Grandma Regina was a great cook. Before major holidays she would cook for days. My grandfather would wrap her food, pack it, and put it in his car to transport it to our house. The sight of his backing the car into our driveway just so, then unloading speckled blue pans, is relived every time I make this sweet-savory chicken.

SEASONING PASTE

¼ teaspoon mustard powder

2 tablespoons apricot preserves

½ teaspoon dried thyme or poultry seasoning (see page 13)

¼ to ½ teaspoon ground ginger

2 garlic cloves, pressed

½ teaspoon sweet paprika

One 4- to 5-pound chicken, washed,
rinsed, and trimmed of all visible fat

Freshly ground black pepper

3 medium onions, cut into thin wedges

½ cup sliced celery, plus 1 stalk cut
into 4 pieces

1 bunch fresh herbs, such as thyme,
or 1 cup basil leaves, fennel fronds,
or parsley

2 teaspoons olive oil or margarine

2 garlic cloves, pressed

¼ cup Chicken Stock (page 61), or good
instant or low-sodium canned broth

1. Preheat the oven to 425°F. To make the paste, in a small bowl, combine the mustard powder, preserves, thyme, ginger, garlic, and paprika and set aside.

2. Pepper the chicken inside and out. Stuff its cavity with some of the onion wedges, the sliced celery, and fresh herbs, without packing it too tightly. Truss the chicken securely (see page 25).

3. Rub the chicken all over with the olive oil and the garlic. Place it breast side down on a roasting rack set in a roasting pan. Pour the stock into the pan and roast 30 minutes.

4. Remove the chicken from the oven. Place the thyme sprigs, carrots, and remaining onions and celery in the pan under the rack and add the orange juice. Brush the chicken with the paste.

5. Reduce the heat to 375°F. Turn the chicken breast side up and roast it, basting as necessary, until the skin is brown and crisp, and the juices run clear when a joint is pierced with a fork, 30 to 40 minutes.

6. Transfer the chicken to a platter and allow it to rest for a few minutes for easier carving. Remove the rack from the pan, tilt

4 sprigs fresh thyme, or 1 teaspoon dried

½ cup sliced peeled carrots

1 cup fresh orange juice

Serves 4 to 6

the pan, and spoon off the fat. Remove any herb sprigs and discard. Using a slotted spoon, place half the cooked vegetables in a food processor. Process by pulsing while adding the pan juices gradually. Carve the chicken and transfer to a platter. Spoon the remaining vegetables around the chicken and serve with the pan sauce.

Honey Ginger Chicken

My children adore this tantalizing baked chicken. Marinated in a soy and honey bath, it cooks to a caramelized sweetness that's irresistible. To produce this delicious taste and deep color, make sure to give the chicken the full roasting time; it won't be overcooked, I promise you.

Serve this bird with rice and a platter of steamed green vegetables such as snow peas, broccoli, and spinach. It's also wonderful cold for lunch with Warm Fennel Slaw (page 185) or buckwheat noodles tossed with Wasabi Sauce (page 46), garnished with cucumber slices and snipped chives.

One 6-inch piece fresh ginger, peeled and coarsely chopped (about ½ cup)

12 garlic cloves, minced

16 medium scallions, white and green parts, coarsely chopped

¾ cup low-sodium soy sauce

¾ cup honey

¼ teaspoon five-spice powder

Freshly ground black pepper

Two 3-pound chickens, trimmed of all visible fat and cut into eighths, or 6 pounds chicken parts of your choice

Serves 6 to 8

1. Preheat the oven to 350°F.

2. Place the ginger, garlic, scallions, and half the soy sauce in a food processor and process 2 minutes. Add the remaining soy sauce, the honey, and five-spice powder. Season to taste with the pepper and process to blend.

3. In a large bowl, combine the chicken with the marinade and toss. Line a large 1¹/₂- to 2-inch deep baking dish with foil and add the chicken skin side down in a single layer. Spoon over the marinade and bake for 45 minutes. Turn the pieces over, baste with the sauce from the pan, and bake another 45 minutes. Serve the chicken hot or cold.

Oven-Poached Coriander Chicken Breasts

Boneless chicken breasts are delicate and low in fat. They also cook in a flash. For this dish, perfect for a buffet, rolled breasts are poached in a thickened coriander and saffron-scented broth. Finished with mushrooms and olives, the breasts are as beautiful to look at as they're great to eat.

Couscous is the perfect mate for this dish. To start the meal, I usually serve a tart and tempting watercress salad with Orange Onion Dressing (page 237).

3 pounds medium chicken cutlets, lightly pounded

¼ cup chopped parsley

1 tablespoon olive oil

1 cup chopped onion

5 garlic cloves, minced

2 tablespoons flour

¼ teaspoon ground coriander

2 tablespoons coriander seeds, coarsely crushed

Pinch of saffron threads (optional)

1 to 2 tablespoons minced rind of Preserved Lemons (page 243), optional

½ cup chopped fresh coriander (cilantro) or parsley

1½ cups Chicken Stock (page 61), or good instant or low-sodium canned broth

Salt and freshly ground black pepper

1½ lemons, thinly sliced and seeded, plus juice of ½ lemon

½ pound small white mushrooms, quartered

½ cup pitted green olives

Serves 6 to 8

1. Place the cutlets, smooth side down, on a flat surface. Sprinkle with the parsley, roll to enclose it, and secure with a toothpick. Place the rolled cutlets seam side down in a deep oven-to-table baking dish; they should fit snugly. Set aside.

2. Preheat the oven to 350°F.

3. In a medium skillet, heat the olive oil over medium heat. Add the onion and garlic and sauté until lightly golden, 3 to 5 minutes. Add the flour, stirring, and sauté for 2 minutes to combine. Add the ground coriander, coriander seeds, saffron, preserved lemon, if using, and fresh coriander. Stir and remove from the heat.

4. Spoon one-quarter of the skillet mixture into a small bowl and set aside. Add the chicken stock to the remaining mixture and stir to incorporate. Pour this over the rolled chicken breasts in the baking dish. Season to taste with the salt and pepper and drizzle over the lemon juice.

5. Cover the dish and oven-poach for 15 minutes. Shift the rolls to ensure even cooking and continue to poach until the cutlets are two-thirds done, about 10 minutes more. Uncover, and transfer the cutlets to a cutting board. Remove the dish from the oven and gently stir the mushrooms, lemon slices, and the reserved onion mixture into the poaching liquid. Gently stir in the olives.

6. Remove the toothpicks from the rolls and cut the rolls into $^1/_2$-inch slices. Transfer the slices to the dish and continue to cook until just done, 5 to 10 minutes. Serve hot.

Sylvia's Autumn Chicken

My friend Sylvie, a passionate cook, provided the inspiration for this savory chicken dish. Featuring a marinade made with prune juice and curry powder, and including carrots and sweet potatoes, the dish sounded marvelous as she described it one day. When I set about making it, I added red lentils, which make the dish more memorable still. It's full of the flavors of autumn, but good any time.

Use Red Garnet sweet potatoes for this, if you can find them.

¾ cup prune juice

1 tablespoon curry powder

1 teaspoon turmeric

⅛ teaspoon freshly ground black pepper

2 sprigs fresh thyme, or ¼ teaspoon dried

One 3½- to 4-pound chicken, cut into eighths, skin removed

1 large Vidalia or other sweet onion, halved and very thinly sliced

1 pound carrots, peeled and thinly sliced on the diagonal

2 sweet potatoes, peeled and thinly sliced on the diagonal

½ cup red lentils, soaked in 1 cup boiling water 30 minutes to 1 hour

¼ cup chopped Italian parsley

Serves 4

1. In a roaster with a cover, combine the prune juice, curry powder, turmeric, pepper, and thyme. Add the chicken and marinate for 1 hour. Preheat the oven to 400°F.

2. Place the onion, carrots, and sweet potatoes under the chicken, cover, and bake 20 minutes. Baste the chicken and rearrange the vegetables so they cook evenly. Bake 15 minutes more, baste again, and add the lentils, stirring them into the pan juices. Bake until the chicken is done and the vegetables have fallen apart, creating a thick sauce, about 20 minutes. Remove the chicken from the oven, stir in the parsley, and serve.

Vineyard Chicken

Sole véronique is a French classic that pairs the fish with fresh grapes. This rolled chicken breast version is an Empire favorite. Fresh basil and tarragon flavor the breasts, which are oven-poached, sliced, and served with a glistening sauce containing red and green grapes. The result is a dish that's both beautiful and delicious. Serve this with a wild rice pilaf or over spinach fettuccine that's been tossed with a bit of olive oil and chopped parsley.

3 tablespoons olive oil

1 cup chopped shallots

½ cup dry white wine

1 cup fresh orange juice

2 cups Chicken Stock (page 61), or good instant or low-sodium canned broth

1 cup packed fresh basil leaves, washed, well-dried, and finely chopped

2 tablespoons fresh tarragon leaves, washed, well-dried, and finely chopped

Salt and freshly ground black pepper

6 medium chicken cutlets (about 2½ pounds total), lightly pounded

1 tablespoon softened margarine

2 teaspoons kudzu, or 1 teaspoon cornstarch

1 teaspoon raspberry vinegar

1½ cups red seedless grapes

1½ cups green seedless grapes

Serves 4 to 6

1. Preheat the oven to 350°F.

2. In a small saucepan, heat 1 tablespoon of the olive oil over low heat. Add the shallots and sauté gently until soft and lightly colored, about 10 minutes. Add the wine, orange juice, and stock and simmer to reduce by half, about 30 minutes. Reserve.

3. In a small bowl, combine the basil and tarragon with the remaining 2 tablespoons of oil. Season to taste with the salt and pepper and stir. Set one-quarter of the mixture aside.

4. Arrange the cutlets on your work surface, smooth sides down. Spread some of the remaining herb-oil mixture over each. Roll each cutlet starting at the small ends and tucking in the sides as you go. Secure the rolls with toothpicks and place the rolls, touching, seam side down in a 8 x 8-inch oven dish.

5. Combine the remaining herb-oil mixture with the margarine. Scrape the mixture onto an 8-inch piece of waxed paper and use the paper to form the mixture into a log. Wrap the log in the paper and place in the freezer to chill.

6. Pour 1 cup of the reserved orange-stock mixture over the rolls, cover tightly, and poach until the chicken is opaque and springy to the touch, 30 to 45 minutes. Uncover and pour the poaching liquid into the saucepan with the remaining orange-stock mixture. Cover the rolls and keep them warm. Alternatively, for a buffet, cut the rolls into $1/2$-inch slices, reform the slices into logs, and return them snugly to the pan.

7. In a small dish, dissolve the kudzu in 1 tablespoon of cold water. Add some of the orange-stock mixture to the kudzu mixture to dilute it further and return this to the saucepan. Heat this mixture over medium-low heat, reduce the heat to low, and simmer gently until the sauce is very lightly thickened, about 10 minutes. Stir in the raspberry vinegar. Slice the chilled log into 4 pieces and whisk it 1 piece at a time into the hot sauce. Allow each piece to dissolve before adding the next. Stir in the grapes and allow the sauce to warm completely.

8. To serve, place the whole chicken rolls or the slices on a warm platter. Spoon some sauce over and around the chicken and offer the remaining sauce separately.

Crisp Lemon Chicken

This lemon-scented roast chicken will remind you of those glorious birds served at French bistros—crisp-skinned, juicy, and full of flavor. The secret, which I discovered one night when I had to make dinner fast, is roasting at a high temperature. Following this method, the chicken cooks quickly and to perfection.

Serve this tart, herby bird with Mashed Potatoes with Leeks and Garlic (page 197), sautéed broccoli rabe, and Oven-Roasted Beets (page 207).

One 4- to 5-pound chicken, rinsed and trimmed of all visible fat

Freshly ground black pepper

2 tablespoons olive oil

4 garlic cloves, pressed

2 lemons, 1 very thinly sliced, 1 juiced

5 sprigs rosemary, or 1 teaspoon dried

1 cup very thinly sliced onion

1 celery stalk with leaves, sliced into ½-inch lengths

½ cup Italian parsley sprigs

1 bay leaf

2 cups Chicken Stock (page 61), or good instant or low-sodium canned broth

Serves 4 to 6

1. Preheat the oven to 425°F.

2. Pepper the chicken inside and out and rub with the oil, then the garlic. Place half the lemon slices, 2 rosemary sprigs (or ½ teaspoon dried), half each of the onion slices, celery with leaves, and parsley inside the cavity. Truss the chicken tightly (see page 25).

3. Place the chicken breast side down on a roasting rack set in a roasting pan. Place the bay leaf and the remaining lemon, rosemary, onion, celery with leaves, and parsley under the rack. Add 1 cup of the chicken stock.

4. Roast the chicken for 30 minutes. Remove from the oven, baste with the pan juices, and turn the chicken over. Pour over the lemon juice, return to the oven, and roast until the skin is crisp and brown and the juices run clear when a joint is pieced with a fork, 30 to 40 minutes.

5. Transfer the chicken to a warm platter and allow it to rest for a few minutes for easier carving. Remove the rack from the pan. Tilt the pan and spoon off the fat. Add the remaining stock to the pan and heat on the stove top, scraping up the brown bits, until the stock is somewhat reduced, about 5 minutes. Remove the bay leaf and rosemary fronds, if using.

6. Carve the chicken and discard the cavity vegetables. Remove the pan vegetables and place them in a strainer, pressing on them with a wooden spoon over the pan to extract as much liquid as possible. Discard the solids. Serve the chicken with the pan juices.

Chicken in a Clay Pot

SEASONING PASTE

1 tablespoon apricot preserves

½ teaspoon freshly ground black pepper

1 teaspoon sweet paprika

3 garlic cloves, pressed

1 teaspoon dried basil

2 medium onions, cut into ¼-inch dice

3 garlic cloves, thinly sliced

½ cup whole canned tomatoes, drained and chopped

One 3½- to 4-pound chicken, rinsed and trimmed of all visible fat, wing tips removed (save for stock making)

Handful of whole mixed fresh herbs, such as Italian parsley, rosemary, and thyme, or ¼ teaspoon each dried rosemary and thyme

¼ cup fresh orange juice

½ cup sliced celery stalks, leaves chopped and reserved

3 medium potatoes, peeled and cut into 1-inch dice

3 medium carrots, peeled and cut into 1-inch pieces

1 tablespoon chopped fresh rosemary leaves, or ¼ teaspoon dried

Serves 3 to 4

Clay-pot chicken cookery is fast and no fuss, and produces a juicy, delectable bird. You can put everything in the pot the night before, stick it in the refrigerator, pop it in the oven the following evening, and dinner is ready two hours later. And because everything cooks together in a sealed casserole, flavors are deliciously blended.

Clay pots come in various shapes and sizes. For this dish and others like it you want one with a 2½-quart capacity. You have to do some preliminary pot seasoning (follow the manufacturer's instructions); soak the pot before each use and you're ready to go. This dish, which features an herby chicken cooked with apricot preserves, garlic, potatoes, and carrots, makes the perfect clay-pot specialty.

1. Soak the clay pot in cold water to cover for about 20 minutes.

2. Meanwhile, prepare the seasoning paste by combining the preserves, pepper, paprika, garlic, and basil in a small bowl.

3. Place the onion, garlic, and tomatoes in the bottom of the pot. Rub the chicken inside and out with the paste. Place the whole herbs in its cavity. Place the chicken on top of the vegetables and pour in the orange juice.

4. Distribute the sliced celery, chopped leaves, potatoes, carrots, and chopped rosemary around the chicken. Cover.

5. Place the pot in a cold oven, turn the heat to 450°F., and bake until done, 2 to 2½ hours. The chicken juices will run clear when a joint is pierced. Remove the chicken from the oven and drain the juices into a bowl. Defat the juices and pour into a sauce boat. Serve the chicken surrounded by the vegetables and pass the juices separately.

Chili-Rubbed Chicken and Corn Ragout

Seasoned with a chipotle chili puree and served with a lively poblano-corn ragout, this chicken is a festive take on the Southwest cooking approach.

Poblanos, used in the ragout, are similar to green bell peppers but hotter and more aromatic. If poblanos are unavailable, use a mixture of green pepper and minced jalapeño (see below). Remember, though, that the jalapeño's heat is in its seeds, so unless you like really spicy foods, omit the seeds.

The complete dish is heavenly, but you can make the chicken alone if you're pressed for time. In that case, serve the chicken with your favorite salsa combined with cooked corn kernels or with chopped cucumber.

RAGOUT

1 tablespoon olive oil

5 garlic cloves, minced

¼ cup chopped red onion

⅓ cup seeded, cored, and julienned poblano pepper, or 1 small julienned green bell pepper mixed with ½ to 1 chopped jalapeño pepper

2 cups julienned red bell peppers

3½ cups corn kernels, fresh or frozen and defrosted

1 cup Chicken Stock (page 61), or good instant or low-sodium canned

12 mustard green leaves or 24 watercress sprigs

1 cup peeled, seeded, and coarsely chopped tomatoes

⅓ packed fresh basil leaves

1. To make the ragout, in a large skillet, heat the olive oil over medium heat. Add the garlic and onion and sauté until soft, about 4 minutes. Add the hot and bell peppers and sauté until softened slightly, about 2 minutes.

2. Add the corn and cook, stirring, about 2 minutes. Add the stock and bring to a boil. Reduce the heat and simmer for 5 minutes. Remove from the heat.

3. Stir in the greens, tomatoes, and basil and allow to come to room temperature. Reserve.

4. To prepare the chicken, remove the tip and second joint from each chicken wing (reserve for stock). Pat the chicken pieces dry.

5. In a shallow bowl, combine the cornmeal, chili powder, cumin, and oregano. In a blender or food processor, puree the chipotle pepper and liquid. Brush the puree on the chicken and dredge evenly on all sides with the cornmeal mixture. Preheat the oven to 500°F.

CHICKEN

6 large whole chicken breasts, halved and boned but with wings attached (reserve remaining bones for stock)

1 cup coarse yellow cornmeal

1 tablespoon chili powder, preferably ancho chili powder

1 tablespoon ground cumin

¼ teaspoon dried oregano

1 ounce canned chipotle pepper (about 2 tablespoons, chopped), plus 2 tablespoons liquid

3 tablespoons olive oil

Serves 6

6. In a large, heavy skillet, heat the olive oil over medium-high heat. Add the chicken and sauté, skin side down, until the skin begins to brown, about 5 minutes. Turn and sauté 2 more minutes. Cook in batches if necessary.

7. Transfer the chicken to a baking sheet. Bake the chicken until the coating is evenly brown and crisp and the juices run clear when the thickest part is pierced with a fork, about 15 minutes.

8. Meanwhile, gently reheat the ragout. When the chicken is done, ladle $^{1}/_{2}$ cup of the ragout on each plate. Place chicken on top and serve.

Roast Cranberry Chicken with Shallots

This dish never fails to elicit praise, as well as those satisfied sounds that mean people are loving their food.

It couldn't be simpler. You make a seasoning paste with spices, herbs, mustard, and maple syrup and rub it on the chicken, which is then roasted with plumped dried cranberries and shallots. The shallots soften and become crispy on the outside; the cranberries cook down to perfect tart-sweetness. The finished dish is tangy, spicy, and sweet all at once.

Buy only natural, minimally sweetened cranberries. If you see sugar crystals on the berries, shop for them elsewhere.

1 cup dried cranberries

1 cup fresh orange juice

One 4½-pound chicken, trimmed of all visible fat, giblets and neck reserved

1 lemon, halved

2 tablespoons coarse-grained mustard

2 tablespoons maple syrup

2 teaspoons ground ginger

⅛ teaspoon ground allspice

1 teaspoon dried thyme, or 3 sprigs fresh

Salt and freshly ground black pepper

6 sprigs fresh herbs: a mixture of rosemary, parsley, thyme, or oregano

16 shallots, peeled

1 large tart green apple, peeled, cored, and diced

2 medium onions, quartered

1½ cups Chicken Stock (page 61), or good instant or low-sodium canned broth

Serves 4

1. Preheat the oven to 425°F. In a small bowl, combine the cranberries and orange juice. Allow to plump, about 20 minutes.

2. Meanwhile, rinse the chicken and pat dry. Squeeze the lemon over the chicken and into its cavity.

3. In a small bowl, combine the mustard, maple syrup, ginger, allspice, and thyme. Add salt and pepper and rub this mixture over the chicken. Place the herb sprigs in the cavity. Put the chicken in a roasting pan that allows about 2 to 3 inches of room around the bird, breast side down.

4. Drain the cranberries, reserving the juice. Scatter the shallots, cranberries, and the apple in the pan. Roast for 30 minutes.

5. While the chicken is roasting, combine the giblets and neck, the onions, reserved orange juice, and the chicken stock in a medium saucepan over high heat. When the mixture boils, reduce the heat and simmer 25 minutes. Set aside.

6. Reduce the oven temperature to 400°F. Add $^3/_4$ cup of the reserved broth mixture to the roasting pan. Turn the chicken and roast 30 minutes more, basting 2 or 3 times with the pan juices.

7. Strain the remaining broth, discarding the solids. Add $^3/_4$ cup of the broth to the roasting pan and roast 30 minutes more, basting.

8. Remove the chicken from the pan and allow to rest for 10 minutes. Using poultry shears, cut the chicken into serving pieces. Discard the herbs. Pour the pan juices into a small bowl and skim off the fat.

9. Return the chicken to the pan. Pour the pan juices and the remaining broth over the chicken. Scatter the shallots, cranberries, and apple over the chicken, cover, and bake for 10 minutes. Place the chicken on a large platter, surround it with the shallots, cranberries, and apple, and serve.

Whimsical Chicken Pot Pie

This easy chicken pie, with its top crust of cookie-cutter figures, is a tradition in my family. You prepare it with frozen pie crust (or make your own). You'll need cookie cutters, of course, in animal, star, alphabet, or number shapes (great for birthday-dinner pies) or whatever strikes your fancy. The cut shapes should overlap slightly to form a latticework-like top crust.

2½ cups Chicken Stock (page 61), or good-quality instant or low-sodium canned broth

2 cups sliced peeled carrots

2 sprigs fresh rosemary, or 1 teaspoon dried

¼ pound sugar snap peas, cut in half diagonally

½ cup green peas, fresh or frozen and defrosted

1 cup fresh cooked corn kernels, cut off cob (about 3 ears), or 1 cup frozen kernels, defrosted

2 teaspoons margarine or vegetable oil

4 teaspoons flour

1 pound cooked chicken breast, cut into 1 x 2-inch strips (about 4 cups)

Cornmeal, for dredging

2 frozen 9-inch prepared pie crusts, defrosted

1 egg white

Makes 4 pies

1. In a small saucepan, bring the stock to a boil. Add the carrots and rosemary and cook until the carrots are tender-crisp, about 4 minutes. Remove the carrots and reserve. Reserve the stock over the heat.

2. Prepare a small bowl of ice water. Add the sugar snaps to the stock and cook until tender-crisp, about 2 minutes. Remove to the ice water. When cold, drain and add to the carrots. Add the peas and corn. Reserve the cooking stock.

3. In a small saucepan, melt the margarine or heat the oil over medium-low heat. Add the flour and cook, stirring, until the flour starts to turn golden, about 4 minutes. Add the reserved stock and whisk the sauce until thickened. Remove the rosemary, if using fresh, and discard. Cover the sauce and set aside.

4. Preheat the oven to 475°F. Coat the insides of four 1¹/₂-cup baking dishes with vegetable oil spray. Spoon in the reserved vegetables and the chicken. Pour the sauce over.

5. Sprinkle a work surface with the cornmeal. Remove the dough from the pans and flatten it gently with a rolling pin. Roll the dough out into 2 circles, ¹/₄ inch thick. Using cookie cutters, cut out shapes and place them overlapping slightly on top of the fillings. In a small bowl, combine the egg white with 1 teaspoon water and mix well. Brush the shapes with the mixture. Place the dishes on a cookie sheet and bake until the tops are golden, 15 to 20 minutes. Cool slightly and serve.

Pungent Shabbat Chicken
with Dried Fruit

This is my most requested dish. Years after people try it, they still ask me for the recipe. It's exactly what you want for a festive Friday night supper or Rosh Hashanah feast, and it couldn't be easier to make: marinate the bird overnight, bake it the next day. Kids in particular enjoy the chicken's lightly caramelized goodness, its orange-gingery taste. (When making it for them, I often include extra drumsticks.) It's also a great buffet dish, hot or cold, and a perfect Passover specialty—but please don't wait for a holiday to try it.

MARINADE

1 cup dried apricots and prunes, or a combination including apricots, prunes, cherries, or currants

½ cup orange juice

12 garlic cloves, peeled and minced

One ½ x ½-inch piece fresh ginger, peeled and finely chopped

2 tablespoons dried oregano

1 tablespoon dried thyme

⅓ cup red wine vinegar

2 tablespoons olive oil

Juice of ½ lemon

3 bay leaves

Two 3½-pound chickens, all visible fat and backbones removed, cut into eighths

Salt and freshly ground black pepper

½ cup dark brown sugar

½ cup dry white wine

¼ cup chopped Italian parsley

Serves 6 to 8

1. To make the marinade, combine the dried fruit and orange juice in a bowl and allow fruit to plump for 15 minutes.

2. Combine the plumped fruit, juice, garlic, ginger, oregano, thyme, vinegar, olive oil, lemon juice, and bay leaves in a large bowl. Add the chicken and season to taste with the salt and pepper. Toss to coat, cover, and marinate, refrigerated, from 4 hours to overnight.

3. Preheat the oven to 375°F. Arrange the chicken in a single layer in 2 large roasting pans and spoon the marinade over. Sprinkle the chicken with the brown sugar, and drizzle over the wine. Bake until juices run clear when a joint is pierced with a fork, about 1 hour. Pour off the pan juices into a serving bowl and skim off the fat. Discard the bay leaves. Sprinkle the chicken with the parsley and serve. Pass the pan juices separately.

Oven-Fried Chicken

Everyone loves fried chicken, but no one likes all the calories and the mess of frying. This oven-fried chicken is the answer. It's so deliciously crisp, you won't believe it isn't fried, and that it uses only two tablespoons of oil. Spicy (omit the red pepper flakes if you're serving it to children) and touched with oregano, the chicken is perfect for picnics or other informal gatherings. Serve it with Honey-Banana Chutney (page 238) or Apple Tomato Chutney (page 240).

One 3½-pound chicken, all visible fat and wing tips removed, cut into eighths

Freshly ground black pepper

½ teaspoon dried oregano

2 tablespoons vegetable oil

¾ cup flour

½ teaspoon paprika

¼ teaspoon red pepper flakes (optional)

Serves 4

1. Preheat the oven to 450°F. Season the chicken with the pepper and half the oregano.

2. Add the oil to a baking dish large enough to hold chicken in one layer. Add the chicken and turn to coat with the oil.

3. In a large, flat dish or large resealable plastic bag, blend the flour with the remaining oregano, the paprika, and red pepper flakes, if using. Dredge the chicken in the flour mixture, or add it to the bag and shake to coat. Shake off excess flour mixture.

4. Return the chicken skin side up to the baking dish. Bake without turning until golden and the juices run clear when a joint is pierced, about 40 minutes. If the chicken hasn't browned sufficiently, spray it lightly with a little vegetable oil cooking spray and cook a little longer. Serve the chicken hot or at room temperature.

Home-Roast Turkey Breast

On Friday afternoons, before the house is full of weekend guests, I roast this easy apple jelly–glazed turkey breast. It pleases everyone—especially white meat lovers—and provides great leftovers for Saturday and Sunday sandwiches and other dishes (see page 246). Cooks who would prefer not to worry about producing equally moist white and dark turkey meat (difficult to achieve when you're cooking a whole bird), love this dish, too.

Save the turkey carcass for stock.

One 7-pound unboned turkey breast

1 lemon

Salt and freshly ground black pepper

5 shallots

½ cup apple jelly or red currant jelly

¾ cup apple cider

½ teaspoon ground ginger

1 teaspoon dried thyme

1 teaspoon canola or other vegetable oil

1 medium onion, quartered

1 celery stalk, cut into 4 equal pieces

1 bunch Italian parsley or fresh coriander (cilantro), tied together with kitchen twine

1 cup Chicken Stock (page 61), or good instant or low-sodium canned broth

2 tablespoons crushed juniper berries

1 bay leaf

Serves 8

1. Place the breast in a baking pan. Squeeze the juice of the lemon inside and over the outside of the breast. Season with the salt and pepper.

2. Chop the shallots in a food processor. Add the apple jelly, ¹/₄ cup of the apple cider, the ginger, and thyme. Pulse to blend.

3. Preheat the oven to 425°F. Brush the underside of the breast with the glaze. Place the breast skin side up in a roasting pan and rub the skin with the oil. Tuck half the onion under the breast and half in the neck pocket of the breast. Tuck the celery and parsley under the cavity.

4. Place the breast in the oven and roast 20 minutes. Remove from the oven and brush with some of the glaze. Add the remaining cider, the stock, juniper berries, and bay leaf to the pan. Cover with foil and roast for 1 hour, basting twice. Remove the foil and brush with the remaining glaze. Lower the heat to 375°F. and roast uncovered until the meat is a lovely caramel color and the juices run clear when the breast is pierced with a fork, 20 to 30 minutes. (The internal temperature at the thickest part of the roast will be 160°F.) Allow to rest 20 minutes before carving. Discard the bay leaf. Serve with the pan juices passed separately.

Roast Turkey with Fennel-Cornbread Stuffing

This is the best stuffed turkey ever, period. Fennel, mushrooms, and sun-dried tomatoes make the cornbread stuffing unusual; the bird itself, glazed with apricot preserves and soy sauce, and served with a sherry-orange sauce, is luscious. (Other stuffing possibilities appear on pages 212–213.)

I've gone into detail about roasting—consider this method basic text. You can prepare the turkey without the stuffing if you like, omitting the fennel for the pan, and you'll still have a festive bird.

STUFFING

½ cup dry-packed sun-dried tomatoes, chopped or snipped with scissors

½ cup dry sherry

2 tablespoons olive oil

4 medium onions, very thinly sliced

6 garlic cloves, minced

2 fennel bulbs, chopped (about 4 cups), fronds reserved for garnish

2 pounds mushrooms, 1 pound sliced, 1 pound finely chopped (about 4 cups)

4 cups cubed day-old French bread with crusts

Orange Cornbread (recipe follows), cubed

2 to 3 teaspoons fresh thyme leaves, or 1 to 2 teaspoons dried

1 teaspoon dried sage

1 cup chopped Italian parsley

1 teaspoon crushed fennel seeds

Salt and freshly ground black pepper

2 cups Chicken Stock (page 61), or good instant or low-sodium canned broth

1. To make the stuffing, combine the sun-dried tomatoes and sherry in a small bowl, and allow the tomatoes to plump for about 15 minutes.

2. In a large skillet, heat the olive oil over low heat. Add the onions, minced garlic, and fennel without the fronds and sauté until the vegetables have softened, about 10 minutes. Add the sliced and chopped mushrooms and sauté until the mushrooms have begun to soften, about 2 minutes.

3. Transfer the vegetables to a large bowl. Add the bread cubes, cornbread, thyme, sage, parsley, fennel seeds, and tomatoes with their soaking liquid. Season to taste with the salt and pepper and toss lightly. Add the chicken stock and toss again, lightly.

4. Preheat the oven to 400°F. Rinse the turkey well and remove all visible fat. Pat the turkey dry and fill the cavity loosely with the stuffing. Stuff the neck area and secure with the neck skin by tucking it under the bird (see page 24). Put any remaining stuffing in an ovenproof baking dish and set aside.

TURKEY

One 18- to 20-pound fresh turkey, or frozen and completely defrosted, fat from cavity removed, neck and gizzard reserved

2 medium carrots, peeled and quartered

1 medium onion, quartered

1 fennel bulb, cut into sixths, cored, trimmed, and fronds reserved for garnish

1 tablespoon vegetable oil

2 cups Chicken Stock (page 61), or good instant or low-sodium canned broth, plus extra

8 garlic cloves, pressed

1 cup apricot preserves

1 to 2 tablespoons soy sauce

1 teaspoon dried thyme leaves

½ cup fresh orange juice

Freshly ground black pepper

½ cup dry sherry

½ teaspoon cornstarch

Salt

Serves 18

5. In the bottom of a large roasting pan, arrange the carrots, onion, and fennel without the fronds. Place the turkey on top gently, breast side up. Rub the bird with the oil. Pour 1 cup of the stock into the pan and roast the turkey for 30 minutes.

6. Meanwhile, prepare the basting glaze. In a medium bowl, combine the garlic, preserves, soy sauce, thyme, and orange juice. Season to taste with the pepper.

7. After 30 minutes, brush the turkey with the glaze. Cover the turkey with a loose tent made with 2 large pieces of foil, reduce the oven to 350°F., and roast the turkey for 4 hours, basting every hour with the glaze and the pan juices. Uncover the turkey and allow it to brown completely, about 1 hour, basting 2 to 3 times. The turkey is done when a thigh joint is loose and juices run clear when a joint is pierced. If you have extra stuffing, stir in about ¹/₂ cup additional stock or pan juices, loosely cover the dish, and bake along with the turkey for the last 40 to 50 minutes of the roasting time. Heat a large platter.

8. Transfer the turkey to the platter, cover loosely with foil, and allow it to rest 15 to 20 minutes before carving. Meanwhile, strain the pan juices into a saucepan, reserving the vegetables, and remove the fat; you should have 4 cups (add stock if necessary). Bring to a simmer over medium heat.

9. In a small bowl, combine the sherry and cornstarch and whisk into the pan juices. Simmer until the gravy is lightly thickened, 5 to 7 minutes. Season to taste with salt and pepper. Empty the cavity of the stuffing. Carve the turkey, garnish with the fennel fronds, and serve with the pan-roasted vegetables and sauce.

Orange Cornbread

This tasty orange-flavored cornbread is made without the usual enrichments. Its relative dryness makes it ideal for stuffings.

1 cup yellow cornmeal plus 2 teaspoons for pan

⅔ cup all-purpose flour

2 teaspoons baking powder

1 tablespoon sugar

½ teaspoon salt

¼ teaspoon poultry seasoning (see page 13), optional

2 egg whites

2 tablespoons canola or other vegetable oil plus 2 teaspoons for pan

¾ cup fresh orange juice

One 9 x 11-inch cornbread (5 cups cubed)

1. Preheat the oven to 425°F.

2. In a large bowl, combine the cup of cornmeal, the flour, baking powder, sugar, salt, and poultry seasoning.

3. In a small bowl, beat the egg whites with the 2 tablespoons of oil and the orange juice until well blended. Add the wet mixture to the dry and stir just to combine. Do not overmix.

4. Grease a 9 x 11-inch pan with the remaining oil. Sprinkle the pan with the remaining cornmeal and shake out excess. Spoon the batter into the pan and shake to spread the batter. Bake until golden on top, about 25 minutes. Cool on a wire rack, then cut into cubes.

Turkey Meatloaf

This turkey-based meatloaf is as savory and comforting as the traditional dish, but lower in fat and calories and healthier to eat. You can make an extra loaf and freeze it to have on hand, or make turkey meatballs (the recipe follows) using the basic loaf mixture. If you make and freeze the meatballs in bags beforehand, they're ready when you want them. No need to brown them before cooking; just add them to your favorite tomato sauce, serve over cooked pasta, and enjoy.

2 pounds ground turkey and/or chicken meat

¾ cup very finely chopped onion

½ cup bread crumbs or rolled oats

¾ cup peeled and very finely chopped carrots

½ cup very finely chopped celery

¾ cup best-quality ketchup

1 tablespoon Dijon mustard

¼ cup chopped Italian parsley

1 egg or 2 egg whites

1 cup tomato juice

Serves 8

1. Preheat the oven to 350°F.

2. Using your hands or a large 2-tined fork, lightly combine the turkey, onion, bread crumbs, carrots, celery, $\frac{1}{2}$ cup of the ketchup, the mustard, parsley, and egg in a large bowl. Form into 1 large or 2 small loaves.

3. Place in one 8 x 8-inch loaf pan or two $7\frac{1}{2}$ x 4-inch loaf pans. Combine the remaining ketchup with the tomato juice and pour over the loaf or loaves. Bake until firm and the tomato topping has set, about 1 hour for the large pan, 45 minutes for the smaller ones. Alternatively, shape a free-form loaf and place in a large pan that allows room for sauce to coat and surround the meat during cooking. Unmold the loaf or loaves and serve.

VARIATIONS

TURKEY MEATBALLS

Meatloaf mixture (above recipe)

4 cups tomato sauce

¼ cup chopped Italian parsley

1. Cover a cookie sheet with waxed paper. Using the meatloaf mixture, shape 2-inch balls. Place on the cookie sheet and place in freezer to chill, but not freeze, about 40 minutes. Alternatively, freeze the meatballs completely and store them in plastic bags or containers between layers of waxed paper for up to 3 months.

2. In a large, deep skillet, bring the sauce to a simmer over medium-low heat. Drop the chilled or frozen meatballs one at a time into sauce, reduce the heat, cover, and simmer until cooked through, 10 to 15 minutes for chilled meatballs, 15 to 20 minutes for frozen. Sprinkle with chopped parsley and serve with hot pasta.

BARBECUE TURKEY MEATOAF

To make a great turkey meatloaf for sandwiches, follow the master recipe, substituting $\frac{1}{2}$ cup tomato juice and $\frac{1}{2}$ cup barbecue sauce (your own or good-quality store-bought), combined, for the whole amount of tomato juice and the remaining $\frac{1}{4}$ cup ketchup (see step 3). Pour this mixture over the loaves, bake as directed, chill, and slice.

Five-Spice Roast Turkey Breast with Pear-Garlic Sauce

A turkey breast makes a delicious roast and is prepared more easily than a whole bird. The breast used for this dish is flavored with five-spice powder, the wonderful Chinese seasoning. It's readily available, but for this recipe I like to make my own. It's easy to do and produces a more fragrant roast.

In addition to the spices, apple juice and a touch of molasses create exciting flavor. Add pear-garlic sauce and the roast is sublime. (You can, however, omit the sauce, substituting natural apple sauce; you'll still have a feast.)

This is a great buffet dish and one that keeps on giving. Next day, try the breast sliced on whole wheat bread with chutney—a great sandwich. Or cube the turkey and combine it with spinach leaves, thinly sliced pear, and scallions for a fine salad.

TURKEY

1 teaspoon ground cinnamon

2 teaspoons ground allspice

1 teaspoon grated nutmeg

2 teaspoons ground coriander

½ teaspoon ground cloves

6 large garlic cloves

½ medium onion, halved

½ cup packed fresh Italian parsley, leaves chopped

6 fresh sage leaves, or ½ teaspoon dried

1½ teaspoons coarsely ground black pepper

One 6-pound turkey breast, boned, skinned, and tied (have your butcher do this; a boned roast will weigh approximately 3½ pounds)

2 tablespoons apple juice

2 tablespoons soy sauce

1 tablespoon molasses

1. Eight hours or up to 2 days in advance, start the turkey. Place the cinnamon, allspice, nutmeg, coriander, cloves, garlic, onion, parsley, sage, and pepper in a food processor. Pulse the mixture until it forms a granular paste.

2. With a paring knife, make X-shaped incisions about 1½ inches deep in the meat at 3-inch intervals. With your fingers or a small brush, press the paste into each X. Spread any remaining paste over the surface of the meat. Wrap the meat tightly in plastic wrap, and refrigerate to season.

3. About 3 hours before serving, preheat the oven to 375°F. Place the turkey in a roasting pan and drizzle over it the apple juice, soy sauce, and molasses. Allow the turkey to come to room temperature (about 30 minutes), and place it in the oven. Reduce the heat to 325°F. and roast the turkey for 2 hours, basting and turning the turkey 3 or 4 times. The turkey is done when the juices run clear when the breast is pierced.

PEAR-GARLIC SAUCE (OPTIONAL)

6 ripe pears, any variety, peeled, cored, and roughly cubed

2 tablespoons sugar

2 large garlic cloves

¼ teaspoon salt

3 tablespoons fresh lemon juice

¼ teaspoon white pepper

¼ cup extra-virgin olive oil

1 cup Chicken Stock (page 61), or good instant or low-sodium canned broth

Serves 6 to 8

4. Meanwhile, prepare the sauce, if using. In a large saucepan, combine the pears, sugar, and ½ cup water. Cook over medium heat until the pears are soft, about 10 minutes. Puree the mixture in the food processor and return it to the saucepan over low heat. Reduce the puree to about 1 cup.

5. Chop the garlic with the salt, mashing it with the back the knife until it forms a smooth puree. Transfer it to the processor and add the pear puree, lemon juice, and pepper. With the processor running, drizzle in the oil in a thin stream, until the sauce is thickened. Transfer to a bowl and reserve.

6. When the turkey is done, place it on a board and keep warm. Add the stock to the roasting pan and scrape up all the brown bits to incorporate them. Pour into a small saucepan and, over medium heat, reduce the liquid to 1 cup. Slice the turkey and serve with the reduced juices and the pear-garlic sauce, if using.

Duck with Honey Glaze

This delicious roast duck is made with a garlic-laced soy and honey glaze. Besides imparting a delicious taste, the glaze gives the ducks a golden color. Serve the ducks as directed with sliced scallions and fresh tangy orange sections.

Two 5-pound ducks, fresh or frozen and completely defrosted, trimmed of all visible fat, wing tips removed and reserved along with neck

½ cup dry sherry

4 lemons, 2 halved, 2 thinly sliced

1½ teaspoons freshly ground black pepper

1 medium onion, finely chopped

2 medium carrots, peeled and finely chopped

2 celery stalks, finely chopped

2 bay leaves

3 black peppercorns

1. A day in advance, bring 6 quarts of water to a boil in a large pot. Carefully drop in the ducks one at a time. Leave each in the pot until its skin whitens, about 3 minutes, remove, and drain in a colander. Using paper towels, dry the ducks inside and out.

2. Rub the ducks inside and out with the sherry. Place a wire rack in a shallow pan and arrange the ducks breast side down on it. Refrigerate the ducks loosely draped with waxed paper for 10 to 12 hours.

3. Preheat the oven to 400°F. Remove the ducks from the refrigerator and rub each inside and out with the juice of the halved lemons. Prick the skin all over with the tines of a fork. Sprinkle the inside and out with the pepper. Place 1 sliced lemon in each cavity.

4. Return the ducks to the rack breast side down. Pour 1 cup water into the pan and roast 30 minutes. Meanwhile, place the wing tips and reserved neck into a saucepan with 2 cups water, the onion, carrots, celery, bay leaves, and peppercorns. Bring to a boil, reduce the heat, and simmer until well flavored and reduced, about 30 minutes. Strain the stock; you will have about ¹/₂ cup. Reserve.

5. To make the glaze, in a medium bowl, combine the soy sauce, ketchup, honey, garlic, ginger, and rosemary. Mix well.

6. Reduce the oven temperature to 350°F. Remove the pan from the oven, drain the water and fat, and turn the ducks over. Prick the ducks again, pour the glaze over them, and using a brush, spread and baste the ducks with the glaze that collects in the pan. Pour the orange juice into the pan.

1¼ cups soy sauce

1¼ cups best-quality ketchup

½ cup honey

2 garlic cloves, pressed

1 tablespoon ground ginger

2 tablespoons chopped fresh rosemary,
or 1 tablespoon dried

2 cups fresh orange juice

2 scallions including 3 inches of the
green, trimmed and sliced diagonally into
thin segments

1 orange, sectioned, white pith removed

Serves 4 to 6

7. Roast the ducks, basting frequently, until the ducks are just done, 1 to 1½ hours (an instant-read thermometer thrust into a thigh, not touching the bone, will register 155° to 160°F.).

8. Remove the ducks from the oven and let them rest for 15 minutes. Skim off any fat from the combined pan juices and glaze. In a small saucepan, combine the juices and the reserved stock and reheat. Cut each duck in half, remove the backbones, and cut again to separate the thighs and breasts. Garnish with the sliced scallions and orange sections. Drizzle the sauce over, or transfer it to a sauce boat to pass separately, and serve.

Slow-Roast Crispy Duck

The secret of duplicating the crisp-skinned roast ducks you see in Chinatown lies in a preliminary blanching with beer and boiling water that opens the duck's pores, allowing maximum fat drainage. The duck is then cooked slowly, raising the temperature as you go, to rid it of its fat and crisp its skin magnificently.

Though the duck is delicious as is, you could also gild the lily (and the duck) by serving it with Every-Way Cherry Sauce (page 244) or Winter Fruit Relish (page 226).

4 cups beer, preferably dark

Two 5-pound ducks, fresh or frozen and fully defrosted, trimmed of all visible fat, neck and wing tips removed

Freshly ground black pepper

2 tablespoons olive oil

12 garlic cloves, crushed

2 tablespoons soy sauce

2 apples

Serves 4 to 6

1. A day in advance, bring 6 quarts of water to a boil in a large pot and add the beer. Return the mixture to a boil. Carefully drop in the ducks one at a time. Leave each in the pot until its skin whitens, about 3 minutes, remove, and drain in a colander. Dry the ducks thoroughly with paper towels.

2. Rub the pepper inside and on the outside of the ducks. In a small bowl, combine the olive oil, garlic, and soy sauce and rub inside and on the outside of the ducks. Wrap the ducks with plastic wrap and refrigerate for 24 hours.

3. Remove the ducks from the refrigerator and allow to come to room temperature, about 1 hour. Unwrap the ducks and place an apple in each duck. Prick the ducks all over with the tines of a fork. Make sure the tines of the fork penetrate the flesh.

4. Preheat the oven to 275°F. Place the ducks, breast side down, on a rack set in a roasting pan or shallow sheet pan with sides. Pour 2 cups of water into the pan and roast the ducks for 1 hour. Remove the ducks from the oven and pour off all the water and fat. Replace it with 1 cup of water and turn the ducks over.

5. Raise the temperature to 300°F. and roast 1 hour. Remove the ducks from the oven and repeat draining fat and water and replacing it with 1 cup of water. Turn the ducks over. Increase the temperature to 350°F., return the ducks to the oven, and roast another 30 minutes.

6. Once again, remove the ducks, drain the fat and water, and replace it with 1 cup water. Increase the oven temperature to 400°F., turn the ducks over, breast side up, and roast until the juices run clear when the thighs are pierced, about 30 minutes. The ducks' skin should be crispy.

7. Remove the ducks from the oven, discard the apples, and set aside to rest for 15 minutes. Cut each duck in half, remove the backbones, and cut ducks to separate thighs and breasts. Serve warm.

Roast Chicken in Cinnamon-Scented Plum Sauce

This dish is a happy marriage of chicken, purple plums, cinnamon, and other sweet spices. It's gorgeous to look at, too—the rosy plums tint the skinless chicken pieces delicately. Prepare it around Rosh Hashanah; it's so delightful to have the smells of cinnamon and clove wafting through the house when the weather is changing, and then to have this chicken to eat. Serve this with basmati rice, a perfect accompaniment to the fragrant bird.

7 large purple plums (preferably Santa Ana or other juicy, dark-skinned plums), or 12 Italian prune plums, pitted

½ cup Chicken Stock (page 61), or good instant or low-sodium canned broth

2 tablespoons plus 1 teaspoon olive oil

One 3½- to 4-pound roasting chicken, all visible fat removed, cut into eighths, wing tips and skin removed

9 garlic cloves, minced

One 1½-inch piece peeled fresh ginger, grated (1½ to 2 tablespoons)

2 medium onions, finely chopped

½ teaspoon ground cinnamon

⅛ teaspoon ground cloves

2 teaspoons ground cumin

⅛ teaspoon cayenne pepper

1 bunch watercress, for garnish

Serves 4 to 5

1. Combine 4 of the large or 6 of the small plums with the stock in a food processor and purée. Preheat the oven to 425°F.

2. Heat a large nonstick skillet over medium-high heat. Add 1 teaspoon of the oil. Add the chicken pieces and brown on all sides, about 5 minutes. With a slotted spoon remove them to a baking dish large enough to hold all the pieces snugly in a single layer.

3. In the same skillet, heat the 2 table-spoons of oil over high heat. Reduce the heat to medium and add the garlic, ginger, and onions. Cook, stirring, until the vegetables are lightly colored, about 4 minutes. Add the cinnamon, cloves, cumin, and cayenne and cook to blend well, about 3 minutes. Stir in plum puree.

4. Thinly slice the remaining plums and arrange over the chicken. Pour the plum sauce over chicken pieces. Cover the dish loosely with foil and place it in the oven. Reduce the heat to 375°F. and bake for 30 minutes. Uncover, baste with the pan juices, and bake uncovered until done, about 20 minutes. The juices will run clear when a joint is pierced with a fork.

5. Line a serving dish with the watercress. Place the chicken pieces over it, spoon the plums and cooking juices over, and serve.

Dillydally Stew

This lovely turkey stew earns its name twice over. First, it's flavored with a good quantity of dill, half of which is cooked with the meat, and the rest added as a final, freshening enhancement. To dillydally is to dawdle, and there's something leisurely about this dish, which bakes in the oven while you go about your business. People think of stews as hearty —many are, but the nice thing about this one is its delicacy. Serve it with steamed new potatoes or parslied rice.

4 tablespoons (½ stick) margarine

3 pounds well trimmed skinned turkey thigh meat, cut into 1-inch cubes

4 tablespoons flour

1 teaspoon grated nutmeg

½ to 1 teaspoon salt

1½ teaspoons freshly ground black pepper

1 cup packed dill leaves, chopped

3 cups peeled carrots cut diagonally into ⅛-inch slices

3 cups coarsely chopped onion

3 cups Chicken Stock (page 61), or good instant or low-sodium canned broth, or turkey stock

1 bay leaf

Two 9-ounce boxes frozen artichoke hearts, defrosted, well drained, and dried

Serves 6

1. Preheat the oven to 350° F.

2. In a heavy ovenproof casserole or Dutch oven, melt the margarine over medium heat. Add the turkey and cook, turning frequently, until all appearance of rawness is gone, about 10 minutes. Try not to brown.

3. In a small bowl, combine the flour, nutmeg, salt, and pepper. Sprinkle the mixture over the turkey, reduce the heat to low, and continue to cook, stirring, about 5 minutes. Add half the dill, the carrots, onion, stock, and bay leaf. Raise the heat to medium, bring the mixture to the boil, cover, and bake in the oven until the meat is fork-tender, about 1 hour.

4. Remove the stew from the oven, uncover, and stir in the artichoke hearts and remaining dill. Remove the bay leaf. Correct the seasonings if necessary and recover to allow the artichokes to heat through, about 3 minutes. Serve.

Sherry-Marinated Chicken with Caramelized Balsamic Onions

This simple baked chicken features the elusive, slightly woody taste of sherry and sweet-tart balsamic caramelized onions. Because most of the work can and should be done a day in advance, it's a good last-minute dish. I serve it when I'm entertaining during the week; it's finished in about an hour, and delights everyone with its sophisticated flavor.

Serve grilled vegetables and a bulgur wheat pilaf as accompaniments to the chicken.

CHICKEN

2 medium onions, peeled and quartered

1 cup dry sherry

2 tablespoons fresh lemon juice

2 bay leaves

2 teaspoons molasses

¼ teaspoon dried oregano

Salt and freshly ground black pepper

Two 3- to 3½-pound chickens, all visible fat, skin and wings removed (reserve the wings for another use), cut into eighths

1. A day in advance, prepare the chicken. Place the onions in a food processor or blender and process until liquefied; set one-third of the mixture aside for preparing the pearl onions. In a large nonreactive bowl, combine the remaining onion mixture with the sherry, lemon juice, bay leaves, molasses, and oregano. Season to taste with the salt and pepper. Add the chicken, turn to coat, cover, and marinate refrigerated for 24 hours. When ready to cook, allow 30 minutes for the chicken to come to room temperature.

2. Meanwhile, prepare the pearl onions. Fill a medium saucepan two-thirds full with water and bring to a boil. Add the onions and boil to loosen their skins, about 3 minutes. Drain under cold water and peel.

3. Place the pearl onions in a 9 x 13 x 1-inch glass or ceramic baking dish. Toss the onions lightly with the olive oil. Pour over the balsamic vinegar and the reserved onion puree and add the thyme. Stir to coat. Sprinkle over the brown sugar and set aside.

4. Preheat the oven to 375°F. Turn the chicken to coat it evenly. Transfer the chicken and marinade to 2 oven-to-table baking dishes each about 1 inch deep. Arrange the chicken bone side up in a single layer. Place the chicken and pearl onions in the oven. Bake the chicken for 35 minutes, remove from the oven,

ONIONS

1 pint pearl onions

1 tablespoon olive oil

½ cup balsamic vinegar

¼ teaspoon thyme leaves

½ tablespoon brown sugar

3 tablespoons sherry wine vinegar
(see page 14)

¼ cup fresh orange juice

¼ cup chopped Italian parsley

Serves 6 to 8

turn, and drizzle the vinegar and orange juice over. Return the chicken to the oven and continue to bake, turning several times while baking to ensure even cooking. Baste the chicken once with the pan juices, return to the oven, and bake until done, 15 to 20 minutes. The onions should be soft and caramelized. Remove the bay leaves from the chicken.

5. Garnish the chicken with the parsley, surround with the caramelized onions, and serve.

Chicken Pinwheels with Black Beans, Cashews, and Leeks

This dish of oven-poached chicken cutlets rolled around a Chinese-inspired stuffing with black beans is perfect for parties. Once baked, the cutlets are sliced into pinwheels and served over soba noodles with a delicate citrus sauce and orange segments—a beautiful mix of colors. It sounds like a big deal, but it isn't, and all the flavors come together in a totally satisfying way.

The chicken and sauce can be prepared almost entirely ahead, so all you have to do before serving the dish is finish the pinwheels and cook the noodles. I use canned black beans for this; they work well.

One 15-ounce can cooked, firm black beans, rinsed and well drained

1 tablespoon margarine

1½ teaspoons dark sesame oil

4 leeks, cleaned and the white parts sliced very thin (about 1½ cups; reserve the greens for another use)

3 tablespoons chopped roasted unsalted cashews

¼ teaspoon five-spice powder

1 to 2 shakes hot sauce, or ½ teaspoon chili oil

2½ pounds chicken cutlets, lightly pounded

2 oranges, peeled, all pith removed and sectioned

Salt and freshly ground black pepper

½ cup dry sherry

½ cup Chicken Stock (page 61), or good instant or low-sodium canned broth

1. Place half the beans in a food processor and pulse to chop roughly. Reserve.

2. Preheat the oven to 375°F. In a heavy, medium skillet, heat the margarine and ½ teaspoon of the sesame oil over medium heat. Add the leeks and sauté until soft, about 10 minutes. Add the cashews, chopped black beans, and five-spice powder. Stir to combine. Remove from the heat, add the hot sauce, and stir. Using a spoon or spatula, separate the mixture in the pan into 6 equal portions. Reserve.

3. Place a cutlet on your work surface, smooth side down with the large end near you. Place one portion of the stuffing on the large end, cover with 1 or 2 of the orange sections, and roll up the cutlet tightly. Secure the cutlet with a toothpick and place it seam side down in a baking dish large enough to hold all the cutlets. Repeat the procedure with the remaining cutlets. Season to taste with salt and pepper. (The dish may be prepared ahead up to this point, covered, and refrigerated for up to 1 day.)

SAUCE

1 tablespoon margarine

1¼ cups chopped shallots

2 cups fresh orange juice

1 cup dry white wine

1 cup Chicken Stock (page 61), or good instant or low-sodium canned broth

2 teaspoons balsamic vinegar

Salt and freshly ground black pepper

½ pound dried buckwheat noodles

½ cup snipped chives

Serves 4 to 6

4. Pour the sherry and chicken stock over the rolls, and cover the dish tightly with foil. Oven-poach the rolls for 20 minutes. Rearrange the rolls to ensure even cooking, cover, and continue to poach until done, about 25 minutes. Remove the toothpicks and keep the rolls warm.

5. Meanwhile, prepare the sauce. Add the margarine to a small saucepan and heat it over low heat. Add the shallots and sauté until just beginning to brown, about 10 minutes. Add the orange juice, wine, and stock. Bring to a boil, lower the heat, and reduce by half, about 30 minutes. Add the vinegar, stir in the remaining beans, and season to taste with the salt and pepper. Remove from the heat and keep warm.

6. Cook the noodles in 4 quarts of salted water until al dente, 2 to 3 minutes. Drain and, using 2 forks, toss with the remaining 1 teaspoon of sesame oil. Make sure the noodles are well separated.

7. Place the noodles on a large platter. Slice the rolls into 5 or 6 pinwheels each and place on top of the noodles. Arrange the remaining orange segments around the noodles and spoon the sauce over all. Garnish with the chives and serve.

Turkey Roast à la Grecque

This delicious dish uses an unskinned boned and butterflied turkey breast, sometimes called a London broil. You can have a butcher prepare the breast for you or you can do it yourself (see the Note). The boned breast is seasoned à la Grecque, sealed in a foil pouch, and baked. The result is a juicy, flavorful roast that is wonderful served with orzo or roasted potatoes. In summer, the London broil is excellent with warm potato salad and raw spinach tossed with Victoria Dressing (page 235). It's also great the next day in sandwiches accompanied by Eggplant Salad with Currants (page 191).

One 4-pound turkey breast with skin, boned and butterflied

2 tablespoons olive oil

½ teaspoon freshly ground black pepper

Salt

18 pearl onions

3 garlic cloves

¼ cup packed fresh dill leaves, chopped

¼ cup packed parsley leaves

4 whole scallions, trimmed

1 teaspoon dried oregano

Grated zest and juice of 1 lemon

½ cup dry white wine

2 bay leaves

Serves 8

1. Preheat the oven to 400°F. Rub the turkey breast with 1 teaspoon of the olive oil. Sprinkle with the pepper and season with the salt. Arrange 2 pieces of heavy-duty foil, each about 18 inches long, across one another on a sheet pan with sides.

2. In a large, heavy skillet, heat 2 teaspoons of the olive oil over medium-high heat. Add the breast skin side down and sear until nicely browned, turn over and sear the second side, about 7 minutes total. Remove the breast and place it skin side up to the center of the foil. Reserve the skillet.

3. Bring a saucepan of water to a boil, add the pearl onions, and cook 2 minutes. Drain the onions and when cool enough to handle, peel.

4. Heat the reserved skillet over medium heat. Add the onions and brown on all sides, about 10 minutes. Using a slotted spoon, remove the onions from the pan and place around the turkey.

5. Add the garlic, dill, parsley, scallions, oregano, and the remaining tablespoon of oil to a food processor and chop the vegetables finely. Scatter the mixture over and around the breast. Sprinkle the breast with the lemon zest and juice and pour the wine over. Place the bay leaves under the breast. Insert a standard meat thermometer in the thickest part of the breast, gather up the foil to enclose it, and crimp the foil to seal, or use an instant-read thermometer later.

6. Place the roast in the oven and bake until it is just cooked through (to an internal temperature of 160°F.), about 1 hour. If using an instant-read thermometer, begin testing at 40 minutes. Remove the breast from the foil, reserving all the juices in a serving bowl. Discard the bay leaves. Slice the turkey and serve it with the onions and the juices drizzled over all.

Note: To bone the breast, use a small, sharp knife and cut closely against the carcass to remove the meat, then spread the breast halves (save the bones for the stockpot).

Asian Butterflied Turkey Breast

Here is another marinated "London broil" turkey breast and, like its predecessor, it's a great company dish. After bathing in Asian flavorings (marinating for ten hours minimum is key), the breast is grilled or broiled briefly, then baked until done. The roast is deliciously juicy and has a tantalizing sweet-sour flavor; it's also low in fat. Most of the work can be completed ahead, so you get to enjoy your guests and don't have to worry about cooking.

Serve the London broil with a cucumber salad, Mashed New Year's Potatoes (page 194), and steamed asparagus for a memorable meal. It's also good sliced and served cold.

One 7-pound turkey breast with skin, boned and butterflied (a London broil; your butcher will do this, or see Note, page 145)

2 teaspoons dark sesame oil

6 scallions, white and green parts, finely sliced

½ cup hoisin sauce

½ cup dry sherry

2 tablespoons Dijon mustard

1 teaspoon five-spice powder

Salt and freshly ground black pepper

1 tablespoon chopped Italian parsley or fresh coriander leaves (cilantro)

Serves 8

1. Place the breast in a large nonreactive container with a cover. In a small bowl, combine the sesame oil, scallions, hoisin sauce, sherry, mustard, and five-spice powder. Using a fork, mix well and pour over the turkey breast. Turn the meat to coat it thoroughly and season with salt and pepper. Allow to marinate, refrigerated, at least 10 hours or, preferably, for a day.

2. Prepare a grill or preheat the broiler. Remove the breast from the container, reserve the remaining marinade, and grill the breast over medium heat, 2 to 3 inches from the heat source, until the skin is browned and the meat seared, 7 to 10 minutes per side. Alternatively, broil the breast until browned and seared, 7 to 10 minutes per side.

3. Preheat the oven, or reduce the oven heat if the breast was broiled, to 400°F. Arrange 2 pieces of heavy-duty foil, each about 18 inches long, across one another on a sheet pan with sides. Place the breast at the center and pour over the reserved marinade. Insert a standard meat thermometer in the thickest part of the breast, gather up the foil to enclose it, and crimp the foil to seal, or seal and use an instant-read thermometer later. Place the roast in the oven and bake until it is just cooked through, about 1 hour. If using an instant-read thermometer, begin testing at 40 minutes. The internal temperature of the roast will be will be 155° to 160°F. (You can also cook the roast entirely on the grill, searing it as above, double wrapping it in foil and finishing it, covered, over low heat. Turn the roast once and cook it to an internal temperature of 170° F., about 20 minutes per side.)

4. Unwrap the turkey and allow it to rest for 15 minutes. Drain off and defat the cooking juices. Slice and serve the breast garnished with the parsley and pass the cooking juices separately.

Turkey London Broil with Shiitake Mushrooms

This dish rivals elegant veal roast and makes a distinctive entree for parties or special dinners. Guests will be surprised to discover that homey butterflied turkey breast—a turkey "London broil"—is the basis of the feast.

As with the other London broil recipes in this chapter, the breast is first broiled (or grilled), then baked until done. The London broil is then surrounded with fragrant marinated shiitake mushrooms that have also been broiled and combined with a piquant dressing. The result is a royal treat that goes particularly well with steamed asparagus and Roast Potatoes with Seltzer (page 192), made with a combination of russet white potatoes, sweet potatoes, and Yukon Gold potatoes.

One 7-pound turkey breast with skin, boned and butterflied (a London broil; your butcher will do this or see Note, page 145)

TURKEY MARINADE

1 tablespoon olive oil

4 garlic cloves, pressed

1 teaspoon dried sage or poultry seasoning (see page 13)

½ cup dry white wine

¼ cup soy sauce

¼ cup balsamic vinegar

3 tablespoons grainy mustard

1 teaspoon cracked black peppercorns

1 pound shiitake mushrooms, stems removed (reserve for stock making), heads sliced into thirds

¼ cup olive oil

2 garlic cloves, pressed

Salt and freshly ground black pepper

1. Place the breast in a nonreactive dish or container with a cover.

2. To make the marinade, in a small bowl, combine the olive oil, garlic, sage, white wine, soy sauce, balsamic vinegar, mustard, and peppercorns. Pour the marinade over the breast and turn it to coat completely with the marinade. Cover and refrigerate the breast overnight, turning it at least once.

3. In a second nonreactive dish or container with a cover, toss the mushrooms with the olive oil and garlic and season to taste with the salt and pepper. Cover and refrigerate the mushrooms overnight.

4. Meanwhile, make the dressing. In a small bowl, combine the olive oil, vinegar, mustard, soy sauce, and honey. Reserve.

5. Remove the breast and the mushrooms from the fridge. Preheat the broiler, or prepare a grill. If using a grill, preheat the oven to 400°F.

MUSHROOM DRESSING

3 tablespoons olive oil

¼ cup balsamic vinegar

1½ teaspoon Dijon mustard

1½ teaspoons soy sauce

1½ teaspoon honey

1 tablespoon chopped parsley

Serves 8

6. Spread the mushrooms in a single layer on a broiler pan and broil 2 to 3 inches from the heat until brown and sizzling, turning as needed, about 10 minutes. Alternatively, grill the mushrooms directly on a grilling rack over medium heat, 2 to 3 inches from the heat source, turning as needed, about 10 minutes. Reserve.

7. Place two 18-inch sheets of foil across one another on a baking sheet with sides. Remove the breast from the marinade (reserve the marinade) and place in the center of the foil. Broil the breast until the skin side is browned and the meat side is seared, 7 to 10 minutes per side. Alternatively, grill until browned and seared, 7 to 10 minutes per side.

8. If oven has not been preheated, reduce the oven temperature to 400°F. Pour the reserved marinade over the breast. Insert a standard meat thermometer in the thickest part of the breast, gather up the foil to enclose it, and crimp the foil to seal, or seal and use an instant-read thermometer later. Place the roast in the oven and bake it until just cooked through, about 1 hour. If using an instant-read thermometer, begin testing at 40 minutes. When done, the internal temperature of the roast will be 160°F.

9. Toss the broiled mushrooms with the dressing and the parsley. Remove the roast from the foil and allow it to rest for 15 minutes. Reserve any cooking juices, defat them, and keep warm.

10. To serve, slice the roast and surround it with the mushrooms. Pass the cooking juices separately.

6. On the Grill

The pleasures of grilling are many, indeed.
First, there's the taste of the food—
that smoky intensity of flavor, the juiciness.
Then there's the ease and speed of grilling.
And the ritual—the communal fun of gathering
around a fire with family and friends,
anticipating the food and then eating.

But grilling needn't be seasonal. Though purists insist that the only grilling worth the name occurs outdoors over live coals, the gas grill, broiler, and grill pan also produce charred flavor. My own discovery of the grill pan occurred recently, and I now sing its praises. The trusty broiler can do magic as well, provided you've preheated it sufficiently and allow some circulation of air within it (by keeping its door slightly open) so your food doesn't bake.

Grilling can also be combined with other cooking methods. When grilling for a crowd, it's advantageous to prebake to make the cooking process more manageable and to avoid a dry result. The preliminary cooking also helps marinades penetrate food. With dishes such as Georgian Cinnamon Citrus Chicken or Be-All and End-All Barbecue Sauce Chicken, prebaking allows flavors to come through more immediately. Besides saving time, prebaking also curbs charring, which can mask delicate tastes.

Marinades are at the heart of my grilling approach. Master their use, and you've got flavor at your fingertips. Nothing could be easier than preparing marinades and using them with chicken and other poultry. One of the great pleasures of dishes such as Thai Peppered Chicken with Chili Sauce or Minted Mustard Chicken is the ease with which they're put together. Poultry grilling is one-two-three: Marinate the bird, grill it, enjoy it!

KEYS TO SUCCESSFUL MARINATING

Most marinades contain an acid—wine, citrus juice, or vinegar. These acids tend to break down poultry protein, allowing seasonings to infuse the bird. Always refrigerate marinating poultry if it is to remain in its flavoring bath more than an hour. It may seem obvious, but it's a good idea to cover marinating poultry—you don't want to flavor the fridge or have the bird lose moisture.

Turn marinating food. You want all food surfaces to have a chance to absorb maximum flavor and to remain well coated (to maintain moisture). You can often put a bird and its marinade in heavy resealable bags; all you have to do is shake the bag now and then and the bird receives a perfectly even distribution of the marinade. The bags are also perfect for transporting marinating chicken to grilling destinations. Or marinate food in containers with tight-fitting lids. Just shake the containers, and your food is bathed in the marinade.

Generally speaking, drain marinating food well before grilling it. Foods that have marinated in an oil-containing bath can go right on the grill or under the boiler. Spice-rubbed or other dry-marinated poultry can't be grilled or broiled until the grill—or the bird—is lightly coated with oil to prevent sticking and ensure browning. (Some grill pans are nonstick; even so, they must be oiled lightly or sprayed with a vegetable spray before preheating.)

Cut-up marinated birds—as opposed to breasts—should be turned often when grilling for even cooking. The white meat cooks more quickly than the dark and should be removed as soon as it's done. Boneless breasts are relatively thin and cook quickly. Always pay attention to birds that have marinated in a bath containing sugar, which can burn quickly.

Many of the marinades that follow can be prepared beforehand—a real time saver—and they're versatile. The marinade used with Grilled

Chicken Paillard with Pepper-Leek Topping, for example, is great to have on hand for meat or fish. As you read the recipes that follow, think of the marinades as independent of the dishes they're used in. That should increase your sense of their usefulness while sparking your cooking imagination.

GREAT GRILLING

The first consideration is the grill itself. If you're the owner of a gas grill, you have little to worry about when it comes to firing the grill—you just turn it on. Know, though, that a gas grill will never get as hot as its briquette-burning alternative. You must therefore preheat your gas grill for 10 to 15 minutes. This preheating rule also holds for the broiler and for the grill pan. Oil, then preheat your grill pan until it sizzles, about 5 minutes.

Gas is convenient, but you get tastier results with live coals; they get hotter and sear better. To prepare a briquette-burning grill, you must first choose the briquettes. For additional flavor, add hickory or mesquite chips to real charcoal briquettes.

Following the traditional method, I pile the briquettes in the grill in a layer that's about 6 inches thick. First, wad up old newspaper, place it in the center of the grill, and mound the charcoal around it. Avoid chemical fire starters of any kind; instead, soak a few coals with ordinary cooking oil and arrange them strategically in the mound. Light the paper and the oily coals do the rest.

Another alternative is to use a pail or chimney starter—it's fussless. Fill the urn with newspaper and briquettes, ignite the newspaper, and when the briquettes have caught, dump them onto the grill bed. Put unlit briquettes on top and allow them to catch. Let all the coals burn until you've got glowing, ash-covered embers. Then, using a large barbecue spatula, redistribute the embers across the fire bed.

To test the heat of the fire, put your hand about 3 inches above it. If you can tolerate the heat for only 2 to 3 seconds, the fire is hot; 3 to 4 seconds means the fire is medium-hot to medium; 5 seconds, low.

Put the grate on the grill to let it get very hot; that ensures attractive grill marks and also aids in cooking. When you're ready to cook, adjust the grill to the height you need, and you're ready to go.

Make sure the food you're grilling is at room temperature before it's cooked and well drained to avoid flare-ups. Vegetables and other small pieces of food are best grilled on grilling racks or screens. These perforated metal cooking surfaces go right on top of the grill (those with handles are easier to use).

Remember—never grill over flaring coals; embers are hotter than flame. If your food begins to burn when you start to cook, remove it from the grill immediately, allow the fire to subside, and change the height of the grill, using asbestos gloves or other protection. If you're using a gas grill, simply change the temperature setting. It's usually best to cover the grill when cooking poultry; heat is concentrated and there's less smoke.

Indoors, just remember to preheat the broiler. And sit down to delectable grilled poultry, any time of year.

Thai Peppered Chicken with Chili Sauce

For this delicious dish, chicken cutlets are marinated in a pungent bath containing garlic and ginger, grilled, and served with a hot Thai sauce. This marinade incorporates a soy mixture with herbs and spices that provides authentic flavor. Presented on a bed of fresh greens and served with Sushi Rice (page 211), the cutlets make a light but flavorful entree, great for a simple supper. You can marinate the cutlets up to two days in advance, which makes the final dish assembly a breeze.

4 large chicken cutlets (about 2 pounds total), lightly pounded

4 whole garlic cloves, plus 2 crushed

One 1-inch piece peeled fresh ginger

1 teaspoon cracked black peppercorns

¼ cup fresh coriander leaves (cilantro)

2 tablespoons chopped fresh lemongrass

2 tablespoons light soy sauce

1 tablespoon peanut or canola oil

1 small fresh red chili pepper, seeded if less heat is desired, and finely chopped

⅔ cup white vinegar

Pinch of salt

1 tablespoon sugar

4 cups shredded greens, such as romaine, Boston, or red leaf, singly or in combination; mint and/or basil leaves can be included

Serves 4

1. Place the chicken in a medium nonreactive bowl.

2. Turn on a food processor and with the machine running, drop the 4 garlic cloves and ginger through the feed tube. When chopped, stop the machine and add to the work bowl the peppercorns, coriander, lemongrass, soy sauce, and oil. Pulse until the coriander is chopped. Pour the mixture over the chicken and toss to coat. Cover and refrigerate for at least 3 hours and up to 2 days.

3. In a small saucepan, combine the chili pepper, vinegar, salt, sugar, and the crushed garlic. Simmer for 3 minutes. Cool.

4. Prepare a grill or preheat the broiler or a grill pan. If using a grill pan, spray it first with olive oil spray. Grill the chicken outdoors over medium heat about 4 inches from the heat source until just cooked through and lightly browned, 6 to 7 minutes per side. Alternatively, broil or cook the chicken in a grill pan about 2 to 3 minutes per side.

5. Divide the greens among 4 plates. Fan each cutlet by slicing it diagonally 1 inch from the narrow end through the opposite side and spreading the meat slightly. Divide the cutlets among the plates. Serve with the chili sauce.

Grilled Coriander Citrus Chicken

Cooks use almost every part of the coriander plant. The musky-tasting leaves—sometimes called cilantro or Chinese parsley—flavor a wide range of Latin and Asian dishes. The seeds, whose taste is subtly floral, are used whole, often in pickling, or ground. This savory dish uses the whole seeds, which should be crushed first with a mortar and pestle to release their fragrance.

The marinade for this chicken, which features the bright, tangy tastes of fresh grapefruit and lime juices, also works well with meaty fish. It can be made in advance and stored refrigerated for up to two weeks.

Serve the chicken with Corn and Pepper Relish (page 219) and roasted potatoes.

MARINADE

1½ cups fresh grapefruit juice
(from 2 grapefruits)

½ cup fresh lime juice

¼ cup canola or other light vegetable oil

5 garlic cloves, crushed

1 bunch scallions, white and green parts
thinly sliced, green parts reserved
for garnish

Scant tablespoon crushed coriander seeds

½ cup soy sauce

¼ teaspoon freshly ground black pepper

Two 3½-pound chickens, all visible fat
removed and cut into eighths

Serves 6

1. To make the marinade, in a large non-reactive bowl, combine the grapefruit juice, lime juice, oil, garlic, scallion whites, coriander seeds, soy sauce, and pepper. Whisk to blend.

2. Place the chicken in the marinade and turn to coat. Marinate, refrigerated, 3 hours or overnight. Remove the chicken from the refrigerator 20 minutes before cooking.

3. Prepare the grill or preheat the broiler. Grill the chicken over medium heat about 4 inches from the heat source, turning as needed, until the juices run clear when the meat is pierced with a fork, 30 to 40 minutes, or broil, turning once, about 10 minutes per side. Allow to cool slightly, garnish with the reserved scallion greens, and serve.

Grilled Chicken Panzanella

My first encounter with panzanella, the rustic Italian bread and tomato salad, was in central Italy, at a small-town cafe. A couple was enjoying a big bowl of panzenella at the next table and the look of pleasure on their faces convinced my husband and me to order the salad. It was fresh and light, full of pure, simple flavors—magnificent.

This version captures the sparkle of that salad (be sure to make it when tomatoes are at their peak), and adds tangy grilled chicken strips. You can prepare and store the salad ingredients separately beforehand—you can even grill the chicken in advance. Then toss everything together just before serving.

This makes a perfect summer-fall Shabbat lunch.

CHICKEN

¼ cup fresh lemon juice

2 tablespoons olive oil

4 garlic cloves, coarsely chopped

1 teaspoon freshly ground black pepper

Kosher salt

6 medium chicken cutlets (about 2 pounds total)

SALAD

8 cups crustless bread cubes (about 1 inch) from good, firm country-style bread

8 large, ripe tomatoes, cut into medium dice

1 small cucumber, peeled and finely diced

1 large red onion, peeled, cut into small dice

4 garlic cloves, minced

1 cup chopped Italian parsley

1. To prepare the chicken, in a medium nonreactive bowl, combine the lemon juice, olive oil, garlic, and pepper. Season to taste with the salt. Add the chicken, stir to coat, cover, and marinate, refrigerated, for 2 to 4 hours.

2. To make the salad, place the bread in a large bowl. Drizzle the bread with enough water to moisten but not soak it, ¹/₂ to ³/₄ cup; toss and allow the bread to absorb the water fully, about 5 minutes. Add the tomatoes, cucumber, onion, garlic, parsley, and rosemary. Mix in the olive oil, lemon juice, and vinegar and season to taste with the salt and pepper. Set aside.

3. Prepare a grill or preheat a grill pan. If using a grill pan, spray it first with olive oil spray. Grill the chicken outdoors over medium heat about 4 inches from the heat source until just done, 6 to 7 minutes per side, or 2 to 3 minutes per side if using a grill pan. Fan each breast by slicing diagonally 1 inch from the narrow end through the opposite side and spreading the meat slightly.

2 tablespoons chopped fresh rosemary

2½ tablespoons extra-virgin olive oil

Juice of 1 lemon

1 tablespoon red wine vinegar

Kosher salt and freshly ground
black pepper

½ cup fresh basil leaves, 6 leaves left
whole, the rest cut into thin strips

Serves 6

4. Divide the salad among 6 plates. Place a fanned cutlet on each portion and season with the salt and pepper. Garnish with the basil leaves and strips and serve immediately.

Grilled Chicken Paillard with Pepper-Leek Topping

This dish of grilled chicken paillard—lightly pounded cutlets—on arugula with a red pepper and leek compote is simple but exciting. The tart-sweetness of the marinated chicken is perfectly balanced by the leeks; the fresh arugula adds bite and character.

I love the balsamic vinegar-based marinade used for this dish. It also works well with firm-fleshed fish or vegetables you intend to grill. The topping is equally versatile—you can use it to make a wonderful omelet, frittata, or open-face turkey sandwich. This colorful dish is also great for a buffet.

TOPPING

2 tablespoons vegetable oil

3 red bell peppers, seeded and cut into thin strips

4 leeks, white and light green parts, washed and thinly sliced

½ cup dry white wine

1 cup Chicken Stock (page 61), or good instant or low-sodium canned broth

2 tablespoons chopped parsley

Freshly ground black pepper

MARINADE

⅓ cup olive oil

¼ cup balsamic vinegar

3 garlic cloves, chopped

2 shallots, finely minced

1 tablespoon fresh oregano leaves, or ½ teaspoon dried

1 tablespoon fresh rosemary leaves, or 1 teaspoon dried

¼ cup dry white wine

1. To make the topping, in a medium skillet, heat the oil over medium-high heat. Add the peppers and leeks and sauté until soft, about 4 minutes. Do not allow to color. Add the wine and stock. Cook until slightly reduced, about 3 minutes. Add the parsley and pepper. Set aside.

2. To make the marinade, in a medium nonreactive bowl, combine the olive oil, vinegar, garlic, shallots, oregano, rosemary, white wine, salt, and pepper and blend.

3. Add the chicken. Cover and refrigerate at least 4 hours and up to overnight.

4. When ready to cook, drain the chicken. Prepare a grill or preheat the broiler or a grill pan. If using a grill pan, spray it first with olive oil spray. Grill the chicken outdoors over medium heat about 4 inches from the heat source until just cooked through, 6 to 7 minutes per side. Alternatively, broil or cook the cutlets in a grill pan, 2 to 3 minutes per side.

Pinch of salt

¼ teaspoon freshly ground black pepper

6 large chicken cutlets
(about 3 pounds total), pounded to
¼-inch thickness

3 bunches arugula, washed and dried,
leaves separated

3 large beefsteak tomatoes, cut into
medium dice

Serves 4 to 6

5. Arrange the arugula and tomatoes on plates. Top with the chicken, spoon over the pepper-leek compote, and serve.

Georgian Cinnamon Citrus Chicken

The Russian region of Georgia is famously fertile. Grapes and wheat have been cultivated in its eastern half for thousands of years; its western part is known for citrus and tea farming. The Georgians love robust, spicy food and are famous for their hospitality. This grilled chicken dish celebrates the Georgian passion for spice and two prized Georgian products, oranges and lemons.

The marinated chicken is baked before grilling to intensify flavor, cut down on time, and ensure even cooking. The baking can be done early in the day so the final preparation goes quickly (refrigerate the chicken if you're staggering its preparation, then grill it without bringing it to room temperature first). The tangy marinade is also great for chicken cutlets or steaks from firm-fleshed fish like tuna or halibut. If using the marinade for chicken cutlets or fish, the marinating time shouldn't exceed 2 hours.

2 cups fresh orange juice
(about 5 oranges)

½ cup fresh lemon juice (about 3 lemons)

½ cup dry white wine

3 cinnamon sticks

Grated zest of 1 orange

Grated zest of 1 lemon

4 garlic cloves, minced

1 tablespoon minced peeled fresh ginger

1 cup minced onion

½ teaspoon fenugreek (optional)

3 tablespoons paprika

1 teaspoon cracked black peppercorns

¼ teaspoon freshly grated nutmeg

1 tablespoon blackstrap molasses

2 tablespoons olive oil

Two 3-pound chickens, all visible fat removed, cut into eighths and skin removed (optional)

Serves 6 to 8

1. In a small saucepan, combine the orange and lemon juices, wine, and cinnamon. Boil until ¹/₂ cup liquid remains. Cool.

2. Place the orange and lemon zests in a medium nonreactive bowl. Add the garlic, ginger, and onion. Stir in the juice mixture, fenugreek, if using, paprika, peppercorns, nutmeg, molasses, and oil. Place the chicken pieces in 1 or 2 nonreactive baking dishes. Brush the chicken on all sides with the marinade. Cover the pans with plastic wrap and marinate, refrigerated, at least 2 hours or up to overnight. Turn the pieces once. Thirty minutes before cooking, remove the chicken from the refrigerator.

3. Preheat the oven to 350°F. and prepare a grill. Baste the chicken with the marinade and bake flesh side down 20 minutes. Remove the chicken and grill it over medium heat about 4 inches from the heat source, or broil, turning as needed, until the juices run clear when the meat is pierced with a fork, 15 to 20 minutes. Serve.

Spiedini di Pollo

Spiedini are the kebabs of Italy and are prepared throughout the country. They are, however, most typical of Apulia, which is known for its spiedini of young lamb. These delicious spiedini contain chicken, red peppers, lemon, and tomato. What gives them their special liveliness is the contrast among the texture of the chicken, the softness of the tomato, and the tart-smoky flavor of grilled lemon. Serve these with grilled polenta for a feast.

2 pounds chicken cutlets, cut into 1½-inch cubes

2 bell peppers, preferably yellow, cored, seeded and cut into 2-inch cubes

⅓ cup extra-virgin olive oil

1 tablespoon balsamic vinegar

1 garlic clove, pressed

1 tablespoon fine, dry toasted bread crumbs

½ teaspoon crushed fennel seeds

Kosher salt and freshly ground black pepper

3 small, firm ripe tomatoes, quartered and seeded

1 large lemon, cut into ¼-inch slices

Four 12-inch wooden skewers, soaked in water for 30 minutes to avoid burning, or metal skewers

Serves 4

1. Put the chicken and peppers in a bowl. Add the olive oil, vinegar, garlic, bread crumbs, and fennel seeds. Season with the salt and pepper, mix well, and marinate at room temperature 20 to 30 minutes.

2. Prepare the spiedini two at a time, threading the ingredients on the skewers in this order: pepper, tomato, lemon, chicken, lemon, tomato, pepper, and so on. Try to end with a piece of pepper. If using wooden skewers, cover any bare wood with strips of foil to prevent coloring during cooking.

3. Prepare a grill or preheat the broiler. Brush the spiedini with the marinade. Grill over medium heat, about 4 inches from the heat source, or broil, 5 to 6 minutes. Turn the spiedini, baste with the marinade, and cook until the chicken is just done, 5 to 6 minutes. Serve immediately.

Rosemary Chicken with Vegetables and Tomato Cumin Sauce

SAUCE

2 tablespoons canola or other light vegetable oil

2 cups chopped onions

One 28-ounce can whole peeled plum tomatoes, drained, their liquid reserved

½ teaspoon ground cumin

¼ cup Italian parsley leaves

Salt and freshly ground black pepper

6 large chicken cutlets (about 3 pounds total), pounded to ¼-inch thickness

16 garlic cloves

2 teaspoons fresh rosemary leaves, or 1 teaspoon dried

⅓ cup dry sherry

¼ cup sherry wine vinegar (see page 14)

⅓ cup canola or other light vegetable oil

Freshly ground black pepper

1 teaspoon crushed cumin seeds

3 medium zucchini, cut lengthwise into thirds

2 red or yellow bell peppers, cored, seeded, and cut into 1-inch strips

24 small shiitake or domestic mushrooms

Serves 4 to 6

If you love the taste of rosemary, you'll adore this dish. Redolent of the herb, cumin-laced and full of fresh vegetables, it's delicious, all-in-one eating. If you have sprigs of the beautiful, spiny rosemary, do use them as a garnish.

1. To make the sauce, in a large skillet, heat the oil over medium heat. Add the onions and sauté until soft and just beginning to brown, about 10 minutes.

2. In a food processor or blender, combine the onions, tomatoes, cumin, and parsley and puree. Thin the sauce if necessary with the reserved tomato liquid. Season to taste with the salt and pepper. Reserve.

3. Place the chicken in a large bowl. In the food processor or blender, combine the garlic, rosemary, sherry and vinegar, oil, pepper to taste and cumin seeds and process to blend well.

4. Pour two-thirds of the marinade over the chicken, toss, and reserve. Place the vegetables in a medium bowl, brush with the remaining marinade, and set aside. Marinate both the chicken and the vegetables, covered and refrigerated, for at least 1 hour and not more than 4 hours.

5. Prepare a grill or preheat the broiler. Oil the grill or a grilling rack and grill the vegetables over high heat, 4 inches from the heat source, until just cooked through, or broil, about 4 minutes for the mushrooms, 2 to 3 minutes for the zucchini and peppers, turning to cook evenly. Remove and keep warm. Grill the chicken over medium heat about 4 inches from the heat source until just done, 6 to 7 minutes per side, or broil, 2 to 3 minutes per side. Place the chicken on a platter, surround with the vegetables, and serve with the sauce drizzled over or on the side.

Minted Mustard Chicken

We Americans neglect mint in our cooking. A symbol of hospitality, it is used widely in Middle Eastern and North African cooking, perhaps most famously in Moroccan tea. This dish glorifies fresh, peppery mint in collaboration with mustard—the dominant ingredients in a piquant marinade for the chicken.

Yes, the recipe calls for both fresh and dried mint; depending on your source and time of year, one may be more pungent than the other. Together, they make this dish special. By the way, this recipe calls for lemonade concentrate. Made basically from lemon juice, water, and a sweetener (buy a preservative-free brand with as few additional ingredients as possible), it's perfect in recipes requiring a greater depth of flavor than lemon juice alone can provide. A good trick to know.

Two 2½- to 3-pound chickens, all visible fat removed, cut into eighths, or 6 large chicken cutlets (about 3 pounds total)

3 garlic cloves

¼ cup Dijon mustard

2 tablespoons olive oil

1 tablespoon frozen lemonade concentrate

2 teaspoons dried mint

½ cup fresh mint leaves, plus additional sprigs for garnish

½ cup parsley leaves

Juice of 1 lemon

Serves 6

1. Place the chicken in large nonreactive bowl. In a food processor, combine the garlic, mustard, oil, concentrate, dried and fresh mint, and lemon juice. Process until well mixed.

2. Pour the marinade over the chicken and marinate, covered, in the refrigerator, for at least 30 minutes or up to 3 hours.

3. Prepare a grill. Drain the chicken, reserving the remaining marinade. For chicken pieces, preheat the oven to 350°F. Place the pieces skin side down on large baking sheets with rims and bake for 20 minutes, reserving the pan juices. Finish cooking on the grill over medium heat about 4 inches from the heat source, or broil, turning as needed, until juices run clear when the meat is pierced with a fork, 15 to 20 minutes. Grill chicken cutlets over medium heat 4 inches from the heat source until just done, 6 to 7 minutes per side, or broil, 3 to 4 minutes per side.

4. Put the remaining marinade in a small saucepan (add ¼ cup water if using cutlets). Add any pan juices, bring to a boil, and boil for 2 minutes. Turn off heat and spoon off fat. Pour over the cooked chicken, garnish with the mint sprigs, and serve.

Mexican Chicken Fajitas

Fajitas are great fun and delicious when homemade. Though you can wrap the grilled chicken strips and peppers for these before serving them, people love assembling fajitas at table. Just put out the tortillas, fillings, and accompaniments, and everyone digs in.

The marinade for the chicken is good used with almost anything. To be more specific, try the marinade with steak or kebabs made with turkey; it will keep refrigerated for a week or two.

This is really an easy dish that's a whole meal; great for entertaining.

MARINADE

Juice of 4 limes

2 teaspoons olive oil

4 garlic cloves, crushed

½ teaspoon ground cumin

¼ teaspoon salt, or to taste

¼ teaspoon pepper, or to taste

1½ pounds chicken cutlets

2 Vidalia onions (or other sweet onions), peeled and quartered

1 red bell pepper, cored, seeded, and quartered

1 yellow bell pepper, cored, seeded, and quartered

2 packages 6-inch flour tortillas, at room temperature

FILLINGS AND ACCOMPANIMENTS

3 cucumbers, peeled and cut into ¼-inch dice

6 plum tomatoes, cut into ¼-inch dice

2 cups shredded romaine or iceberg lettuce

1 cup Red Table Salsa (page 224)

¼ cup fresh coriander leaves (cilantro), snipped

1½ cups Guacamole (page 221)

Serves 6 to 8

1. To make the marinade, in a large nonreactive bowl, combine the lime juice, olive oil, garlic, cumin, salt, and pepper and mix well. If broiling the chicken (rather than grilling it), cut the peppers into $^1/_2$-inch strips (precut peppers would be too difficult to handle on the grill). Add the chicken, onions, and the peppers to the marinade, cover, and marinate, refrigerated, 2 to 3 hours.

2. Preheat the oven to 200°F. Wrap the tortillas in foil and place in the oven to warm, about 30 minutes. Remove and keep warm.

3. Meanwhile, prepare a grill. Drain the chicken, onions, and peppers and grill over medium heat 4 inches from the heat source until both are just done, 4 to 5 minutes per side. Remove and cut the chicken and peppers into $^1/_2$-inch strips. Alternatively, turn the oven control to broil after the tortillas have been removed and allow the broiler to preheat. Cut the drained chicken and peppers into $^1/_2$-inch strips and place in a pan. Broil until just done, 2 to 3 minutes per side.

4. Place the chicken and peppers, fillings, and accompaniments in separate bowls or on plates. Put the tortillas on a platter or in a basket. Each diner fills and rolls his or her own tortillas and chooses accompaniments.

Be-All and End-All Barbecue Sauce Chicken

Everyone needs a great all-American barbecue sauce in their repertoire. The marvelous sauce used here for grilled chicken is truly the be-all and end-all of its kind—pungent-sweet with a fine burnished flavor note.

Besides being delicious, the sauce is healthier than those you can buy. Instead of corn syrups, fructose, colorings, and who can say what glop, this one contains molasses, honey, and tomato paste. Decidedly peppery, the sauce can be made even kickier with additional jalapeño or shakes of hot sauce.

You can also make the sauce ahead—it keeps refrigerated for up to three weeks; keep it on hand. The chicken is baked before grilling or broiling to ensure deep flavor and even cooking; you may, however, grill or broil it from start to finish (see Note).

Serve the chicken with Warm Fennel Slaw (page 185), baked beans, and Skillet White Cornbread (page 214).

1 tablespoon olive oil

1 large onion, chopped

6 garlic cloves, minced

1 jalapeño pepper, seeded and minced, or 1 teaspoon hot sauce

¼ cup tomato paste

½ cup blackstrap molasses

½ cup honey

⅔ cup cider vinegar

¾ cup Dijon mustard

1 teaspoon dried thyme

1 tablespoon soy sauce

Two 3½-pound chickens, all visible fat removed and cut into eighths

Serves 6 to 8

1. In a large saucepan, heat the oil over medium heat. Add the onion, garlic, and jalapeño and cook, stirring well, until the onion is soft but not brown, 3 to 4 minutes.

2. Stir in the tomato paste, molasses, honey, vinegar, mustard, thyme, and soy sauce. Simmer for 10 minutes. Cool.

3. Place the chicken in a medium bowl. Add 1¹/₂ cups of the sauce, coat the chicken well, and marinate, covered, in the refrigerator for 2 hours or up to overnight. Reserve the remaining sauce for brushing the chicken.

4. Prepare a grill and preheat the oven to 400°F. (see Note). Place the chicken skin side down on trays and bake for 20 minutes. If finishing the chicken in the broiler, turn oven control to broil.

5. To finish the chicken, grill over medium heat about 4 inches from the heat source, or broil, turning as needed, until the juices run clear when the meat is pierced with a fork, 15 to 20 minutes. Brush the chicken as needed with the remaining marinade and watch carefully to prevent burning. If the chicken browns too quickly, move the grill or broiler rack farther from the heat source. Serve immediately or at room temperature.

Note: If not prebaking, grill or broil the chicken, turning as needed, about 40 minutes.

Grilled Turkey Burgers on Pita Bread with Red Onion Confit

If you like the idea of light, lean turkey burgers better than you've liked the reality, these are for you. Made with onion, a bit of ketchup, and egg white, these burgers are moist and savory, as well as easy on the calories. They're served with a tart-sweet red onion confit on pita bread and make a fine meal.

The dish is easiest if you prepare the confit ahead. It keeps for up to six weeks refrigerated in a covered container and is also great with steak or on turkey sandwiches.

I serve the burgers with assorted mustards and good half-sour pickles, a bowl of lettuce, and a plate of sliced tomatoes.

RED ONION CONFIT

¼ cup olive oil

2 pounds red onions, thinly sliced

⅓ cup sugar

⅛ teaspoon salt

¼ teaspoon freshly ground black pepper

2 bay leaves

½ cup red wine vinegar

½ cup raspberry vinegar

1. To make the confit, in a large nonreactive saucepan, heat the oil over medium-low heat. Add the onions, sugar, salt, pepper, and bay leaves. Cover and cook until the onions are soft and translucent, about 30 minutes.

2. Uncover and add the vinegars. Turn the heat to high and cook, stirring constantly, until most of the liquid is gone, about 15 minutes. Allow to cool.

3. To make the burgers, in a large bowl, thoroughly combine the turkey, bread crumbs, ketchup, mustard, onion, egg white, and parsley with 2 tablespoons of hot water. Season with the salt and pepper. Shape the mixture into 8 patties and place on a waxed paper-lined tray. Cover and chill at least 1 hour.

BURGERS

2 pounds lean ground turkey

¼ cup bread crumbs

2 tablespoons best-quality ketchup

2 tablespoons mustard

½ red onion, minced

1 egg white

½ cup chopped parsley

Salt and freshly ground black pepper

Four 8-inch pocketless pita breads or
eight 6-inch pita breads with pockets

Serves 8

4. Prepare a grill or preheat the broiler. Grill the burgers over medium heat about 4 inches from the heat or broil until cooked through, 4 to 6 minutes per side. Warm the pita bread on the grill, or sprinkle it lightly with water to keep it moist and warm it in the oven. Halve the pocketless pitas, if using, and place one half on each plate. Top the pitas with the confit and burgers. Alternatively, fill each of the pocketed pitas with a burger and some of the confit. Serve.

Marge Rosenthal's Grilled Chicken with Penne and Roast Vegetables

For this dish you make a pasta "sauce" with roasted tomatoes and garlic, caramelized asparagus, and peppers. Then grilled chicken breasts are sliced and combined with room-temperature penne and the sauce. The result is spectacular, and makes a perfect summer dinner or Shabbat lunch.

12 plum tomatoes, quartered lengthwise

$1/2$ teaspoon salt, plus additional

$1/2$ teaspoon sugar

1 teaspoon dried oregano

10 tablespoons olive oil

2 heads garlic, 2 cloves removed, peeled, and crushed

2 pounds fresh asparagus, trimmed and cut into 1-inch lengths

2 yellow bell peppers, cored, seeded, and cut into 1-inch dice

6 ounces portobello mushrooms stemmed and cut into 1-inch dice

1 pound penne

2 tablespoons fresh lemon juice

Freshly ground black pepper

2 pounds chicken cutlets, lightly pounded

Serves 4

1. Preheat the oven to 350° F.

2. In a mixing bowl, combine the tomatoes, the $1/2$ teaspoon salt, sugar, $1/2$ teaspoon of the oregano, 2 tablespoons of the olive oil, and the crushed garlic cloves. Toss gently.

3. Cut off the tops (about $1/2$ inch) from the garlic heads and put each head in the center of a square of aluminum foil. Pour 1 tablespoon of the olive oil over each and seal the foil squares by gathering the tops and twisting them gently.

4. Pour the tomato mixture into half a baking pan and place the wrapped garlic in the other half. Bake 30 minutes.

5. Meanwhile, in a mixing bowl, toss together the asparagus, yellow peppers, mushrooms, the remaining $1/2$ teaspoon oregano, and 2 tablespoons of the oil. Reserve.

6. After 30 minutes, add the asparagus mixture to the pan next to the garlic pouches. Continue to cook an additional 15 minutes, then remove the garlic. Turn off the oven, keeping the pan mixtures warm. Allow the garlic to rest for 10 minutes.

7. Bring a large pot of salted water to a boil. Prepare a grill or preheat the broiler or a grill pan.

8. Add the pasta to the water and cook until al dente, 8 to 10 minutes. While the pasta is cooking, unwrap the garlic and squeeze the softened cloves into a small nonreactive bowl. Mash with a fork, add the lemon juice, and 2 tablespoons of the olive oil. Season to taste with the pepper and reserve.

9. Coat the chicken with the remaining 2 tablespoons olive oil. Season lightly with the salt and pepper. Grill the breasts outdoors over medium heat, about 4 inches from the heat source, turning once, until just cooked through, 6 to 7 minutes per side, or broil or cook in the grill pan, 3 to 4 minutes per side. Cut the chicken diagonally into $1/2$-inch-thick slices.

10. Drain the pasta and toss with the mashed garlic mixture until well combined. Gently fold in the tomatoes, vegetables, and any juices that may have accumulated in the pan. Fold the chicken into the pasta, adjust the seasonings, and serve.

Tuscan Barbecued Chicken

This dish has its roots in the open-spit-grilled specialties of the Tuscan countryside. You can watch chickens turning slowly on spits there, becoming golden and sending the most incredible smells into the great outdoors.

You can recapture some of that pleasure with this garlicky, tomato-laced version, which is simple to make. The little bit of molasses in the marinade adds no sweetness of its own, but it effectively counteracts the acidity of some of the other ingredients, which is a good technique to keep in mind.

Serve this with grilled Polenta (page 193).

MARINADE

2 shallots, peeled

2 teaspoons molasses

2 tablespoons tomato paste

8 garlic cloves, peeled

1 tablespoon chopped fresh rosemary

2 teaspoons fresh oregano,
or 1 teaspoon dried

12 fresh basil leaves, or
2 teaspoons dried

1 tablespoon red wine vinegar

½ cup dry red wine

Two 2½- to 3-pound chickens, all visible
fat removed, cut into eighths

¼ cup dry red wine

Serves 6 to 8

1. To make the marinade, in a food processor, combine the shallots, molasses, tomato paste, garlic, rosemary, oregano, basil, vinegar, and wine. Pulse until the vegetables are finely chopped.

2. In a large bowl, combine the chicken and the marinade. Stir to coat the chicken well, cover, and refrigerate for 4 to 6 hours or overnight.

3. Prepare a grill or preheat the broiler. Remove the chicken from the marinade and drain; reserve the marinade. Grill the chicken over medium heat about 4 inches from the heat source, turning frequently, until the juices run clear when the meat is pierced with a fork, 30 to 40 minutes, or broil, turning once, 10 to 12 minutes per side.

5. Meanwhile, in a small saucepan, combine the remaining marinade with the wine. Bring to a boil, turn down the heat, and simmer to reduce, about 10 minutes. Serve the chicken immediately or at room temperature with the sauce.

Tennessee Barbecued Chicken

Folks from Tennessee prize "dry" barbecue, which is unsauced during cooking. This Tennessee-style barbecued chicken celebrates that preference. Its marinade uses apple juice concentrate, which provides just the right amount of sweet-tart flavor. The finished dish, which has a delicate barbecued savor, is the perfect antidote to the many "red" barbecues people often make.

Serve this chicken with Skillet White Cornbread (page 214), Warm Fennel Slaw (page 185), or potato salad.

MARINADE

One 12-ounce can frozen apple juice concentrate, thawed

½ cup best-quality ketchup

2 tablespoons cider vinegar

2 teaspoons dried thyme

8 garlic cloves

2 small onions, quartered

1 tablespoon olive oil

1 teaspoon celery seed

¼ cup Dijon mustard

¾ cup parsley leaves

Few shakes hot sauce, or a bit of harissa (see page 11), optional

Two 2½- to 3-pound chickens, all visible fat removed and cut into eighths

Serves 6 to 8

1. To make the marinade, in a food processor, combine the apple juice, ketchup, vinegar, thyme, garlic, onions, oil, celery seed, mustard, parsley, and hot sauce. Process until smooth.

2. In a large bowl, combine the chicken and the marinade and marinate, covered, in the refrigerator for 2 hours.

3. Prepare a grill (alternatively, the chicken can be broiled; see step 4). Preheat the oven to 400°F. Remove the chicken from the marinade and place the marinade in a small saucepan. Place the chicken skin side down in a baking pan. Bake the chicken for 20 minutes.

4. If not grilling the chicken, turn up the oven control to broil. Remove the chicken from the oven and grill over medium heat about 4 inches from the heat source, or broil, turning as needed, until the juices run clear when the meat is pierced with a fork, 15 to 20 minutes.

5. Meanwhile, bring the marinade in the saucepan to a boil, turn down the heat, and simmer to reduce slightly for 10 minutes. Serve the chicken with the marinade warm or at room temperature.

Grilled Chicken Breasts with Cider Sauce and Sautéed Apples

It's fall, the air is crisp, the leaves are turning, and you have bowls of just-picked apples from the farmer's market. Friends are coming for dinner—what do you serve?

This elegant dish, a true apple celebration. In it, apples appear in a tart-sweet cider-based sauce and a luscious fruit accompaniment for grilled chicken breasts. The dish is ideally made with Jonagold apples, Pippins, or any of the great heirloom apple varieties available in the fall—but it works beautifully, too, with everyday types. Serve the chicken with wild rice or Basmati Rice (page 210) and steamed green beans—and enjoy the warm apple aromas that fill the house when you make it.

1 tablespoon margarine or vegetable oil

2 garlic cloves, crushed

3 tablespoons sugar

3 cups apple cider

4 whole cloves

One ½-inch piece cinnamon stick, or ⅛ teaspoon ground cinnamon

2 tablespoons fresh lemon juice

¼ cup sweet white wine, such as Sauternes

1 tablespoon plus 1 teaspoon arrowroot

2 tablespoons Chicken Stock (page 61), or good instant or low-sodium canned broth, or water

Salt and freshly ground black pepper

3 large, firm apples, peeled, cored, and cut into ½-inch slices

1 tablespoon Dijon mustard

½ teaspoon fresh thyme leaves, or ¼ teaspoon dried

6 medium chicken cutlets (about 2½ pounds total)

2 tablespoons chopped Italian parsley

Serves 4 to 6

1. In a heavy 3-quart saucepan, heat the margarine over medium heat. Add the garlic and sauté until it has softened, about 3 minutes. Add the sugar and cook, stirring, until the sugar turns golden brown, 3 to 5 minutes. Remove from the heat and add the cider (stand back, the mixture can splatter). Add the cloves, cinnamon, lemon juice, and wine.

2. Return the pan to the stove. Increase the heat and bring the mixture to a boil, stirring to dissolve the caramel. Lower the heat and simmer until the mixture is smooth and slightly reduced, about 20 minutes.

3. In a small bowl, dissolve the arrowroot in the stock. Whisk it into the sauce and return the sauce to the heat. Simmer, whisking, until the sauce is clear and lightly thickened, about 1 minute. Season to taste with the salt and pepper, strain out the solids, and keep warm.

4. Lightly coat a large skillet with vegetable oil spray. Warm it over low heat and in it arrange the apple slices in a single layer. Sauté gently, turning once, until lightly browned, 5 to 8 minutes. Carefully remove the apples with a spatula and set aside.

5. Prepare a grill or preheat the broiler or a grill pan. If using a grill pan, spray it first with olive oil spray.

6. In a small bowl, combine 6 tablespoons of the sauce with the mustard and the thyme and brush the chicken cutlets with the mixture. Grill the cutlets over medium heat about 4 inches from the heat source until golden, 6 to 7 minutes per side. Alternatively, broil or cook in the grill pan, about 3 minutes per side. Serve the cutlets with the sliced apples, drizzle the sauce over both, and sprinkle with the parsley. Pass additional sauce separately.

Butterflied Grilled Rock Cornish Chickens with Chinese Marinade

Unstuffed rock cornish chickens (Empire's designation for these small birds) have a delicate but pronounced flavor, and are easy to grill when butterflied. For this dish, the chickens are first marinated in a classic Chinese marinade that is good also with lamb chops or flank steak. Serve the birds with Sesame Coriander Sauce (page 242) and fresh sugar snap peas for an elegant meal that's particularly nice for summer.

MARINADE

2 tablespoons frozen orange juice concentrate

½ cup low-sodium soy sauce

½ cup hoisin sauce

½ cup honey

¼ cup fresh lemon juice

6 garlic cloves

One 1- to 2-inch piece fresh ginger, peeled

½ teaspoon dried thyme

½ teaspoon freshly ground black pepper

2 bay leaves

4 rock cornish chickens, 2½ to 3 pounds each, rinsed and soaked (see page 20), trimmed of all visible fat, backbone removed, and butterflied if 2½ pounds or under, otherwise split in half

Serves 4 to 6

1. To make the marinade, in a food processor, combine the concentrate, soy sauce, hoisin sauce, honey, lemon juice, garlic, ginger, thyme, and pepper. Pulse to chop the garlic and ginger roughly. Add the bay leaves.

2. Place the chickens in a nonreactive pan or container with a fitted cover. Add the marinade, cover, and marinate, refrigerated, for at least 2 hours or as long as overnight. Turn the chickens twice while marinating.

3. Bring the chickens to room temperature, about 20 minutes. Drain the marinade, place it in a small saucepan, and simmer 20 minutes to reduce. Reserve.

4. Prepare a grill or preheat the oven to 400°F. if broiling. To grill, cook the chickens over medium heat about 4 inches from the heat source, bone side down, about 20 minutes. Brush with the marinade, turn, and cook until the juices run clear when the chickens are pierced at the joints, about 20 minutes more. To broil, place the chickens in a pan and prebake them skin side down 20 minutes. Turn the chickens and brush with marinade. Turn the oven control to broil and broil the chickens until the juices run clear when the joints are pierced with a fork, 8 to 10 minutes. Serve half a chicken per person or quarter the chickens and pass them on a large platter.

Grilled Sesame Gourmettes

Gourmettes are Empire's name for the small drumsticklike parts of chicken wings. It's a pleasure to be able to buy them in four-pound bags—they're succulent mouthfuls that work perfectly for all sorts of informal meals (I love to serve them for picnics). Here, gourmettes are marinated in a tahini- and honey-flavored bath, grilled, and served—simple and good.

You could also use chicken parts for this or a three-pound bird cut into eighths. I like to accompany the dish with a tabbouleh or cucumber salad or coleslaw.

MARINADE

One 2-inch piece of fresh ginger, peeled and put through a garlic press

¼ cup soy sauce

½ cup toasted sesame tahini

1½ tablespoons honey

1 tablespoon sesame seeds

6 garlic cloves, peeled

4 pounds gourmettes (see Headnote)

¼ cup chopped fresh coriander leaves (cilantro), snipped chives, or sliced scallions, for garnish

Serves 6

1. To make the marinade, in a food processor or blender, combine the ginger, soy sauce, tahini, honey, sesame seeds, and garlic. Process until well blended.

2. Place the chicken in a large nonreactive dish about 2 inches deep. Make no more than 2 layers. Pour the marinade over, making certain that the pieces are evenly coated; use a brush if necessary. Cover and refrigerate for 2 to 3 hours at least, or as long as overnight.

3. Prepare a grill or preheat the broiler. Remove the gourmettes and shake off excess marinade. Grill over medium heat about 4 inches from the heat source, turning as needed until brown and crispy, or broil, about 15 minutes total. Garnish with the chopped coriander and serve.

African Spice-Rubbed Drumsticks with Banana Boats

Recipes can begin with an idea—or a bag of groceries. This one started with bananas and the wish to pair them, African style, with chicken. I decided to grill banana halves in their skins and serve them with drumsticks that had been rubbed with black pepper, spices, and a touch of sugar to "open up" the flavors. The result was this utterly tantalizing dish, African in its play of heat, sweet, and warm fruitiness.

For a portable meal, serve the grilled drumsticks with Honey-Banana Chutney (page 238) instead of the boats. The dish relies on good chili powder; keep trying brands until you find one that rings the bell. Multiply that ring by two or three if you like things spicy!

RUB

¼ teaspoon ground cumin

2 tablespoons paprika

2 tablespoons chili powder

1 tablespoon dark brown sugar

1 tablespoon cracked or very coarsely ground black peppercorns

2 tablespoons dried oregano

3 pounds chicken drumsticks

4 firm, barely ripe bananas, unpeeled

½ to 1 tablespoon canola or vegetable oil spray

Serves 6 to 8

1. To make the rub, using a fork, combine the cumin, paprika, chili powder, brown sugar, peppercorns, and oregano in a bowl. Mash any lumps.

2. Oil the drumsticks lightly. Roll the drumsticks in the rub, place on a pan or in a dish, and refrigerate, covered, at least 2 hours or as long as overnight.

3. Twenty minutes before cooking, remove the drumsticks from the refrigerator. Prepare a grill or preheat the broiler. Grill the drumsticks over medium heat about 4 inches from the heat source, turning as needed, until brown and crisp, about 30 minutes, or broil, turning once, about 12 minutes per side.

4. Meanwhile, slice the unpeeled bananas in half lengthwise. Coat or spray the flesh with the vegetable oil. About 5 minutes before the chicken is done, place the bananas on the grill or under the broiler, flesh side towards the heat, and cook until the flesh has softened and is sizzling, 3 to 5 minutes. If there is insufficient room to cook the chicken and bananas simultaneously, finish the chicken, keep warm, and grill the bananas. Serve the bananas and chicken together.

Grilled Chicken with Melon Salsa and Tender Greens

MARINADE

1 tablespoon fresh lime juice

3 small garlic cloves, pressed

Pinch of kosher salt

¼ teaspoon freshly ground black pepper

1 tablespoon canola or other vegetable oil

4 medium chicken cutlets (about 1½ pounds total)

SALSA

1½ cups ripe honeydew melon cut into ¼-inch dice

1½ cups ripe cantaloupe cut into ¼-inch dice

1½ teaspoons grated peeled fresh ginger

5 tablespoons minced scallion, white and green parts

1 teaspoon seeded and minced jalapeño pepper

Juice of 1 lime

¼ teaspoon kosher salt

Leaves from 1 head Boston lettuce or other tender greens

1 teaspoon walnut or hazelnut oil

8 fresh mint leaves, cut into thin strips

Serves 4

A salsa need not be red, coriander-spiked, and incendiary. A gingery salsa made with honeydew melon, cantaloupe, and a touch of jalapeño is a brilliant accompaniment, and perfect with lightly charred grilled chicken.

Use only ripe melons for the salsa. The fruit you want has no greenish cast, a stem end that yields slightly to pressure, and a fragrant melon smell. This dish is a summertime treat; serve it with Skillet White Cornbread (page 214) or—even better—fresh Gingerbread Madeleines (page 215).

1. To make the marinade, in a medium bowl, combine the lime juice, garlic, salt, pepper, and oil. Add the chicken, turn to coat well, and marinate, refrigerated, 15 to 20 minutes.

2. To make the salsa, in a second medium bowl, combine the melons, ginger, scallion, jalapeño, lime juice, and salt. Refrigerate until cold.

3. Prepare a grill or preheat the broiler or a grill pan. If using a grill pan, spray it first lightly with vegetable oil. Grill the breasts outdoors over medium heat, about 4 inches from the heat source, turning as necessary, until just cooked through, 6 to 7 minutes per side, or broil or cook it in the grill pan, about 3 minutes per side.

4. Toss the lettuce leaves with the oil and divide among 4 plates. Cover with the chicken and top with the salsa. Garnish with the mint and serve.

Turkish Chicken with Grilled Pita

The merchants in the Istanbul spice market sell a wonderful spice mixture in large cellophane tubes, which are unlabeled. Each spice in the blend is arranged separately in the tube and combines with the others only when the tube is emptied. After buying and cooking with the delicious blend, I was determined to solve the mystery of its composition. Three different spice vendors were consulted and, at last, the spice code was cracked: cumin, turmeric, sweet paprika, oregano, black pepper, and sumac. Eureka!

The blend is featured in this pungent grilled chicken dish served with grilled pita. You'll love its flavor so much, you'll want to add Turkish spice to everything you cook. For a very special meal, serve the chicken and pita with grilled vegetables and Skordalia (page 245).

MARINADE

Juice of 6 lemons

¼ cup Turkish spice (see Note)

1 cup Dijon mustard

14 garlic cloves, peeled

4 sprigs rosemary, chopped,
or 2 teaspoons dried

¼ cup olive oil

1 tablespoon molasses

3 tablespoons lemonade concentrate

1 tablespoon tomato paste

Two 3-pound chickens, all visible fat
removed and cut into eighths

4 pocketless 8- to 10-inch pita breads,
for serving

Serves 6 to 8

1. To make the marinade, in a nonreactive bowl, combine the lemon juice, Turkish spice, mustard, garlic, rosemary, oil, molasses, concentrate, and tomato paste. Add the chicken, turn to coat well, and marinate, refrigerated and covered, 2 to 3 hours or overnight. When ready to cook, bring the chicken to room temperature.

2. Prepare a grill or preheat a broiler. Grill the chicken over medium heat about 4 inches from the heat source, turning as necessary, until the juices run clear when the meat is pierced with a fork, about 40 minutes, or broil, turning once, 10 to 12 minutes per side.

3. Five minutes before the chicken is cooked, add the pita breads to the grill and allow to warm and char slightly. If broiling, moisten the pita with water, wrap in foil, and warm in the oven. Slice the pita into wedges and serve with the chicken.

Note: To make Turkish spice, combine in a glass jar with lid ¼ cup ground cumin, ¼ cup turmeric, 3 tablespoons sweet paprika, ¼ cup oregano leaves, 1 teaspoon freshly ground black pepper, and ¼ cup sumac. Shake and use or store in the freezer for up to 1 year.

Chicken Gourmettes with Lekvar

Chicken gourmettes—chicken-wing "drumsticks"—are versatile, bite-size morsels. They're great for an informal dish like this, which features lekvar, or sweet-tart prune butter. The lekvar-based sauce is used to baste the chicken and as an accompanying dip. I love double-duty sauces like this one, which provides a double depth of flavor.

Serve the gourmettes with coleslaw, Summer Corn and Cucumber Salad (page 186), or Sushi Rice (page 211). Any unused sauce can be kept under refrigeration for two weeks.

½ cup lekvar (prune butter; available at specialty food markets) or apple butter

½ cup dry sherry

2 tablespoons soy sauce

One 1-inch piece fresh ginger, peeled

2 scallions, green and white parts, cut into 2-inch pieces

1 tablespoon peanut oil

4 garlic cloves

1 tablespoon honey

½ cup fresh coriander leaves (cilantro), plus 1 tablespoon chopped coriander leaves, for garnish

½ to 1 jalapeño pepper, seeded

4 pounds chicken gourmettes

Serves 6 to 8

1. In a food processor, combine the lekvar, sherry, soy sauce, ginger, scallions, oil, garlic, honey, and 2 tablespoons of hot water. Pulse 4 to 5 times to chop the vegetables and process to blend, about 1 minute. Add the $^1/_2$ cup coriander leaves and jalapeño, and pulse 2 to 3 times to combine. Scrape down the work bowl and divide the mixture into 2 parts.

2. Dry the gourmettes well and brush them with some of the lekvar mixture. Turn the pieces to coat them completely. (At this point, you can refrigerate the gourmettes overnight and finish them later.)

3. Prepare a grill or preheat the broiler. Grill the gourmettes over medium heat about 4 inches from the heat source or broil, turning as needed, until the gourmettes are nicely browned and cooked through, about 15 minutes. Garnish the gourmettes with the chopped coriander and pass with the reserved lekvar sauce. (Do not serve with any sauce used for brushing the uncooked gourmettes.)

7. Side Dishes

Side dishes are
more than supporting players.
Which one of us hasn't considered
an herby cornbread, tempting coleslaw,
or a sweet and savory stuffing
the real point of a meal?

It's in this sides-are-best spirit that the following dishes were developed. Designed to complement poultry dishes, they work equally well with meat and fish entrees and, often, on their own.

Take salads. With the abundance of exciting, fresh produce now available to us and condiments of all kinds, we're no longer caught in yesterday's iceberg-lettuce-with-Russian-dressing fix. My salads also contain interesting fruit and vegetable pairings. The Watercress Orange Salad and the Peach and Pepper Salad are intriguing examples of this sweet-pungent kind; so is the Summer Corn and Cucumber Salad. Served with crusty bread, these salads are great as is; they work equally well as preludes or accompaniments to barbecues or other meals featuring grilled, broiled, or roasted poultry.

Slaws are always welcome—provided they have heart. Warm Fennel Slaw, a wok-cooked dish highlighting the lusty taste of fennel, and Annual Beach Barbecue Coleslaw, crunchy with slivered almonds, are stand-up-

and-be-counted slaws. They make great outdoor fare but work indoors too, year-round. These are reborn classics.

Also provided are definitive versions of old favorites such as kasha varnishkes (the secret of this dish involves a pre-toast of the groats), and a wonderful spinach kugel made with matzo that's perfect for Passover. Crispy skillet cornbread, herbed popovers, and ratatouille are other basic but beloved sides that can make a cook's reputation.

So can stuffings. I've always felt that stuffings deserve a richer place in our dining lives than they usually occupy. Don't wait for a holiday to make stuffing—and vary the kinds you serve. Though everyone enjoys the time-honored stuffings of family tables, there are new kinds to try. The fennel-cornbread stuffing (see page 128) is a good place to start, and a good place to learn a savory cornbread stuffing base. Sweet and Savory Stuffing, rich with currants, apples, and pine nuts, is an opulent accompaniment, as is Wild Rice, Mushroom, and Cherry Stuffing. You'll find basic stuffing information on page 24, but here are additional stuffing suggestions:

Cook stuffing outside as well as inside the bird. I always include some pan-heated stuffing with holiday birds. Not only is the stuffing's flavor more distinctive when cooked this way but it will also contain less fat. Ladle a spoonful or two of broth over the stuffing before cooking it to prevent it from drying out.

A caterer's trick: cook and serve stuffing in ramekins, especially if you're doing a preplated meal. Or serve the stuffing unmolded—coat ramekins lightly with oil and bread crumbs before adding the stuffing, bake, and invert onto plates. Offered either way, the servings look great, and are tidier than the usual stuffing presentations.

Add fresh herbs to stuffings just before they're served. This freshens stuffing taste enormously. Also, don't let stuffing linger in the bird. Slow cooling is not optimal, and can be hazardous. Take the stuffing out right away to ensure best taste.

Bread stuffings can be wonderful, but don't neglect stuffings based on root-vegetables like sweet potatoes or leeks, or stuffings made with rice, wild rice, barley, or kasha. And add contrast to these stuffings with dried fruit like apricots or cherries and nuts, including pecans or hazelnuts. Imagination is key. Once you see the rich potential of stuffings (and other sides), your culinary horizons will expand excitingly.

Annual Beach Barbecue Coleslaw

Coleslaw is definitely a subject for debate. There are probably as many versions as there are cooks, and everyone has his or her favorites. I've made many coleslaws over time—and this one, prepared annually for a potluck beach barbecue, is the hands-down best. Perfectly tart-sweet, with the nutty flavor of sesame and crunch of almonds, it's the ideal accompaniment to grilled poultry. It's also a cinch to make—an easy dish for big parties.

1 small red cabbage, finely shredded

1 small green cabbage, finely shredded

4 scallions, white and green parts, finely chopped

⅓ cup canola or other vegetable oil

2 tablespoons dark sesame oil

6 tablespoons brown rice vinegar

4 tablespoons sugar

1 teaspoon salt

Cracked black peppercorns

1 cup toasted slivered almonds

¼ cup toasted sesame seeds

Serves 8

1. In a large bowl, combine the cabbages and scallions and mix.

2. In a small bowl, combine the canola and sesame oils, vinegar, sugar, and salt and mix. Season with the pepper. Pour the mixture over the cabbage mixture and toss well. Refrigerate several hours, tossing occasionally.

3. Right before serving, add the almonds and sesame seeds. Toss.

Warm Fennel Slaw

Fresh fennel absolutely deserves to be more popular in America. Doted on by the Italians, this bulbous vegetable with its feathery leaves and licorice-like taste is wonderful braised as a side dish, or shredded, as here, in coleslaw. This delicious slaw, which happens to be low in fat and cholesterol, is served warm, which brings out the perfume of the fennel and the fresh herbs in the dressing. Serve this simple-to-make slaw with roast chicken and mashed potatoes; it's also great with Spiedini di Pollo (page 161), on a buffet table.

2 tablespoons olive oil

4 cups thinly sliced onions

1 small fennel bulb, fronds removed and reserved, outer tough leaves removed, the remainder cored and slivered

6 cups packed finely shredded savoy or green cabbage

½ cup seasoned rice wine vinegar (see page 14)

1 tablespoon fennel seeds, crushed

1 cup packed mixed fresh herb leaves, such as chives, coriander (cilantro), Italian parsley, including the fennel fronds

Salt and freshly ground black pepper

Serves 4

1. In a wok or very large skillet, heat the olive oil over medium heat. Add the onions and fennel and sauté until the onions begin to soften, 10 to 15 minutes.

2. Add two-thirds of the cabbage, turn up the heat to high, and stir-fry until the cabbage has just begun to wilt, 3 to 4 minutes. Remove the mixture to a large bowl. Add the remaining cabbage and toss. Reserve.

3. In a food processor, combine the vinegar, fennel seeds, and herbs. Process until the mixture is pureed.

4. Pour the dressing over the cabbage and onions. Season to taste with the salt and pepper, toss, and serve.

Summer Corn and Cucumber Salad

Because this salad features raw corn kernels, make it only when the corn season is at its height. Choose the freshest, sweetest ears you can get your hands on, scrape off the kernels, and you're ready to go. (You can blanch the corn, if you like, but try it raw the first time.) Cucumber, sweet onion, and a light mustardy dressing complete this sprightly summer delicacy.

4 ears fresh corn

2 cucumbers, peeled, halved, and seeded

½ Vidalia or other sweet onion, sliced paper-thin

2 to 3 tablespoons distilled white vinegar

1 tablespoon canola or other vegetable oil

1 tablespoon coarse-grain mustard

Salt and fresh ground pepper

12 fresh basil leaves

Serves 4 to 6

1. Slice the kernels off the cob and place in a large bowl.

2. Slice the cucumbers thinly on the diagonal, creating "crescent moons." Add to the corn along with the onion and toss.

3. In a small bowl, whisk together the vinegar, oil, and mustard. Season to taste with the salt and pepper. Pour the dressing over the vegetables and toss. Just before serving, snip the basil leaves to make irregular pieces and add to the salad. Mix lightly and serve.

Red Salad

I call this salad red because of the tomato and crisp radicchio (which is actually purple-veined, but allow a cook some culinary license!). It was created for a Fourth of July picnic, where it was accompanied by grilled chicken with blueberry chutney and Skillet White Cornbread (page 214)—my bid for a red, white, and blue celebration. The salad's citrus-accented balsamic vinaigrette also contains chicken stock, an intriguing flavor enrichment and partial oil substitute. This is tantalizing and ridiculously easy to make.

1½ pounds Italian plum tomatoes, quartered

½ cup mixed fresh herb leaves, such as basil, Italian parsley, summer savory, thyme

6 cups torn radicchio leaves

2 tablespoons chopped shallots

¼ cup balsamic vinegar

¼ cup Chicken Stock (page 61), or good instant or low-sodium canned broth

1 teaspoon Dijon mustard

1 teaspoon sugar (optional)

2 teaspoons extra-virgin olive oil

1 tablespoon fresh orange juice

Salt and freshly ground black pepper

Serves 6

1. In a large bowl, toss together the tomatoes, herbs, and radicchio.

2. In a small bowl, whisk together the shallots, vinegar, stock, mustard, sugar, if using, olive oil, and orange juice. Season to taste with the salt and pepper. Pour the dressing over the salad, toss, and serve.

Watercress Orange Salad

I'm a big watercress fan. Too long relegated to garnishing status, peppery watercress is marvelous when allowed to take center stage, as here. This salad also features orange segments, a perfect foil for the watercress, sliced onion, and a cumin-laced vinaigrette.

2 bunches fresh watercress, washed

3 seedless oranges, peeled and all pith removed, divided into sections, juice reserved

2 tablespoons red wine or balsamic vinegar

½ small onion, halved and thinly sliced

¼ cup olive oil

2 teaspoons Dijon mustard

¼ teaspoon ground cumin

Salt and freshly ground black pepper

Serves 5 to 8

1. In a large bowl, toss together the watercress and oranges.

2. In a small nonreactive saucepan, over medium heat, bring the vinegar to a simmer. Add the onion and turn off the heat. Allow to sit until cool (this mellows the onion).

3. Drain the vinegar from the onion and reserve both. In a small bowl, whisk together the olive oil, reserved vinegar, mustard, cumin, and reserved orange juice. Season to taste with the salt and pepper.

4. Add the reserved onion and the dressing to the salad. Toss and serve.

Peach and Pepper Salad

This is my desert island salad, a must to accompany grilled dishes in summer. The peach and red pepper combination is inspired; a vinaigrette made with lime juice, chili pepper, and a bit of molasses glorifies the fruit, which must be summer-ripe. Friends who have had this have asked me for the recipe of "that delicious fresh relish you made." Call it what you like, you must try it.

3 garlic cloves, peeled

1 to 2 chili peppers, such as jalapeños or serranos, seeded if less heat is desired

½ cup packed Italian parsley leaves

⅓ cup olive oil

1 tablespoon molasses

⅓ cup fresh orange juice

Juice of 3 limes

4 large firm-ripe peaches, pitted and sliced

2 red bell peppers, cored, seeded, and julienned

1 large red onion, very thinly sliced

Salt and freshly ground black pepper

Serves 6

1. Through the feed tube of a food processor with the machine running, add the garlic and chili peppers. When chopped, stop the machine and add the parsley. Pulse to chop. Add the olive oil, molasses, and orange and lime juices. Pulse to blend. Pour into a large bowl.

2. Add the peaches, bell peppers, and onion. Toss, season to taste with the salt and pepper, and serve.

Cold String Beans with Wasabi Vinaigrette

This lively salad, with its pungent wasabi dressing, makes a perfect accompaniment for fried chicken. If you can find Romano beans—a flat pole bean with superb flavor—do use them for this. Just make sure to marinate whatever beans you've chosen in the vinaigrette for an hour before serving.

These go very well with grilled chicken breasts in addition to fried chicken.

1½ pounds fresh bush string beans or Romano pole beans, stringed and trimmed

1 red onion, finely minced

¼ cup chopped fresh basil leaves

¾ cup Wasabi Sauce (page 46)

1 teaspoon low-sodium soy sauce

Several grinds of black pepper

Serves 6

1. Cut the beans into bite-size pieces, about $1^1/_2$ inches long. Fill a 3-quart saucepan with water and bring to a boil. Add the beans, let the water return to a boil, and cook for 15 seconds. Drain the beans and run under cold water to stop the cooking process. Drain well.

2. In a large bowl, combine the onion, basil, Wasabi Sauce, soy sauce, and pepper. Add the beans and stir to coat. Refrigerate, allowing the beans to marinate for about 1 hour. Serve chilled.

Eggplant Salad with Currants

This recipe is a vegetarian favorite. It's a caperless caponata that works equally well as a salad or a condiment and is also great with grilled meats or served as a dip with toasted pita bread for entertaining; I present it in chilled endive leaves. It tastes best if it has a day to mellow, and keeps refrigerated for a week.

For looks and flavor, peel the eggplant partially. Using a swivel-blade peeler, remove lengthwise strips of peel alternating with unpeeled strips. Make the peeled strips one-third the size of the unpeeled. Try this with other eggplant dishes—it works!

5 to 6 medium eggplants (about 4½ pounds)

½ to 1 teaspoon kosher salt

½ cup olive oil

1½ cups chopped shallots or onions

7 garlic cloves, minced

4 tablespoons tomato paste

5 plum tomatoes, cut into ½-inch cubes

5 teaspoons soy sauce

3 tablespoons red wine vinegar, approximately

½ cup dried currants

Freshly ground black pepper

Makes 7 cups

1. Partially peel the eggplant (see Headnote). Cut into 1-inch cubes and sprinkle thoroughly with the salt. Place in a colander over the sink. Allow the eggplant to drain bitter liquid, about 20 minutes. Blot dry.

2. In a large, deep skillet, heat the olive oil over medium heat. Add the shallots and garlic and sauté until they are translucent, about 5 minutes. Add the eggplant and cook until soft and reduced by half, 15 to 20 minutes.

3. Add the tomato paste and stir. Add the tomatoes and sauté until beginning to break down, about 5 minutes. Remove from the heat.

4. Add the soy sauce, vinegar, and currants. Season to taste with the pepper. Taste and add more vinegar, if desired. Cool and serve or refrigerate.

Roast Potatoes with Seltzer

Yes, seltzer. It's the mystery ingredient sprinkled over the potatoes before roasting them for this dish that makes them always turn out particularly moist and crisp. My friend Phil Gilbert, while he was the executive chef for CBS, introduced me to this wonderful technique. Try it and see for yourself. And do roast a variety of potatoes together for a special dish.

2 pounds potatoes, all-purpose, new, sweet, or Yukon Gold, alone or in combination, scrubbed (see Note)

1 to 2 tablespoons olive oil

Salt

2 teaspoons chopped fresh rosemary

1 tablespoon seltzer

Freshly ground black pepper

Serves 6 to 8

1. Preheat the oven to 500°F.

2. Cut the potatoes into 1-inch cubes, place in a large bowl, and toss with the olive oil, salt, and rosemary (see Note).

3. Turn the potatoes onto a nonstick or foil-lined cookie sheet with sides. Spread the pieces for even browning. Sprinkle the potatoes with the seltzer.

4. Roast the potatoes until brown and crispy, about 30 minutes. Grind pepper to taste over them and serve.

Note: The potatoes can be cubed in advance and held for 1 day, refrigerated, in a bowl of water. Drain and dry them well before proceeding.

Polenta

To quote Italian cooking expert Marcella Hazan, polenta consists of "corn flour, water, and a well-lubricated elbow." Cornmeal becomes polenta—the warm, soft mass that is wonderful with many dishes—when, with constant stirring, it absorbs water or broth. Served with stews or entrees that have enough sauce or cooking juices to flavor it, polenta is a great, earthy alternative to potatoes or rice.

You can chill freshly made polenta quickly for grilling by placing the loaf pan (see Variation) carefully in a bowl of ice water in the refrigerator for about 40 minutes.

6½ cups Chicken Stock (page 61), or good instant or low-sodium canned broth, or vegetable stock

Salt

2 cups coarse-grained yellow cornmeal or imported meal for polenta (not instant)

1 teaspoon extra-virgin olive oil

¼ cup finely chopped Italian parsley

Serves 6

1. In a heavy-bottomed pot, bring the stock to a boil over high heat. Add about a teaspoon of salt and stir. Add the polenta in a thin trickle, letting it stream through the fingers of one hand while stirring with a whisk. When all the polenta is added, reduce the heat to medium-low and begin to stir with a wooden spoon. Stir constantly until the polenta comes away easily from the sides of the pot, about 20 minutes.

2. Stir in the olive oil and parsley, turn the polenta into a large bowl, and serve.

VARIATION

GRILLED POLENTA WITH RED PEPPERS
Prepare the polenta as above. When the polenta is cooked, pour it into an oiled loaf pan, cool, and refrigerate. Prepare a grill or preheat the broiler. Slice 4 red peppers into ¹/₂-inch strips. Lightly spray them with olive oil spray and grill them skin side down over medium heat, about 4 inches from the heat source, or broil them, skin side facing the heat source, 7 to 8 minutes; reserve. Unmold the polenta and cut into ¹/₂-inch slices. Oil the grill or, if broiling, lightly spray or brush the slices with olive oil and grill or broil until lightly browned with crisp edges, 2 to 3 minutes per side. To serve, line a serving platter with arugula, arrange the polenta over it, and top with the peppers. Sprinkle with chopped parsley and additional olive oil and lemon, if you wish.

Mashed New Year's Potatoes

What better dish to welcome the New Year than creamy, comforting mashed potatoes? This version is made with sweet as well as regular potatoes for great nondairy taste. I like my mashed potatoes with a few lumps for textural interest, so I hand-mash; use a ricer or a food mill for a smooth texture. If you want, you can prepare these an hour or so ahead, keeping them warm, covered, in a double boiler or pan over hot water.

1 pound sweet potatoes, peeled and cubed

2 pounds all-purpose potatoes, peeled, cubed, and placed in a bowl of cold water to prevent discoloration

1 tablespoon margarine

¾ to 1 cup Chicken Stock (page 61), or good instant or low-sodium canned broth, heated

Salt and freshly ground black pepper

1 tablespoon chopped Italian parsley

Serves 6

1. Place the potatoes in a large saucepan, cover with cold water, and bring to a boil. Reduce the heat to maintain a simmer and cook until tender, 20 to 30 minutes.

2. Drain the potatoes and return them to the saucepan over low heat. Shake the pan to remove remaining moisture from the potatoes.

3. Transfer the potatoes to a large bowl and begin mashing them with a hand masher; alternatively, put them through a ricer or food mill. Beat them slowly by hand or using an electric mixer. Add the margarine and stock and season to taste with the salt and pepper. Beat well. Stir in the parsley and serve at once or keep the potatoes warm in a pan over hot water.

Kasha Varnishkes

This traditional favorite—buckwheat groats with noodles—often suffers from indifferent cooking. The secret to making a superior dish involves toasting the grain before it simmers. This enhances its nutty flavor and helps to ensure crispy kernels, a nice contrast to the soft noodles. Bow ties have become the noodle of choice for the dish, but you could also use shells or rigatoni.

Kasha varnishkes goes with almost anything. It's particularly nice with dishes that have a delicate sauce—Grandma Regina's Roast Chicken (page 112) and Barbara's "Wild" Balsamic Chicken (page 105) are great possibilities.

2 cups Chicken Stock (page 61), or good instant or low-sodium canned broth, or mushroom broth (from cubes)

2 tablespoons crumbled dried mushrooms, any kind (see Note)

1 tablespoon olive oil

1 cup finely chopped onions

1 egg white

1 cup whole or medium buckwheat groats

1 cup thinly sliced fresh mushrooms

2 cups bow-tie noodles

Serves 4

1. In a medium saucepan, bring the stock to a boil. Add the dried mushrooms and remove from the heat. Allow the mushrooms to soften, about 20 minutes. Using a slotted spoon, remove the mushrooms and reserve. Strain the stock through cheesecloth or paper towels to rid it of any sand from the mushrooms. Return the stock to the saucepan.

2. In a medium skillet, heat the olive oil over medium heat. Add the onions and sauté until they begin to turn golden, about 8 minutes. Remove the onions from the pan and reserve. Reserve the skillet. Return the stock to a boil.

3. In a small bowl, using a fork, combine the egg white and groats. Transfer to the skillet and cook over medium heat, stirring to break up the groats, until brown, about 4 minutes. Return the onions to the skillet and mix until the groats are well separated and dry. Add the dried and fresh mushrooms and stir to mix well, 2 to 3 minutes. Add the boiling stock and mix well. Reduce the heat to low, cover, and cook for 10 minutes.

4. Meanwhile, cook the noodles according to package directions. Drain well and toss with the cooked kasha. Serve.

Note: Broken dried mushrooms, available at many markets, are fine for this.

Matzo Spinach Kugel

Kugel, the traditional pudding made with noodles or vegetables, is one of the joys of sabbath or holiday tables. This savory kugel, made with spinach and farfel (crushed matzo), and lightened with whipped egg whites, is especially good with roast chicken or veal.

To ensure a wonderful kugel crust, preheat the baking dish with added oil before pouring in the kugel mixture.(Be aware of your dish's material; to avoid its cracking, you may have to start the dish in a cold oven to heat.) The kugel is best served hot.

Two 10-ounce boxes frozen chopped spinach, defrosted

3½ cups matzo farfel

3 tablespoons canola or other vegetable oil

1 cup washed and chopped leeks, white and light green parts

1 cup chopped Spanish or other mild onion

1 bunch scallions, white and green parts, chopped

4 egg whites

1 teaspoon sugar

2 egg yolks

½ cup chopped Italian parsley

1 tablespoon chopped fresh dill

¾ teaspoon salt

1 teaspoon finely ground black pepper

Pinch of grated nutmeg (optional)

Serves 6 to 8

1. Preheat the oven to 400°F. Drain the spinach in a colander and squeeze out any extra water. Place in a large bowl and reserve.

2. In a bowl of cold water, soak the farfel until beginning to soften, about 7 minutes. Drain the farfel and reserve.

3. In a heavy skillet, heat 1 tablespoon of the oil over medium heat. Add the leek and onion and sauté until soft, about 10 minutes. Add the scallions and sauté 2 minutes more. Remove from the heat and reserve.

4. In a medium bowl, beat the egg whites until soft peaks form. Add the sugar and continue to beat until the whites are stiff but not dry. Into the spinach mixture stir the egg yolks, the onion mixture, the drained farfel, parsley, and dill.

5. Add the remaining 2 tablespoons of oil to a 12- to 14-inch baking dish, and heat it in the oven until the oil sizzles. Meanwhile, fold the egg whites, salt, pepper, and nutmeg, if using, into the spinach mixture.

6. Carefully remove the baking dish from the oven. Pour the kugel mixture into the dish and smooth it with the back of a spoon. Reduce the heat to 375°F. and bake until the kugel is golden, about 1 hour. With a knife, promptly loosen the kugel from the pan along its edges and invert the kugel onto a large platter. Serve hot or at room temperature.

Mashed Potatoes with Leeks and Garlic

These mashed potatoes are the ultimate. They're luscious and satiny and contain leeks and garlic. Always dry out boiled potatoes before mashing them; that way they'll mash up fluffy and light rather than watery. I like to use olive oil to make these, but margarine works nicely, too. The necessary substitution of milk or cream with chicken stock is a boon in disguise. It adds more complex flavor, and reduces the fat.

3 tablespoons olive oil or margarine

3½ cups washed and finely chopped leeks, white and pale green parts

3 pounds baking potatoes (about 6 large), peeled, cut into 1-inch cubes, and placed in a bowl of cold water to prevent discoloration

6 garlic cloves, unpeeled

½ cup Chicken Stock (page 61), or good instant or low-sodium canned broth, heated

Salt and freshly ground black pepper

Serves 6 to 8

1. In a large, heavy skillet, heat the oil over medium heat. Add the leeks and sauté, stirring occasionally, until very soft and golden, 8 to 10 minutes. Turn off the heat and keep warm.

2. In a large saucepan, combine the potatoes, garlic, and enough water to cover the potatoes by 1 inch. Bring the water to a boil and simmer until the potatoes are easily pierced with a fork, 10 to 15 minutes.

3. Drain the potatoes and garlic into a large colander. Remove the garlic and reserve. Return the potatoes to the saucepan and dry them over medium heat, shaking the pot, about 30 seconds.

4. Transfer some of the potatoes to a small bowl. Peel the reserved garlic and add to the bowl. Mash with the potatoes and return to the pot. Mash the potatoes with a hand masher.

5. In a food processor or using a food mill, puree the leeks, adding the stock. Stir the leek puree into the potatoes and continue mashing until smooth and creamy. Alternatively, put the potatoes, garlic, and leeks through the medium disc of a food mill, add the stock, and mash. Season to taste with salt and pepper and serve.

Pureed Celery Root and Carrots

Knobby brown celery root (or celeriac) is one of the world's more homely vegetables. Don't pass it up, though—its celery-parsley flavor makes luscious eating, especially when pureed with carrots and pears (an intriguing accent), as here. Choose relatively small, firm celery roots with a minimum of rootlets and knobs. Before using, peel the root and soak it in acidulated water (the juice of one lemon to a bowl of water) to avoid its discoloration. Add the peeled pears to the water also. Serve this delicious recipe with roast chicken, fish steaks, or grilled lamb or veal chops.

1 pound celery root, peeled and cut into 1-inch cubes

2 pears, or apples, peeled, cored, and cut into large pieces

1 pound carrots, peeled and cut into 1-inch pieces

1 pound sweet potatoes, peeled and cut into 1-inch cubes

6 sprigs parsley tied together with string

3 cups Chicken Stock (page 61), or good instant or low-sodium canned broth

Grated nutmeg

Salt and freshly ground black pepper

Serves 6 to 8

1. Place the celery root, pears, carrots, potatoes, and parsley in a large saucepan. Add the stock and bring to a boil.

2. Reduce the heat and simmer until the carrots are very tender, about 10 minutes. Drain, reserving $1/2$ cup of the stock.

3. Transfer the mixture to a food processor in small batches and puree until smooth, adding the reserved stock as needed. Season to taste with the nutmeg, salt, and pepper. (At this point, the puree can be refrigerated for a day.)

4. To serve, reheat the puree in a double boiler over low heat, 3 to 5 minutes. Or preheat the oven to 350°F. Transfer the puree to a baking dish, cover, and warm in the oven, 20 to 30 minutes.

Zucchini Potato Latkes

Because of the miracle of the oil in the story of Chanukah, it's traditional to eat something oil-fried for the holiday. Latkes—potato pancakes—are the customary fried dish. This delicious version features zucchini in addition to the potatoes, and makes light, delicate pancakes. Perfect for the Festival of Lights, these are scrumptious as is, or with applesauce or sour cream.

For best latke consistency, half the raw potatoes are grated using the chopping blade of a food processor, half with its fine grating disc. Or use a hand box-grater, grating half the potatoes on the large-hole side, the remainder on the fine-hole. The latkes can be made cocktail size—they're great passed with drinks.

2 medium zucchini

4 large potatoes, peeled, cut to fit a food processor feed tube, and placed in bowl of water to prevent discoloration

4 eggs

2 to 4 tablespoons flour or fine matzo meal during Passover (see Note)

1 large onion, quartered

2 tablespoons chopped fresh dill

Salt and freshly ground black pepper

Canola or other vegetable oil, for frying

Makes thirty-two 2¹/₂-inch latkes or 72 cocktail size

1. In a food processor fitted with a fine grating disk, grate the zucchini. Squeeze out any extra liquid and place in a large bowl.

2. Grate half the potatoes in the food processor with the grating disc, or on the finest side of a box-grater, and squeeze out any liquid. Quickly add the potatoes to the zucchini. Add the eggs and the flour until the mixture is no longer runny and stir to blend.

3. In the processor fitted with a metal blade, pulse-chop the onion and remaining potato finely, or grate the potato only on the large-hole side of a box-grater and combine with the onions. Add to the zucchini-potato mixture. Add the dill and season to taste with the salt and pepper. Stir to blend well.

4. In a large, heavy skillet, heat ¹/₈ to ¹/₄ inch of vegetable oil over medium heat. Stir the batter if it appears to have separated. When the oil is hot (a drop of the potato mixture added to it will sizzle immediately), spoon quarter-cups of the mixture, or tablespoons for cocktail lakes, into the oil. Do not crowd. Brown the pancakes on both sides, about 5 minutes total. Drain them on brown paper or paper towels and keep warm while preparing additional batches. Serve immediately.

Note: To make fine matzo meal, pulse-chop regular matzo meal using a food processor.

Sautéed Pear
with Spinach and Basil

In this simple but fascinating vegetable dish, the pear adds delicious fruit sweetness to the spinach and the basil takes everything to a higher flavor plane. This is great with roast chicken—with roasts of all kinds, actually—and is also low in calories and fat. In other words, the perfect vegetable accompaniment.

2 tablespoons chopped shallots

1 very firm pear, quartered, cored, peeled, and thinly sliced

2 pounds fresh spinach, washed and shaken or partially spun dry (allow some water to cling to leaves)

1 cup fresh basil leaves

2 tablespoons Chicken Stock (page 61), or good instant or low-sodium canned broth

⅛ teaspoon freshly grated nutmeg

Salt and freshly ground black pepper

Serves 4

1. Choose a large skillet with a tight-fitting lid and coat the skillet's interior with vegetable oil spray. Heat the skillet over medium heat. Add the shallots and sauté until softened, 3 to 4 minutes. Add the pear and sauté it until it begins to brown, about 3 minutes.

2. Add the spinach, basil, and stock, stirring. Increase the heat, cover, and cook until the spinach has wilted, 2 to 3 minutes. Add the nutmeg and season to taste with the salt and pepper. Serve.

Winter Vegetable Roast

How often have you enjoyed nibbling pan vegetables without realizing that they could be served as a luscious accompaniment? They can, as this intensely flavored dish of butternut squash and parsnips proves. Oven-caramelized and touched with molasses, these are worthy of your fanciest poultry roasts. Make sure the vegetables aren't over-roasted; a little browning brings out natural sweetness; overcooking will create bitterness.

1 shallot, finely minced

1 teaspoon black strap molasses

4 teaspoons canola or other vegetable oil, plus extra for the pan, or vegetable oil spray

2 butternut squash (about 2½ pounds total), peeled, seeded, and cut into ½-inch cubes

2 parsnips (1 pound total), peeled and cut into ½- inch cubes

Kosher salt and freshly ground black pepper

1 tablespoon chopped fresh thyme or parsley

Serves 8

1. Preheat the oven to 425°F. In a small bowl, combine the shallot, molasses, and oil. With a whisk or fork, blend the mixture until emulsified.

2. Oil a large baking sheet with sides or an 8 x 11-inch roasting pan, or coat with vegetable oil spray. Spread the squash and parsnips on the sheet, not touching, drizzle over the oil-molasses mixture, and toss gently to coat evenly. Distribute the vegetables evenly and season to taste with the salt and pepper.

3. Roast the vegetables until they are thoroughly cooked and have begun to brown nicely, 45 to 55 minutes. Stir them occasionally while cooking with a spatula or wooden spoon to avoid sticking. Do not overcook.

4. Transfer the vegetables to a serving dish (or set them aside to be reheated later). Correct the seasoning, sprinkle with the thyme, and serve.

Grilled Vegetables

Lightly charred and intensely flavored, grilled vegetables are a marvelous accompaniment to virtually any meat entree. They're also beautiful arranged on a large platter for parties. Serve the vegetables hot off the grill or cook and store them for up to three days. (Mushrooms are best prepared and eaten within hours.) Before choosing a vegetable "menu," go to your market and see what looks freshest. Prepare any or a combination of vegetables as follows.

FLAVORED OIL

Garlic cloves, pressed

Olive oil

Dried herbs, such as thyme or oregano (optional)

Baby zucchini (3 to 4 inches), cut in half

Asparagus, blanched 2 seconds in boiling water, cooled in ice water and well drained

Shiitake, oyster, porcini, or other mushrooms, any tough stems removed

Cauliflower, broken into large florets, cooked in chicken broth with saffron (optional) until crisp-tender

Red or yellow bell peppers, peeled, cored, and cut into ½-inch strips

Belgian endive, cut in half

Eggplant, cut into ¼-inch-thick slices, salted with kosher salt, allowed to drain in a colander for about 20 minutes, and dried

Salt and freshly ground black pepper

Servings depend on vegetable quantities

1. To make the flavored oil, add the garlic to the oil in the ratio of 4 cloves to every ½ cup oil. Add the herbs, if using.

2. Brush the vegetables very lightly, doing one type at a time, with the flavored oil. Season to taste with the salt and pepper.

3. Prepare a grill or preheat a broiler or grill pan. Grill the vegetables over medium heat, about 4 inches from the heat source, or broil or cook using the grill pan, turning as needed, until browned, 4 to 8 minutes. If storing, cool, place each type in separate containers and refrigerate. Bring to room temperature before serving.

Ratatouille

Ratatouille, the vegetable stew from Provence, can be utterly delicious or a sorry mush. Now that we have the zucchini and basil needed to make it almost year-round, it behooves us to get the dish right. The secret of a perfect ratatouille is to cook each vegetable no longer than necessary, and to use tomato paste for a rich red "base." Ratatouille is the perfect accompaniment to roast chicken with polenta or mashed potatoes; it's also great tossed with pasta.

2 tablespoons olive oil

2 medium onions, chopped

5 garlic cloves, minced

1 eggplant, partially peeled (see Headnote, page 191), cut into 1-inch cubes, lightly salted, and drained 30 minutes in a colander to remove bitterness

3 tablespoons tomato paste

3 tablespoons dry red wine

1 bay leaf

⅔ cup tomato juice

⅓ cup shredded fresh basil leaves, or 1 tablespoon dried

1 tablespoon chopped fresh rosemary, or 1 teaspoon dried

2 medium bell peppers, 1 red and 1 green, cored, seeded, and thinly sliced lengthwise

1 zucchini, halved lengthwise and cut into ½-inch slices

1 summer squash, halved and cut into ½-inch slices

2 medium tomatoes, cut into ¼-inch cubes

½ cup chopped Italian parsley

Salt

Serves 6 to 8

1. In a large, heavy nonstick pot, heat the olive oil over medium heat. Add the onions and garlic and sauté until golden, about 10 minutes.

2. Squeeze the eggplant in paper towels to dry it and add it to the pot. Sauté for 5 minutes and add the tomato paste, wine, and bay leaf. Stir and add the tomato juice, basil, and rosemary. Simmer for 10 minutes.

3. Add the peppers and simmer, covered, for 5 minutes. Add the squashes, cover, and simmer until crisp-tender, about 10 minutes. Stir in the tomatoes and parsley and season to taste with the salt. Serve hot or at room temperature.

White Vegetable Puree

This delightful puree of white root vegetables including leeks (white parts only), potatoes, parsnips, celery root, and cauliflower makes a luscious accompaniment to roast or grilled chicken and is very easily prepared.

3 leeks, white parts only, washed and cut into 1-inch pieces

2 baking potatoes, peeled and cut into large cubes

2 parsnips, peeled and cut into large cubes

1 celery root (celeriac), peeled and cut into large cubes

1 small head cauliflower, broken into flowerets

¼ cup olive oil

Pinch of grated nutmeg

Salt and freshly ground black pepper

Serves 4 to 6

1. Bring a large pot of water to the boil. Add the leeks, potatoes, parsnips, celery root, and cauliflower and cook until tender, about 20 minutes. Drain thoroughly.

2. Using tongs, transfer the leeks to a food processor and puree. Mash the remaining vegetables with a potato masher and add the leek puree. Add the olive oil and nutmeg and continue to mash until the mixture is fluffy. Season to taste with the salt and pepper and serve.

Moghlai Spinach

This spicy Indian-influenced spinach is a welcome accompaniment to almost any chicken or meat-based entree. I like it particularly with grilled chicken kebabs. Garam masala, the Indian spice mix required for this dish, is easily made. Adjust the heat of the spinach as you like, increasing or decreasing the amount of cayenne, or leave it out entirely.

4 tablespoons canola or other vegetable oil

½ teaspoon whole fennel seeds, crushed

4 cardamom pods

2 medium onions, peeled, cut in half lengthwise, and sliced crosswise into fine half-rings

One 2-inch piece fresh ginger, peeled and julienned

2 pounds spinach, trimmed and washed well

½ to 1 teaspoon salt

½ teaspoon garam masala (page 11)

¼ teaspoon cayenne pepper (optional)

Serves 6

1. In a pan or heavy-bottomed pot large enough to hold the spinach, heat the oil over medium-high heat. Add the fennel seeds and cardamom, stir, and add the onions and ginger. Sauté, stirring, until the onions have browned, about 5 minutes.

2. Add the spinach, stuffing it into the pan in batches if necessary. Cover and allow the spinach to wilt. Uncover, stir, and add the salt, garam masala, and cayenne, if using. Continue to cook, stirring occasionally, until the spinach has cooked to softness, 2 to 3 minutes. Remove the cardamom pods if you wish and serve.

Couscous

A North African staple, couscous is cooked and dried granular semolina pasta. It's a simple, delicious alternative to rice or potatoes, perfect with stews and roast poultry, or cold in salads or with summer entrees. (To serve it cold, follow the directions below, adding the juice of a lemon and a splash of fruity olive oil.)

Couscous is sold in bulk in Middle Eastern markets and some gourmet shops, or packaged in many supermarkets. Its traditional preparation is lengthy, involving multiple steamings to ensure separate grains. I have found that quick-cooking or precooked couscous is not only easy to prepare but also yields a delicious dish. That's the couscous I call for here.

2½ cups Chicken Stock (page 61), or good instant or low-sodium canned broth

1 cinnamon stick

½ teaspoon turmeric

½ cup finely minced carrot (1 large carrot)

2½ cups quick-cooking or precooked couscous

Salt and freshly ground black pepper

Serves 6 to 8

1. In a deep, wide saucepan or skillet with a cover, bring the stock, cinnamon stick, and turmeric to a boil. Turn off the heat.

2. Immediately stir in the carrot and couscous. Cover, remove the pot from the burner, and let sit for 10 minutes. Fluff with a fork and let sit for 5 to 10 minutes. Season to taste with the salt and pepper and serve immediately.

Oven-Roasted Beets

I've noticed a surge in the popularity of beets recently and I couldn't be happier. Well-handled, beets are delicate, delicious vegetables; roasting is one of the best ways I know to maximize their subtle goodness. In this recipe the beets receive the enhancement of a sweet-tart glaze made with raspberry vinegar; fresh herbs complete the flavor picture. Serve these with Chicken Scarpariello (page 103) and roasted potatoes or turnips. They also reheat very well.

2½ pounds (3 to 4 bunches) beets, scrubbed and tops trimmed to 2 inches

1 small red onion or 4 shallots, peeled

¾ cup fresh orange juice

2 tablespoons raspberry vinegar

1 teaspoon honey

1 tablespoon canola or other vegetable oil

Handful of fresh herbs, such as thyme, rosemary, or oregano, or ½ teaspoon crushed anise seed

Pinch of kosher salt

Freshly ground black pepper

Serves 6 to 8

1. Preheat the oven to 400°F. Place the beets in a baking dish, add $^1/_2$ cup of water, cover tightly, and bake until the beets can be pierced with a knife, 45 minutes to 1 hour.

2. Add the onion, orange juice, vinegar, honey, and oil to a food processor. Process until the onion is liquefied and the mixture smooth. Pour the mixture into a large bowl. If using anise, add.

3. When the beets are cool enough to handle, remove their remaining tops and the bottom tails, peel, and cut into $^1/_4$-inch slices. Add to the juice-vinegar mixture and toss. Raise the oven heat to 450°F.

4. In a 9 x 12-inch heavy nonreactive baking dish, scatter the herbs. Place the beets on them, overlapping the slices. Drizzle the remaining juice-vinegar mixture over them and season to taste with the salt and pepper.

5. Bake until the beet edges are well colored and the beets have absorbed all the liquid, about 40 minutes. Serve.

Braised Brussels Sprouts

I know—you can't stand brussels sprouts. I didn't like them much either until I saw them growing so prettily, nestled in a row on the stalk. I realized that the main problem with preparing them was overcooking and inadequate seasoning. These brussels sprouts are braised—not boiled—so their flavor is subtle and delicious. And they're delicately seasoned. Try these and you'll become a brussels sprouts fan for sure.

1 teaspoon olive oil

1 large sweet onion, halved and sliced very thinly

½ to 1 cup Chicken Stock (page 61), or good instant or low-sodium canned broth

2 sprigs fresh thyme, or ½ teaspoon dried

Pinch of saffron threads

2 pints brussels sprouts, trimmed and stem ends scored to make an x about ¼ inch deep

Salt and freshly ground black pepper

Serves 4 to 5

1. In a large nonstick skillet, heat the olive oil over medium heat. Add the onion and sauté until it turns a caramel color, 10 to 12 minutes.

2. Add the stock, thyme, and saffron and simmer 2 minutes. Add the brussels sprouts and season to taste with the salt and pepper.

3. Cover and cook until just tender, shaking the pan occasionally, 10 to 15 minutes, depending on the size of the sprouts. Serve.

Broiled Basil Tomatoes

These have become a much beloved standard in my house. The dish couldn't be simpler—tomatoes, basil, and garlic and a bit of oil baked together and then broiled. But the results are so good that people ask for seconds and thirds. The best dishes, I think, are usually the ones in which a few ingredients end up tasting perfectly like themselves—only more so. This is one.

6 large, firm ripe tomatoes

¼ cup olive oil

½ cup fresh tightly packed basil leaves

5 garlic cloves, pressed

Kosher salt and freshly ground black pepper

Serves 6

1. Preheat the oven to 500°F.

2. Core and cut the tomatoes into eighths. Place them in a heavy baking dish.

3. In a small saucepan, heat the oil over medium heat. Stir in the basil leaves and cook until wilted, about 3 minutes. Toss the basil-oil mixture and the garlic with the tomatoes and arrange the tomatoes in a single layer in the baking dish. Push the basil under the tomatoes and season to taste with the salt and pepper.

4. Bake the tomatoes until they begin to soften, about 20 minutes. Run them under the broiler to brown, about 3 minutes, and serve.

Basmati Rice

Grown in the foothills of the Himalayas for thousands of years—and now produced in Texas as well—long-grain basmati is delicate and delicious. Its perfumy aroma (basmati means "queen of fragrance" in Hindi) and nutlike flavor is a result of aging, which decreases the water content of the kernels. Basmati is, of course, the usual accompaniment to Indian food, but it is also wonderful served with virtually any poultry or meat entree. In this recipe, the rice is prepared with onion and other seasonings, but you can also make it plain for a simple, delightfully textured grain dish.

2 cups basmati rice

4 tablespoons canola or other vegetable oil

1 medium onion, peeled, halved, and thinly sliced crosswise

2 garlic cloves, minced

Seeds from 4 cardamom pods, or whole pods (optional)

½ to 1 teaspoon salt

One ½-inch piece fresh ginger, peeled and minced

One 1-inch piece cinnamon stick

2 bay leaves

2½ cups Chicken Stock (page 61), or good instant or low-sodium canned broth

Serves 4 to 6

1. Wash the rice in several changes of water and drain.

2. In a heavy-bottomed pot with a tight-fitting lid, over medium heat, heat the oil. Add the onion and sauté, stirring, until beginning to soften, 1 to 2 minutes. Add the garlic and cardamom seeds or pods, if using, and sauté until the onion browns, 5 to 7 minutes. Add the rice and salt and stir gently to coat the grains. Lower the heat if the rice begins to stick. Add the ginger, cinnamon, and bay leaves. Stir and add the stock.

3. Bring to a boil. Place a sheet of foil over the pot and cover with the lid. Turn the heat to very low and cook until the stock is absorbed and the rice is fluffy, about 25 minutes. Remove the bay leaves, cinnamon stick and cardomom pods, if using, and serve.

Sushi Rice

Short-grained and moderately sticky when cooked, sushi rice is perfect for preparing rolled and hand-shaped sushi. It's made with less water than other boiled rice so it's delightfully chewy. You'll find sushi rice in Asian markets and many supermarkets.

After cooking, the rice is combined with a sweet-sour dressing made with rice wine vinegar, mirin (a syrupy rice wine), and sugar. It is used for Chicken Nori Rolls with Wasabi Sauce (page 46); you can also add it to chicken soup with great success.

2½ cups sushi rice

2½ cups water

4 tablespoons brown rice vinegar

3 tablespoons sugar

2½ teaspoons salt

2 tablespoons mirin

Makes about 5 cups

1. Wash the rice. Drain it thoroughly in a colander or strainer, about 10 minutes.

2. In a small pot with a tight-fitting lid, combine the water and the rice. Bring to a boil, cover, and turn down the heat to low. Cook for 15 minutes without lifting the lid.

3. Remove from the heat and allow to sit, covered, for 10 minutes.

4. Meanwhile, prepare the dressing. In a small bowl, combine the vinegar, sugar, salt, and mirin. Stir to dissolve the sugar and salt.

Add the dressing to the rice, stir to combine, and allow the rice to cool to room temperature before using.

Sweet and Savory Stuffing

½ cup dried currants

½ cup apple juice

1 tablespoon canola or other vegetable oil

1 pound lean ground turkey

2 cups finely chopped onion

6 garlic cloves, minced

½ teaspoon red pepper flakes

6 celery stalks (including leaves), finely chopped

2 red bell peppers, cored, seeded, and sliced into thin strips

6 cups day-old cubed French bread (see Note)

2 cups coarsely chopped Italian parsley

1 teaspoon poultry seasoning (see page 13)

1 tablespoon chopped fresh rosemary, or 1 teaspoon dried

½ cup chopped fresh basil, or 2 teaspoons dried

4 Granny Smith apples, peeled, cored, and cubed

½ cup pine nuts, toasted

1½ cups Chicken Stock (page 61), or good instant or low-sodium canned broth, plus ½ cup, heated, for moistening the stuffing (optional)

Salt and freshly ground black pepper

Makes about 14 cups

This is a mighty stuffing. Bread-based and using ground turkey, currants, apples, and pine nuts, it's full of wonderful flavors and pleasing textural contrasts. It would work beautifully with any roast turkey recipe; extra stuffing, if any, can be baked in pans with the bird, or after (I like to ladle some stock onto pan-baked stuffing just before serving it for moistness). This is also great the next day served with cold turkey and chutney.

1. In a small bowl, combine the currants and apple juice. Allow the currants to plump, about 25 minutes. Reserve.

2. In a large skillet, heat the oil over medium heat. Add the ground turkey, onion, garlic, red pepper flakes, and celery and sauté, stirring, until the turkey is browned and crumbly, about 10 minutes. Add the pepper strips and cook 5 minutes. Drain any fat.

3. In a very large bowl, combine the turkey mixture, bread, parsley, poultry seasoning, rosemary, basil, apples, currants with any remaining apple juice, and the pine nuts. Toss gently. Add the 1¹/₂ cups stock and season to taste with the salt and pepper. Spoon into the prepared bird or 2 lightly oiled 9 x 13 x 2-inch pans. If using pans, bake at 325°F. until firm, about 40 minutes. For a moister pan-baked stuffing, drizzle the ¹/₂ cup of stock over the baked stuffing just before serving.

Note: Fresh bread that has been dried in a 250°F. oven for 30 minutes may also be used.

Wild Rice, Mushroom, and Cherry Stuffing

This special stuffing contrasts the rich, earthy flavors of brown and wild rice, mushrooms, and whole-grain bread with the spirited tastes of mint, marsala, and dried cherries. It's a welcome alternative to more traditional chicken or turkey stuffings.

½ cup dried cherries

½ cup marsala or dry sherry

1 cup brown rice

¾ cup wild rice

4 cups Chicken Stock (page 61), or good instant or low-sodium canned broth, or more if needed, plus ½ cup, heated, to moisten stuffing (optional)

1 bay leaf

½ cup marsala

1 tablespoon olive oil

6 leeks, white part only, washed and thinly sliced

4 garlic cloves, minced

1 cup chopped celery, leaves included

2 tablespoon tomato paste

¼ teaspoon ground allspice

2 cups sliced fresh mushrooms

1 cup chopped fresh mint leaves

1 cup day-old or dried crumbled whole-grain bread (see Note)

½ cup chopped toasted almonds

Makes 10 to 12 cups

1. In a small bowl, combine the cherries and marsala. Allow the cherries to plump, about 20 minutes. Reserve.

2. In a large Dutch oven or skillet with a cover, combine the brown and wild rice, the 4 cups of chicken stock, bay leaf, and marsala. Bring to a boil, stir, lower the heat, and simmer, covered, until the rice is nearly tender, about 40 minutes.

3. Meanwhile, in a large skillet, heat the olive oil over medium heat. Add the leeks and garlic, reduce the heat to medium-low, and sauté for 5 minutes. Add the celery and sauté until wilted, about 4 minutes. Add the tomato paste and stir to combine. Add the allspice and mushrooms and cook 2 minutes. Reserve.

4. When the rice is tender, stir in the vegetable mixture. Add the mint, bread, cherries with any remaining marsala, and the almonds and combine gently. Moisten the stuffing with more stock, if necessary. Spoon into the prepared bird or 2 greased 9 x 13 x 2-inch pans. If using pans, bake uncovered at 325°F. until firm, about 45 minutes. For a moister pan-baked stuffing, spoon the ¹/₂ cup stock over the baked stuffing before serving.

Note: To dry fresh bread, spread slices on a baking sheet and bake in a preheated 250° F. oven until easily crumbled, about 30 minutes.

Skillet White Cornbread

Most cornbreads made without dairy products lack the fresh corn taste, crispy exterior, and overall light quality this one possesses. The fresh corn kernels added here ensure sweet corn taste. Apple juice takes the place of some of the oil normally used, which means a lighter bread. The skillet does the rest. I use white cornmeal for a crumb that highlights the kernels, but you could use yellow, if you like.

1¼ cups white cornmeal

¾ cup all-purpose unbleached flour

2½ teaspoons baking powder

1 tablespoon sugar

½ teaspoon salt

2 eggs

3 tablespoons vegetable oil

1 cup apple juice

1 cup fresh white corn kernels, cut off cob, or frozen kernels

Serves 6 to 8

1. Preheat the oven to 425°F. Place a 9-inch cast-iron skillet in the oven and let it heat while making the batter.

2. In a large bowl, combine the cornmeal, flour, baking powder, sugar, and salt.

3. In a small bowl, beat the eggs with the oil and apple juice until well blended. Add the egg mixture to the dry ingredients and stir in the corn.

4. Pour a little vegetable oil into the preheated skillet and swirl to coat it. Spoon in the batter and bake until golden on top, about 25 minutes. To serve, cut into wedges.

VARIATION

CORNBREAD WITH HERBS
Prepare the batter as above and add 2 tablespoons chopped red onion and 1 tablespoon chopped fresh dill when adding the corn kernels. Proceed as directed.

Fresh Gingerbread Madeleines

This is a dark gingerbread, sweet and well spiced. Prepared in shell-shaped madeleine molds (available in most kitchen-supply shops), it's fabulous with Mango-Dressed Chicken Salad (page 248) or Indochinese Chicken Salad with Grapefruit, Cashews, and Cucumber (page 252) or other spicy salads. I also like the madeleines as is, or served with strawberries. (Omit the mustard powder and cayenne if you're making these for dessert.) They're also great for dunking.

¾ cup all-purpose unbleached flour

¾ cup whole-wheat pastry flour

1 teaspoon baking powder

¾ teaspoon ground cinnamon

¼ teaspoon ground cloves

¼ teaspoon mustard powder (optional)

¼ teaspoon freshly grated nutmeg

¼ teaspoon salt

Pinch of cayenne pepper (optional)

¼ cup margarine, softened

¼ cup brown sugar, light or dark

3 tablespoons grated peeled fresh ginger

½ cup molasses

¾ teaspoon baking soda

⅔ cup boiling water

2 eggs, beaten

Makes 24 madeleines or one 8-inch round gingerbread

1. Preheat the oven to 350°F. Spray the madeleine pan (or an 8-inch cake pan) with vegetable oil spray. Using a dry brush, go over the madeleine molds to ensure that they are completely oiled.

2. Sift the all-purpose and pastry flours, baking powder, cinnamon, cloves, mustard powder, nutmeg, salt, and cayenne, if using, into a medium bowl. In a separate bowl, cream the margarine and brown sugar and stir in the ginger.

3. In a small bowl, beat together the molasses and $1/2$ teaspoon of the baking soda. Beat until the mixture lightens and small bubbles form. In a measuring cup, combine the boiling water with the remaining baking soda.

4. Add the molasses mixture to the margarine and sugar. Mix thoroughly and add the dry ingredients alternately with the water, ending with the dry ingredients. Combine completely and fold in the eggs.

5. Fill each madeleine mold two-thirds full. Bake until a toothpick inserted into the madeleines comes out clean, 15 to 20 minutes. If using a round pan, bake about 30 minutes. Remove the madeleines from the pan while still hot, coaxing them out with the tip of a knife. Cool on a rack.

Herbed Popovers

The appearance of popovers is always an event. This towering herbed version is easy to make and perfect with entrees like Chicken Salad with Jicama, Asparagus, and Orange (page 249) or with Tomato Rice Chowder (page 261). To ensure perfect popovers, have all the ingredients at room temperature and keep the oven door closed during the first 30 minutes of baking. Really, you mustn't *peek!*

1 cup water or vegetable broth

1 tablespoon margarine, melted

1 cup sifted all-purpose unbleached flour

¼ teaspoon dried dill

⅛ teaspoon salt

⅛ teaspoon mustard powder

2 eggs, beaten

Makes 9 to 10 popovers

1. Preheat the oven to 450°F. Grease and flour 10 popover tins or deep muffin cups. (If using a tin with more than 10 molds, fill the extra with water to prevent burning while baking.)

2. In a medium bowl, combine the water, melted margarine, flour, dill, salt, and mustard powder and beat until smooth. Add the eggs one at a time, blending after each addition, and beat just to combine. The batter should be the consistency of heavy cream.

3. Working quickly, fill the popover tins or muffin cups two-thirds full. Do not overfill; too much batter will result in a muffinlike texture. Bake immediately for 30 minutes without peeking. After 30 minutes, lower the heat to 350°F. and bake until puffed and golden, about 20 minutes. To test for doneness, remove a popover. If it is done, the sides will be firm; if it collapses, return the pan to the oven and bake longer. Prick the popovers with the tip of a knife to release steam after baking and prevent their collapsing. If necessary the popovers can be pierced and held in a 200°F. oven for up to 12 minutes.

8. Chutneys, Dressings, and Salsas

Chutneys, dressings, and salsas
are a cook's bag of tricks.
With them, you can make culinary magic.

Use them, first, to add flavor and dimension to other dishes. Accompaniments like the Apple Tomato Chutney, Fresh Pineapple Salsa, and Sesame Coriander Chutney add immediate excitement to dishes of grilled chicken and other meats. The Winter Fruit Relish and sauces like the garlicky White Bean Puree work wonders on sandwiches. For instant taste, try the Vietnamese Dipping Sauce with grilled gourmettes (mini drumsticks from the wings) or the creamy Mustard Dill Sauce with crudités.

Use these flavor-enhancers also as the jumping-off point for dish creation. Start with a favorite chutney like the apple tomato, add it to a basic vinaigrette, and you've got a marvelous salad dressing for fresh greens or fruit and lettuce mixtures.

Basics are here, too. Best-Ever Tomato Sauce, Victoria Dressing, and Orange Onion Dressing are versatile dish-makers and will become standards on your table. The Grilled Red Pepper Sauce, for example, is marvelous with poached or breaded and sautéed chicken cutlets like grandma Fanny's (page 283) or with Baked Turkey Kibbe (page 56). There's very little you can't serve this sauce with—use it also with grilled eggplant or zucchini.

You can also give salsas and other condiments as gifts. Food-loving friends are enormously pleased to find one of these seasonings, which have a good shelf life, in a prettily wrapped package. Every-Way Cherry Sauce, an accompaniment for both sweet and savory dishes, is the perfect thanks-for-having-me gift.

These condiments are also a way of "canning." You can "put up" tomatoes and other fresh fruit and vegetables when they're freshest, turning them into accompaniments like Fresh Tomato Coulis, Corn and Pepper Relish, and Preserved Lemons, the pungent Moroccan pickle. Putting these condiments in jars or other containers and storing them in the fridge, or freezing them, isn't hard work; making them and having them on hand not only provides a sense of accomplishment but also simplifies daily meal and menu making. A jar or container of the Cumin Tomato Sauce, for example, cooked with fresh string beans, creates a very special dish in minutes. With preserves like these in your pantry, you save time *and* eat imaginatively.

Corn and Pepper Relish

A perfect summer relish, great with cold roast chicken. Use the freshest, sweetest corn you can get your hands on—frozen kernels just won't do. The relish will last four to five days, refrigerated.

6 ears fresh, sweet corn

2 red bell peppers, cored, seeded, and finely diced

1 small red onion, finely diced

Kosher salt and freshly ground black pepper

Shake of hot sauce

4 tablespoons extra-virgin olive oil

1 tablespoon apple cider vinegar

3 tablespoons coarsely chopped fresh dill

Makes 5 cups

1. Husk the corn and cut the kernels from the cobs. Bring a large pot of water to a boil. Place the corn in a strainer and dip it into the water. Blanch the corn for 30 seconds, remove, and drain well.

2. Place the corn in a large bowl. Add the red peppers and onion and season to taste with the salt and pepper. Add the hot sauce, olive oil, and vinegar and stir well. Let marinate for at least 1 hour. Just before serving, mix in the dill.

Fresh Tomato Coulis

Serve this lively coulis with chicken cutlet sandwiches, or as an accompaniment to Oven-Fried Chicken (page 126) or Chicken Fingers (page 41). Note that it depends on ripe tomatoes for its goodness. For color and taste, mix red and yellow tomatoes. The coulis keeps for three days refrigerated.

2 tablespoons extra-virgin olive oil

1 tablespoon chopped garlic

3 cups diced ripe tomatoes

About 10 fresh basil leaves, snipped into pieces

Kosher salt and freshly ground black pepper

Makes 2 cups

1. In a large, heavy skillet, heat the olive oil over medium heat. Add the garlic and sauté until dark golden (but not browned), 3 to 5 minutes.

2. Add the tomatoes and basil, turn up the heat, and cook, stirring constantly, until the tomatoes have softened, about 5 minutes. Season to taste with the salt and pepper. Serve warm.

Minted Apricot Sauce

Made with mint tea, fresh mint, and dried apricots, this lovely sauce goes perfectly with Sesame Minted Meatballs (page 48). The sauce keeps refrigerated a week or longer, but the fresh mint in it loses its punch before that; add more before serving the sauce, if it has been stored. For a touch of fire, shake in drops of hot sauce.

1½ cups boiling water

2 bags mint-flavored tea

¼ pound dried apricots

½ teaspoon sugar

Juice of 1 lemon

Freshly ground black pepper

1 teaspoon chopped fresh mint or Italian parsley

Makes 1 cup

1. In the boiling water, steep the tea bags until the brew is dark and full-flavored, about 15 minutes. Remove the tea bags and add the apricots. Allow them to plump, about 30 minutes. Remove the apricots and reserve the tea.

2. Put the apricots in a food processor. Add 1 cup of the tea, the sugar, and lemon juice. Season to taste with the pepper. Process to make a thick puree. If the puree seems overly thick, add the reserved tea. Add the mint and pulse-chop to combine. Serve.

Guacamole

There are guacamoles and guacamoles; this version is the best of all, I think. Besides using Hass avocados—which ripen and peel evenly and have a rich, delicious flavor—a superior guacamole like this one requires last-minute assembly. You can, if you wish, ready all the vegetables except the avocado beforehand, store them separately, and combine them with the avocado just before serving.

Avocados ripen off the tree. Buy them ahead and allow them to become yielding (but not overly soft) to the touch. The avocado pit inserted in the finished guacamole (or stored with it) helps retard browning, I've found. Try it.

1 ripe Hass avocado

1 garlic clove, pressed

2 teaspoons chopped red or sweet white onion

⅓ cup chopped scallions, white and green parts

2 teaspoons seeded and minced jalapeño pepper

3 tablespoons chopped fresh coriander (cilantro)

2 tablespoons chopped ripe tomato

Juice of ½ lime

Pinch of ground cumin

Kosher salt and freshly ground black pepper

Makes 1¹/₂ cups

1. Just before serving, peel the avocado and scoop its flesh into a medium bowl. Add the garlic, onion, scallions, jalapeño pepper, coriander, tomato, lime juice, and cumin.

2. Blend all the ingredients, mashing the avocado with a fork. Season to taste with the salt and pepper and serve.

Black Bean Puree

Musky with coriander, and with a smoky sherry presence, this simple puree is an excellent accompaniment to dishes of Mexican or Latin American provenance (the Mexican Chicken Fajitas, page 165, for example). It can also be used as a dip. It will keep covered in the fridge for a week.

1 cup dried black beans, preferably soaked (see Note), rinsed, and drained

2 bay leaves

3 garlic cloves

1 bunch coriander (cilantro) including stems, washed and tied with twine

1 cup plus 1 tablespoon dry sherry

½ teaspoon ground cumin

2 shakes of hot sauce

Salt and freshly ground black pepper

Makes 4 cups

1. In a large saucepan or Dutch oven, combine the beans, bay leaves, garlic, coriander, the 1 cup of sherry, and 2 quarts of water. Bring to a boil, lower the heat, and simmer, uncovered, for $1^1/2$ hours.

2. Remove the herbs and discard. Drain the beans, reserving the soaking liquid, and add the beans and garlic to a food processor. Puree, adding 1 to 2 cups of the cooking liquid to create a smooth texture resembling whipped potatoes. Add the cumin, the remaining 1 tablespoon of sherry, and the hot sauce. Season to taste with the salt and pepper. Serve warm, at room temperature, or store.

Note: For best results, soak the beans in water to cover 4 to 6 hours, changing the water once, before proceeding with the recipe.

White Bean Puree

A creamy, garlicky condiment that works wonderfully as a vegetable dip, sandwich filling, or cracker spread. It will last refrigerated for about a week.

¼ cup extra-virgin olive oil

4 to 6 garlic cloves, minced

One 19-ounce can white cannellini beans, drained and rinsed

¼ cup Italian parsley leaves

Juice of ½ lemon

Salt and freshly ground black pepper

Makes 2 cups

1. In a small, heavy skillet, heat the olive oil over medium heat. Add the garlic and sauté just until it begins to turn golden, 1 to 2 minutes. Remove the skillet from the heat immediately.

2. In a blender or food processor, combine the garlic-flavored oil, the beans, parsley, and lemon juice. Process until smooth. Season to taste with the salt and pepper and serve or store.

Fresh Pineapple Salsa

A zippy condiment that's perfect with spicy grilled chicken or other meats, or try it with croquettes. Like other salsas, it is best made a little ahead, but can be prepared as few as two or three hours in advance if you're pressed for time. Use it within a few days.

½ medium cored and peeled fresh pineapple, cut into 2-inch chunks

1 tablespoon fresh lime juice

1 tablespoon sugar

1 teaspoon grated peeled fresh ginger

1 tablespoon fresh coriander leaves (cilantro), finely chopped

Makes 2½ cups

1. Add the pineapple in a food processor and pulse 2 or 3 times to chop it roughly.

2. Transfer the pineapple to a nonreactive bowl. To the bowl add the lime juice, sugar, and ginger. Toss and chill. Just before serving, stir in the coriander.

Red Table Salsa

This is a superior version of the table sauce you dip tortilla chips into or serve with fajitas or just about any other Mexican dish. Try putting this garden-fresh condiment on the table to use like mustard or ketchup—it's light and provides a delicious kick. The salsa keeps refrigerated, five or six days.

1 to 2 jalapeño or chipotle peppers, seeded

1 red onion, peeled

3 garlic cloves

3 very large ripe tomatoes, quartered

½ cup fresh coriander leaves (cilantro), plus additional for serving

½ red or yellow bell pepper, cored, seeded, and cut into 1-inch pieces

¼ to ½ cup fresh lime juice

Kosher salt and freshly ground black pepper

Makes 2 cups

1. In a food processor, combine the jalapeño, onion, and garlic. Chop coarsely, about 3 pulses.

2. Add the tomatoes, coriander, bell pepper, and lime juice and pulse to combine all the ingredients, 2 to 3 times. Do not over-process—the salsa should be chunky. Transfer to a bowl and season to taste with the salt and pepper. Before serving, garnish with additional coriander.

Peach Salsa

This is a delicate, fruit-sweet salsa with heat and a bit of citrus tang. To peel the peaches, place them in a colander and pour boiling water over them, or dunk them in a pot of boiling water for fifteen seconds, let cool, and skin.

This is terrific with simply grilled chicken or as a dunk for tortilla chips. It keeps for five days under refrigeration. Don't try to freeze it; it doesn't work.

½ large red onion

1 jalapeño pepper, seeded

½ red bell pepper, cored, seeded, and cut roughly into pieces

Juice of 1 lemon

2 teaspoons sugar

6 whole fresh peaches, peeled, pitted, and halved, or 12 canned peach halves, drained

Pinch of salt and freshly ground black pepper

¼ cup tightly packed fresh coriander leaves (cilantro)

Makes 4 cups

1. In a food processor, combine the onion, jalapeño pepper, and red pepper. Chop coarsely by pulsing, 4 to 5 times; do not over-process.

2. Add lemon juice, sugar, peach halves, salt, pepper, and coriander. Pulse 5 to 6 times to chop the peaches and combine the ingredients. Taste and adjust the seasonings. Serve chilled or at room temperature.

Orange Cranberry Relish

For best flavor, make this tart-sweet relish, a perfect accompaniment to roast turkey and other fowl, two or three days in advance. Store it tightly covered in the refrigerator.

One 12-ounce bag fresh cranberries, picked over and rinsed

1 seedless orange, peeled (reserve ¼ of peel) and quartered

½ to 1 cup sugar

3 tablespoons fresh lemon juice

Makes 3½ cups

1. In a food processor, combine half each of the cranberries, orange flesh, and peel. Chop by pulsing, 2 to 3 times. Remove to a large bowl.

2. Repeat chopping using the remaining cranberries, orange flesh, and peel. Add to the bowl and combine.

3. Add ¹/₂ cup of the sugar and the lemon juice. Combine well. Taste for sweetness; cranberries vary in tartness. Adjust lemon juice and/or sugar, if necessary.

Winter Fruit Relish

A quickly made dried-fruit relish that's especially nice with roasts and other winter dishes. It's perfect for Thanksgiving, but I serve it for Passover, too. The relish is meant to have a loose consistency. It lasts two weeks, refrigerated.

1 tablespoon olive oil

2 medium onions, sliced

8 ounces mixed dried fruit, coarsely chopped

1 to 1¼ cup Chicken Stock (page 61), or good instant or low-sodium canned broth

2 tablespoons light brown sugar

2 tablespoons cider vinegar

1 tablespoon grated peeled fresh ginger

Makes 2 cups

1. In a medium nonstick skillet, heat the olive oil over medium heat. Add the onions and sauté until soft, about 10 minutes.

2. Stir in the fruit, 1 cup of the stock, the brown sugar, vinegar, and ginger. Simmer until the fruit is soft, about 20 minutes, adding stock if necessary. The relish should be the consistency of a loose chutney. Cool and serve or store.

Spicy Papaya Mustard Sauce

Intriguingly spicy and touched with sweet-tart papaya, this is great with satés, grilled chicken cutlets, or turkey steaks (unboned half-breasts).

It can be made in advance and stored, refrigerated, for four days.

2 tablespoons vegetable oil

1½ teaspoons curry powder

¼ teaspoon ground allspice

¼ teaspoon freshly ground black pepper

One ¼-inch piece of fresh ginger, peeled and minced

1 teaspoon mustard powder

1 cup diced plum tomatoes (3 large tomatoes) or 1 cup drained canned diced

¼ cup fresh orange juice

6 tablespoons red wine vinegar

1 tablespoon honey

1 teaspoon soy sauce

¼ cup Dijon mustard

¼ teaspoon kosher salt

1 jalapeño pepper, seeded and minced

1 large ripe papaya, seeded, peeled, and diced (about 1½ cups)

Makes 2 cups

1. In a medium nonreactive saucepan over medium heat, heat the oil. After 1 minute, reduce the heat to low and add the curry powder, allspice, pepper, ginger, mustard, and tomatoes. Cook, stirring, until the spices become fragrant, about 1 minute.

2. Add the orange juice, vinegar, honey, soy sauce, mustard, salt, jalapeño pepper, and papaya and simmer until the tomatoes are soft if fresh, or have cooked down, about 30 minutes. Remove from the heat, cool until just warm, and puree in a food processor or blender.

Horseradish Mustard Sauce

A simple sauce with a nice horseradish bite. Try it with grilled chicken or fish like salmon or halibut, or corn and chicken Croquettes (page 258). For a dairy sauce, or lightened variation, substitute nonfat yogurt for the mayonnaise. Keeps for one week, refrigerated.

2 tablespoons Dijon mustard

½ cup prepared white (beetless) horseradish

½ cup light or reduced-fat mayonnaise

2 tablespoons snipped chives, dill, or tarragon

Juice of 1 lemon

Salt and freshly ground black pepper

Makes about 1¹/₂ cups

1. In a food processor, combine the mustard, horseradish, mayonnaise, chives, and lemon and process until smooth. Alternatively, whisk the ingredients in a bowl.

2. Season to taste with the salt and pepper. Serve room temperature or chilled.

Mustard Dill Sauce

This simple sauce makes a great dip for crudités of all kinds. You can also use it with poached chicken or as a dressing for chicken salad. It will keep, refrigerated, for about two weeks.

2 heaping tablespoons grainy mustard

1 tablespoon Dijon mustard

½ cup light mayonnaise

¼ cup chopped fresh dill

1 teaspoon lemon fresh juice

Makes about ³/₄ cup

In a small bowl, combine the mustards, mayonnaise, dill, and lemon juice. Stir to blend well. Serve chilled.

Peanut Hoisin Sauce

Plain hoisin really blossoms when combined with the additional ingredients below. Serve this zippy sauce with Rice Paper Rolls (page 281) or use it to marinate chicken or fish.

1 cup hoisin sauce

½ cup minced onion

⅓ cup brown rice vinegar

½ teaspoon hot sauce, or 2 teaspoons chili bean paste

⅛ teaspoon curry powder

1 tablespoon finely chopped roasted peanuts

Makes about 2 cups

1. In a small saucepan, combine the hoisin sauce, onion, vinegar, and ⅔ cup water. Bring to a boil, lower the heat, and simmer until the onion is very soft, about 8 minutes. If the sauce becomes thicker than buttermilk, add more water. Stir in the hot sauce and curry powder. Allow to cool.

2. Place the sauce in a small bowl. Sprinkle with the peanuts and serve.

Tahini Sauce

A creamy, tangy accompaniment made with Middle Eastern tahini (ground sesame seeds). It's important not to over-process the ingredients or the sauce will be too thick; you want a consistency like that of heavy cream. And be sure to mix the tahini well before using it— it tends to separate.

This is great with Sesame Minted Meatballs (page 48). It will last one to two weeks refrigerated.

1 scallion, white and green parts, cut into quarters

1 very small garlic clove

½ cup warm water

⅓ cup plus 2 tablespoons toasted sesame tahini, mixed before using if separated

3 tablespoons fresh lemon juice

1 teaspoon soy sauce

Freshly ground black pepper

⅛ teaspoon sweet paprika

Makes scant 1 cup

1. In a food processor, combine the scallion and garlic and pulse to chop. Add the water and tahini and pulse 2 or 3 times to blend.

2. Add the lemon juice and soy sauce. Season to taste with the pepper and paprika and pulse to combine. Add more water by tablespoons if the sauce seems too thick and blend. Serve or cover and refrigerate.

Grilled Red Pepper Sauce

This simple, naturally sweet sauce is a great favorite of mine. It's wonderful with grilled meats of all kinds, or with grilled eggplant. It goes together in seconds and keeps one to two weeks refrigerated.

3 large red bell peppers

2 to 3 garlic cloves

¼ cup extra-virgin olive oil

2 teaspoons fresh lemon juice

½ teaspoon ground cumin

Kosher salt and freshly ground black pepper

Makes 1½ cups

1. Prepare an outdoor grill. Grill the peppers over medium-hot heat about 2 to 3 inches from the heat source, turning as necessary, until blackened, about 10 minutes. Alternatively, char the peppers over the open flame of a gas stove burner, turning, 5 to 7 minutes.

2. Place the peppers in a paper bag, close, and allow them to steam to loosen their skins, 10 to 15 minutes. When cool enough to handle, remove the peppers and peel them with your fingers or a small knife. Halve the peppers, core, and seed them.

3. In a food processor, combine the peppers, garlic, olive oil, lemon juice, and cumin and pulse to make a thick puree. Season to taste with the salt and pepper, then use or refrigerate.

Best-Ever Tomato Sauce

A good, simple sauce that's my workhorse pasta accompaniment. It's delicious also with Fanny's Chicken Cutlets (page 108)—actually, I use it whenever a recipe calls for tomato sauce. I keep quart containers of this in the freezer, where it lasts for months. I even give it to cooking friends, who sing its praises.

If you're concerned about your fat intake, you can use half the oil called for below with excellent results; just be sure to prepare the sauce in a nonstick skillet.

7 tablespoons olive oil

20 garlic cloves, minced

2 medium onions, finely chopped

One 6-ounce can tomato paste

1 teaspoon dried oregano

2 bay leaves

6 to 10 fresh basil leaves, depending on size, or ½ teaspoon dried

One 28-ounce can whole tomatoes with puree

Two 28-ounce cans crushed tomatoes

Makes 9 to 10 cups

1. In a heavy-bottomed Dutch oven or nonstick deep skillet, heat the olive oil over medium heat. Add the garlic and sauté until just golden, about 3 minutes.

2. Add the onions and sauté until translucent, about 5 minutes. Lower the heat and stir in the tomato paste carefully (it will splatter). Add the oregano, bay leaves, half the basil leaves or the dried basil (or all the basil leaves if making the sauce in advance), the whole tomatoes with the puree, and the crushed tomatoes. Break up the tomatoes with a wooden spoon.

3. Simmer 1¼ hours. When the oil begins to surface along the edges of sauce, it's done. Add water by the half-cupfuls if a thinner consistency is desired. Tear the remaining basil leaves and stir in just before serving.

VARIATION

SUMMER SAUCE
For a delightful fresh sauce, prepare the recipe up to step 3, omitting the basil. In a food processor, combine 5 ripe plum tomatoes, 1 large garlic clove, and 1 cup packed fresh basil leaves. Simmer the sauce for 1¼ hours, as directed, adding the fresh puree during the last 5 minutes of cooking.

Cumin Tomato Sauce

This spicy tomato-based sauce takes the traditional red pasta accompaniment in a Middle Eastern direction. Other than as a pasta sauce, I love to serve this as a dip for appetizers like the Chicken-Stuffed Grape Leaves (page 40); it's good too with Chicken Fingers (page 41). Or try cooking string beans in the sauce (plan to do this before you prepare the sauce, and use half the amount of stock called for to make it).

The sauce will keep for a few days refrigerated.

2 tablespoons olive oil

¼ cup minced garlic

1 cup finely chopped onion

12 ripe plum tomatoes, peeled and pureed, or one 28-ounce can crushed plum tomatoes

1 teaspoon dried oregano

¾ teaspoon ground cumin

12 fresh basil leaves

8 sprigs Italian parsley

2 cups Chicken Stock (page 61), or good instant or low-sodium canned broth

¼ teaspoon salt

Pinch of freshly ground black pepper

Makes about 4 cups

1. In a large, heavy-bottomed pot, heat the olive oil over medium heat. Add the garlic and sauté until just turning golden, 3 to 4 minutes. Add the onions and cook until soft, about 5 minutes.

2. Add the tomatoes, oregano, cumin, and basil. Simmer until the sauce thickens, about 20 minutes. Remove from the heat and transfer the mixture to a food processor. Add the parsley and stock and puree. Add the salt and pepper and serve.

Vietnamese Dipping Sauce

An intriguing sweet-sour sauce flavored with peanuts. Excellent as a dip for grilled gourmettes (chicken-wing "drumsticks") and used with Vietnamese Spring Rolls with Two Dipping Sauces (page 55). The sauce will keep two to three weeks refrigerated.

½ cup brown rice vinegar

¼ cup sugar

1 cup unsalted dry-roasted peanuts

2 tablespoons minced peeled fresh ginger

3 small garlic cloves

2 tablespoons packed coriander leaves (cilantro)

Pinch of red pepper flakes

¼ to ½ teaspoon salt

3 tablespoons soy sauce

1 tablespoon dark sesame oil

Makes 2 cups

1. In a small saucepan, combine the vinegar, sugar, and $1/2$ cup water. Bring to a boil, reduce the heat, and simmer until the sugar is completely dissolved, about 5 minutes.

2. Add the nuts to a food processor and pulse to chop finely. Add the ginger and garlic and pulse to chop. Add the vinegar-sugar mixture and process until pureed. Add the coriander and pulse to chop and combine. Add the red pepper flakes, salt, soy sauce, and sesame oil and process to combine. Serve or store.

Green Sauce

This simple dressing is unusual in the best sense of the word—an unexpected flavor combination that works wonderfully well. It's also beautiful. Use it as an accompaniment to Poached Chicken Breasts (page 95). The sauce will last two to three days, refrigerated.

1 cup tightly packed well-washed spinach leaves

1 cup loosely packed Italian parsley

1 cup packed fresh basil leaves

2 to 3 garlic cloves

1 teaspoon ground cumin

½ cup red wine vinegar

1 cup olive oil

Salt and freshly ground black pepper

Makes 2 cups

1. In a food processor, combine the spinach, parsley, basil, garlic, cumin, and vinegar. Process until well combined.

2. With the motor running, add the olive oil through the feed tube in a slow, steady stream to emulsify the dressing. Season to taste with the salt and pepper.

Victoria Dressing

Victoria is my sister-in-law, and this is her good, basic salad dressing. It's tart with lemon that's mellowed slightly with a touch of sugar. I have this on hand almost all the time. It keeps for ten days under refrigeration, but note that its acidity increases with time.

⅔ cup olive oil

¼ cup balsamic vinegar

Juice of 3 lemons

1 garlic clove, pressed

1 tablespoon Dijon mustard

Pinch of sugar (about ½ teaspoon)

Salt and freshly ground black pepper

Makes 1½ cups

1. In a small bowl, combine the olive oil, vinegar, and lemon juice. Whisk to mix.

2. Add the garlic, mustard, and sugar and whisk until well combined. Season to taste with the salt and pepper.

Balsamic Tomato Vinaigrette

There are few sauces or dressings I think of as basic—this is one. In fact, it's an everything sauce. Use it drizzled over fresh sliced tomatoes or greens; as a sauce for grilled chicken paillards or breasts (serve the chicken in a pool of the vinaigrette); as a sauce for pasta with chunks of cooked chicken and roast vegetables; and more. You'll discover other great uses for this fabulous dressing, which keeps refrigerated for five days. Note that it gets tangier with time.

2 large ripe tomatoes

1 small onion or 8 shallots, peeled

2 small garlic cloves

1 cup tomato juice

1 cup balsamic vinegar

20 to 24 fresh basil leaves

½ cup fruity extra-virgin olive oil

Salt and freshly ground black pepper

Makes about 2 cups

1. In a food processor, combine the tomatoes, onion, garlic, tomato juice, vinegar, and basil and process until a smooth consistency is obtained. With the machine running, dribble the olive oil through the feed tube slowly until blended in.

2. Season to taste with the salt and pepper. If not using immediately, cover and refrigerate. Bring to room temperature before using.

Orange Onion Dressing

A fruity dressing with a bit of bite. Use it to dress a salad made with fennel, watercress, orange segments, olives, and red onions. It's delicious, too, over steamed savoy cabbage.

The recipe makes an ample amount, but the dressing keeps for a month under refrigeration.

1 small red onion, chopped

1¼ cups olive oil

¼ cup cider vinegar

1 tablespoon sherry wine vinegar (see page 14) or balsamic vinegar

½ teaspoon mustard powder

Juice of ½ lemon

½ cup fresh orange juice with pulp

Pinch of sugar

½ teaspoon crushed fennel seeds

½ teaspoon paprika

Salt and freshly ground black pepper

Makes 2 cups

1. Place the onion in a food processor and pulse to chop. You should have about ¹/₂ cup.

2. Add the olive oil, vinegars, mustard, lemon and orange juices, sugar, fennel seeds, and paprika. Process until smooth. Season to taste with the salt and pepper and pulse to blend.

Honey-Banana Chutney

This is the ultimate chutney, a delicious, sweet, and tangy blend that's particularly versatile. It's good with sandwiches, all types of grilled meats, and, of course, curries. This recipe makes quite a bit, but it keeps for months under refrigeration; it also makes a thoughtful and much appreciated culinary gift.

1 cup chopped carrots

1½ pounds mixed fruit, such as apples, pears, and peaches, peeled, cored, or seeded, and cut into ¼-inch slices

2 large onions, finely chopped

2 garlic cloves, minced

1 tablespoon chopped peeled fresh ginger

½ cup fresh orange juice

1 teaspoon ground cloves

¼ teaspoon kosher salt

¼ to ½ teaspoon cayenne pepper

1 cup honey

1 cup cider vinegar

½ cup dried currants

2 pounds firm, not fully ripe bananas, peeled and cut into ¼-inch slices

Makes 6 cups

1. In a large, heavy saucepan, combine the carrots, mixed fruit, onions, garlic, ginger, orange juice, cloves, salt, cayenne, honey, vinegar, and currants. Place over medium-low heat and simmer, uncovered, stirring occasionally, until thickened, about 45 minutes.

2. Stir in the bananas and cook 15 minutes. Cool and serve, can, or pack in jars and refrigerate.

Fresh Coriander Chutney

I enjoyed this special chutney at an Indian wedding celebration. It took a while to secure the recipe, a specialty of the groom's aunt, but here it is. Try this with Chicken Fingers (page 41) or Iraqi Chicken Fritters (page 35). Or mix it with equal parts yogurt and serve it as a dairy condiment with fish.

Refrigerated, the chutney lasts for at least a month.

1 to 2 tablespoons chopped hot red or green chilies, such as Thai peppers, jalapeños, or serranos, seeded (see Note)

¼ cup fresh lemon juice

2 cups tightly packed chopped fresh coriander leaves (cilantro; about ¼ pound whole bunches)

¼ cup chopped onion

One 1½-inch piece peeled fresh ginger, chopped

1 teaspoon salt

1 teaspoon sugar

Freshly ground black pepper

Makes about 2 cups

1. In a food processor or blender, combine the chilies, lemon juice, coriander, onion, ginger, salt, sugar, and ¼ cup water. Process until puréed, 2 to 3 minutes.

2. Season the puree to taste with the pepper. Serve or store tightly covered, refrigerated.

Note: 1 seeded jalapeño pepper equals about 1 tablespoon chopped.

Apple Tomato Chutney

A really fabulous chutney that adds excitement to the simplest dishes. Serve it with kebabs and on turkey sandwiches; it's so good, in fact, you'll want to have jars of it on hand to spread on bread.

Be sure to use fresh spices for this—throw those old ones away!

10 ounces (about 2 cups) dried currants

2 cups unpeeled finely minced Granny Smith or McIntosh apples (about 2 apples)

1 cup minced onion

2 cups canned tomatoes, drained and chopped

2 celery stalks, finely minced

¼ cup grated peeled fresh ginger

½ cup mustard seeds

2 cups dark brown sugar

2 tablespoon molasses

2 cups apple cider vinegar

1 tablespoon kosher salt

1 tablespoon cayenne pepper, or to taste

1 tablespoon turmeric

1 tablespoon ground cardamom

2 tablespoons curry powder

Makes 6 cups

1. Place the currants, apples, onion, tomatoes, celery, ginger, mustard seeds, brown sugar, molasses, vinegar, salt, cayenne, turmeric, cardamom, and curry powder in a large, heavy pot and bring to a boil. Reduce the heat to medium and simmer, covered, stirring occasionally, until slightly thickened, about 30 minutes.

2. Uncover and cool completely. The chutney will thicken as it cools. Serve or transfer to glass jars. Store, tightly covered, in the refrigerator or can.

Fresh and Dried Cranberry Chutney

This mouthwatering chutney, which features a double-whammy of dried and fresh cranberries, should be a staple in every home. Make lots of it at the height of cranberry season and store it in glass jars. It's perfect for Thanksgiving (why not replace the usual cranberry sauce with this superior condiment?), but use it with other roasted poultry dishes too. It's good also with curries, of course.

The chutney keeps three months refrigerated.

1 teaspoon vegetable oil

1 large onion, chopped

5 garlic cloves, chopped

8 whole cloves

Four ½-inch slices peeled fresh ginger

3 celery stalks, chopped

4 cups fresh cranberries, coarsely chopped

2 cups dried cranberries

2 cups dark brown sugar

¼ cup fresh lemon or lime juice

2½ cups cranberry juice

½ cup balsamic vinegar

¼ cup port

1 tablespoon kosher salt

½ teaspoon ground allspice

2 cinnamon sticks

1 teaspoon red pepper flakes

1 tablespoon curry powder

½ cup minced fresh mint leaves

Makes 4 cups

1. In a large, heavy-bottomed saucepan, heat the oil over medium heat. Add the onion and garlic and sauté until translucent, about 5 minutes.

2. Push 2 cloves into each ginger slice. Add them to the pan with the celery, fresh and dried cranberries, brown sugar, juices, vinegar, port, salt, allspice, cinnamon, red pepper flakes, and curry powder. Reduce the heat to low and simmer, uncovered, for 35 minutes. Remove from the heat, stir in the mint, and cool (the chutney will thicken as it cools). Serve at room temperature or pour into clean, dry glass jars, cap, and refrigerate. Before using, remove the ginger.

Sesame Coriander Sauce

This wonderful sauce is an everyday condiment in India, somewhat like ketchup or hot sauce in this country. It's perfect with Butterflied Grilled Rock Cornish Chicken (page 176), lamb, or grilled fish.

½ cup sesame seeds

¼ cup tightly packed fresh coriander leaves (cilantro)

¼ cup tightly packed fresh mint leaves

2 scallions, white and green parts, trimmed

2 to 4 fresh hot green chilies, such as jalapeños, seeded and coarsely chopped

3 tablespoons tamarind paste, or 1 teaspoon tamarind concentrate dissolved in 3 tablespoons water

½ teaspoon salt

5 tablespoons brown rice vinegar

2 tablespoons dark sesame oil

Makes 1 cup

1. Put the sesame seeds in a small cast-iron frying pan. Place over medium heat and toast the seeds, stirring, until golden, 2 to 3 minutes. Transfer the seeds to a spice grinder or food processor fitted with a plastic blade (the metal one won't process the seeds) and grind as fine as possible.

2. If using a spice grinder, transfer the seeds to a food processor. Otherwise, exchange the plastic for a metal blade. Add the coriander, mint, scallions, chilies, tamarind paste, salt, and vinegar to the food processor. With the machine running, add the sesame oil and 5 tablespoons of hot water and process until as smooth as possible.

Preserved Lemons

Preserved, or pickled, lemons are a traditional North African ingredient and condiment. In Morocco they are used in fragrant lamb and vegetable tagines. They are a great addition to Moroccan salads or salads made with chicken, and part of Oven-Poached Coriander Chicken Breasts (page 114). The only "trick" to making these is to be certain that the lemons are well covered with liquid so they can pickle. Only the rind of the lemons is used; discard the pulp.

5 to 6 thick-skinned lemons, preferably organic, rinsed and wiped dry, plus the juice of 3 lemons

½ cup kosher salt

Makes 1 quart

1. Make 1 slit about 2 inches deep at the end of each lemon. The lemons will have been "opened," but not cut apart. Stuff the openings with as much salt as the lemons will hold.

2. Pack the lemons into a clean, dry, wide-mouth 1-quart canning jar. Press down hard on the lemons as you pack them, releasing all their juice. Add the lemon juice. The lemons must be covered with juice and the jar completely filled; add more juice if needed as any air space at the opening will cause the top lemons to mold.

3. Place the jar in a dark, cool nonrefrigerated place for 2 weeks, shaking the jar daily. Once pickled, they are ready to use and can be kept indefinitely in the refrigerator. When using them, discard the pulp and use only the peel.

Every-Way Cherry Sauce

Here's another recipe from Marge Rosenthal, my former catering partner and the vigilant recipe tester for this book. It's her version of a sauce originally served at the New York restaurant The Duck Joint, and it's just marvelous. Perfect with roast duck, it also excels as an accompaniment for roast or grilled chicken. And it's a lovely dessert sauce, great over angel food cake or with ice cream.

The recipe makes a lot, but I promise you you'll use it all. It keeps in the refrigerator for two to three weeks or you can freeze it for months in 8-ounce containers. If it lasts that long.

¾ cup sugar

One 16-ounce can pitted black cherries, strained (reserve the liquid)

½ cup (4 ounces) red currant jelly

½ lemon, thinly sliced

2 whole cloves, or ⅛ teaspoon ground

2 cinnamon sticks

¼ teaspoon salt

¼ teaspoon ground white pepper

½ cup sweet sherry

2 teaspoons arrowroot

¼ cup brandy (optional)

Makes 3½ cups

1. In a medium saucepan, combine the sugar and 1½ cups water. Bring to a boil over medium-high heat and add the cherry liquid, jelly, lemon, cloves, cinnamon, salt, and pepper. Reduce the heat to medium and simmer gently, stirring occasionally, until slightly reduced, about 30 minutes.

2. Meanwhile, in a small bowl, combine the sherry and arrowroot. When the sugar mixture is ready, whisk in the sherry mixture gradually and continue to stir until it is fully incorporated. Simmer the sauce until thickened, about 10 minutes.

3. Remove the sauce from the heat. Strain to remove the lemon and spices. Add the cherries and brandy, if using, and serve, or cool and store.

Skordalia

A traditional Greek condiment that's aromatic with garlic and ideal with grilled foods. You can also use it to make "instant" garlic bread, or try brushing it on pocketless pita before grilling it. It will keep two to three days under refrigeration.

9 garlic cloves, peeled

4 walnuts halves

1 slice crustless French bread

3 tablespoons fresh lemon juice or red wine vinegar

½ teaspoon salt

½ teaspoon freshly ground black pepper

½ cup olive oil, approximately

Makes about 1 cup

1. With a food processor running, add the garlic through the feed tube, clove by clove. Add the walnuts, bread, lemon juice, salt, and pepper.

2. Add 1 to 2 teaspoons of water to make a thin paste. With the machine running, add the oil gradually in a thin stream until the sauce emulsifies and has the consistency of mayonnaise.

9. The Next Day

What do you think of when you hear
the word "leftovers"? Back-of-the-refrigerator food
that's reheated and served? Yesterday's
odds and ends disguised in sauces?

The following recipes ask you to think of leftovers in an entirely new way. Not as second-appearance items, but as components of original dishes with clean, true flavors. Say no to casseroles and other catch-all creations, and yes to delicious entrees, salads, soups, and sandwiches that use stored poultry in exciting ways.

The key to preparing these dishes is to think ahead. Though most of the recipes here are the perfect solution to an excess of cooked chicken or turkey (the Artichoke Chicken Hash, for example), all are done most efficiently with a poultry "pantry." It's easy to create one. When roasting a chicken or poaching or grilling chicken breasts, make extra, with next-day cooking in mind. That way, you'll breeze through the creation of real dishes like Hacked Chicken with Sesame Noodles or Curried Chicken Cakes. When you organize your cooking life this way, with an eye to future meals, you maximize the possibility of best results while saving time and work.

The sandwiches in this chapter are particularly appealing. Basil Chicken Salad on Rosemary Focaccia and Pita Kebab Pockets are small meals made easily with next-day poultry. Expand your next-day sandwich pantry with chutneys and other condiments (see "Side Dishes," Chapter 7) and you're really in business. These condiments keep for months refrigerated, and are often the basis for great sandwich improvisations. Kids will turn their backs on fries or other snack foods when your special sandwiches are offered. Serve them with fresh fruit and children are well fed.

Some other next-day tips:
- Turkey is a trove for next-day cooking. Freeze and store cooked turkey legs, thighs, and any leftover turkey burger. Use the turkey parts to make dishes like White Bean and Escarole Soup, Chiles Rellenos, even Kreplach.
- When possible, for convenience, leave birds whole when storing them. Later, slice or chop their meat for recipes.
- Never throw away any dish leftovers; use them as a part of other creations. Polenta Construzione, a delicious chicken sandwich made with grilled polenta, uses the Grilled Polenta with Red Peppers recipe in its entirety as a sandwich component. Leftover grilled vegetables or mushrooms can be used to make exciting salads or sandwiches. Leftover grain dishes— using bulgur, pasta, or couscous, for example—can reappear in salads, brightened with fresh vegetables or fruit. Leftover salads may seem unpresentable, but they can enliven poultry in a pita pocket or between slices of good bread.

Leftovers are an invitation to creativity—you need just know how to approach them. Think next-day and you'll never produce a repeat culinary performance.

Mango-Dressed Chicken Salad

The elegant, sweet-tart dressing for this chicken salad is made with mango. I love the fruit —its brilliant orange flesh, its delectable, exotic flavor. Look for an unblemished mango with yellow skin, blushing with red. Carve the flesh from the large seed it clings to with a sharp knife.

The salad takes minutes to make but impresses everyone who tries it. It's great for entertaining at lunch, or for an easy supper with whole grain pumpernickel.

1 medium mango, pitted and skinned (½ to ⅔ cup pulp)

¼ cup olive oil

½ cup white wine vinegar

½ cup chopped fresh chives, plus additional for garnish

Salt and freshly ground black pepper

½ pound string beans, or *haricots verts*, stem ends trimmed

10 to 12 cups washed and dried mixed greens, such as spinach, mesclun, arugula, torn lettuce, watercress

4½ cups cooked chicken cut in cubes or julienne strips

Serves 6

1. In a food processor or blender, combine the mango pulp, olive oil, vinegar, and the ¹/₂ cup of chives. Puree until smooth and season to taste with the salt and pepper. Reserve.

2. Bring a pot of water to a boil. Drop in the beans and cook until tender-crisp, 2 to 3 minutes. Drain and run the beans under cold water to stop the cooking. Drain the beans well.

3. In a large bowl or deep serving platter, arrange the greens. Place the beans over and arrange the chicken down the middle. Snip the additional chives on top.

4. At the table, pour on the dressing, toss, and serve.

Chicken Salad with
Jicama, Asparagus, and Orange

I call this my tender salad. Even though it contains crunchy jicama, the overall impression it makes is of plush, luxurious eating. The combination of asparagus, tart orange segments, and chicken is delicate and delightful.

Jicama, for those not familiar with it, is a bulbous root vegetable with a sweetish taste that's a bit like that of an apple crossed with a potato. It's increasingly available in supermarkets. Peel jicama with a sharp knife and it's ready to go. (It can be held, peeled, in water for two to three days in the refrigerator.)

The salad is wonderful served with freshly made popovers (page 216).

1 jicama (about 12 ounces), peeled and julienned

5 navel oranges, peeled, all membrane removed, and separated into sections

16 asparagus, trimmed, peeled, and cut diagonally into ½-inch pieces

1 head Boston lettuce, washed and dried

1 head red leaf lettuce, washed and dried

1 pound cooked chicken or turkey white meat, cut diagonally into ½-inch strips

¼ pecans or roasted cashews

1 small bunch chives

1 cup Orange Onion Dressing (page 237)

Serves 4

1. Place the jicama in the bottom of a large bowl. Arrange the orange sections on top. (The juice from the oranges will prevent the jicama from browning.)

2. Bring a saucepan of water to a boil. Blanch the asparagus until bright green and tender-crisp, about 3 minutes. Drain and run under cold water to stop their cooking. Drain well.

3. Divide the lettuce among 4 plates. Place one-quarter of the chicken in the center of each. Arrange the asparagus evenly around the chicken. Place the orange segments in groups of 3 on each plate, alternating with little piles of the jicama. Sprinkle with the nuts, snip the chives over the top, and drizzle on the dressing. Serve the salad with additional dressing in a separate dish.

Couscous Salad with Cinnamon-Cumin Dressing

Pasta salads were everywhere in the '80s. Their quality varied widely, but when they were good, they were delicious. Like other cooks, I made my share, and soon discovered the pleasure of salads made with couscous—a pasta, after all. This example containing chicken, currants, and zucchini is the best I've devised. It's brilliantly colored and has a delightful medley of tastes and textures. Its Indian-influenced dressing, made with the spice blend garam masala (in a pinch, you can use curry powder), is spectacular.

For a special presentation, serve the salad in a scooped-out pumpkin or gourd. (If you garden, let 2 zucchini grow baseball-bat big, carve them out, and fill them with the salad.) Accompany the dish with fresh, warm pocketless pita bread and a refreshing dessert like mango sorbet with blueberries.

4½ cups Chicken Stock (page 61), or good-quality instant or low-sodium canned broth

1 cinnamon stick

½ teaspoon turmeric

¼ medium onion

One ½-inch slice fresh ginger

4 carrots, peeled and finely chopped

4½ cups quick-cooking couscous

½ cup dried currants

2 small zucchini, halved lengthwise and sliced across very thinly

4 cups cooked chicken cut into ½-inch cubes or pieces

2 cups fresh peas or frozen defrosted

1. In a deep, wide skillet, combine the chicken stock, cinnamon stick, turmeric, onion, and ginger. Bring to a boil, reduce the heat, and simmer very gently for 10 minutes. Using a slotted spoon, remove the onion, cinnamon, and ginger and discard. Stir in the carrots and remove the skillet from the heat. Stir in the couscous, mixing thoroughly. Cover and let stand to absorb the liquid, about 10 minutes. Uncover and fluff with a fork to separate the grains.

2. Stir in the currants and zucchini. Turn the mixture into a large serving bowl and toss in the chicken.

3. If using fresh peas, place them in a colander and pour boiling water over just to brighten them. Run them under cold water, drain, and add them, or the defrosted peas, to the salad.

1 cup olive oil

⅓ cup fresh lemon juice

1½ teaspoons turmeric

1 teaspoon ground cinnamon

½ teaspoon garam masala (see page 11)
or curry powder

¼ teaspoon ground cumin

¼ teaspoon ground ginger

2 tablespoons cider vinegar

Salt and freshly ground black pepper

Leaves of 2 heads Boston lettuce
or other tender lettuce

Leaves of 1 bunch Italian parsley, chopped

½ cup fresh snipped chives
or thinly sliced scallion

Serves 8

4. To make the dressing, in a jar with a tight-fitting lid, combine the oil, lemon juice, turmeric, cinnamon, garam masala, cumin, ginger, and vinegar. Shake well. Season to taste with the salt and pepper.

5. Arrange the lettuce leaves on a serving dish. Just before serving, toss the salad with the dressing, parsley, and chives. Arrange the salad on the leaves and serve.

Indochinese Chicken Salad with Grapefruit, Cashews, and Cucumber

One of the pleasures of Asian cooking is its exuberant use of ingredients. While we in the West keep to a relatively narrow palette of flavors—most of our dishes highlight a single taste— the East has no qualms about bringing the salty, sweet, bitter, and hot together. This light, Asian-influenced salad is a delicious example. Its tangy, slightly bitter grapefruit, crunchy nuts, and tart-sweet soy-laced dressing make it a rainbow of tastes and textures. It also features snow pea sprouts, which are available in Asian markets (or use watercress leaves instead).

Serve the salad for a sophisticated lunch or nice light supper with baguettes or a crusty sour dough ficelle.

4 medium cucumbers, peeled

2 pink or yellow grapefruit, peeled, all pith removed, and cut into sections

2 cups shredded cooked chicken

2 medium carrots, peeled and coarsely grated

2 cups bean sprouts

2 cups snow pea sprouts or watercress leaves

2 tablespoons fresh mint leaves

2 tablespoons fresh coriander leaves (cilantro)

1. Halve the cucumbers lengthwise and using a spoon, scoop out the seeds. Cut the halves into $1/4$-inch slices.

2. In a medium bowl, combine the cucumbers, grapefruit, chicken, carrots, bean sprouts, pea sprouts, mint, and coriander. Refrigerate up to 2 hours.

3. Meanwhile, make the dressing. In a small bowl, combine the water and sugar and stir well until the sugar is dissolved. Let cool. Add the garlic, chilies, vinegar, lime juice, and soy sauce and mix well.

DRESSING

3 tablespoons boiling water

2 tablespoons sugar

4 garlic cloves, chopped

1 to 2 small red or green chilies, such as Thai peppers or jalapeños or serranos, seeded and finely chopped

4 tablespoons brown rice vinegar

4 tablespoon fresh lime juice

2 teaspoons light soy sauce

4 large green cabbage leaves, run briefly under hot water to brighten, then dried

2 tablespoons unsalted roasted cashews

Serves 4

4. Line a serving dish with the cabbage leaves. Just before serving, drizzle the dressing over the salad and mix. Arrange the salad on the leaves, sprinkle with the cashews, and serve.

Grilled Chicken Niçoise Salad

VINAIGRETTE

⅔ cup extra-virgin olive oil

1 garlic clove, minced

Pinch of sugar

2 tablespoons grainy or regular
Dijon mustard

⅓ cup red wine vinegar

Salt and freshly ground black pepper

2 red bell peppers, cored, seeded,
and julienned

1 teaspoon olive oil or olive oil spray

12 small red new potatoes,
washed and quartered

½ pound fresh green beans,
stem ends trimmed

4 medium grilled or broiled chicken cutlets
(about 1½ pounds total)

12 cups (about 1 pound) mesclun or
tender baby spinach leaves,
washed and dried

20 cherry tomatoes, yellow if available,
halved

20 pitted Niçoise olives, or other cured
black Mediterranean olives

4 hard-cooked eggs, sliced,
or 6 hard-cooked egg whites, sliced (discard yolks)

1 teaspoon drained capers

2 tablespoons Italian parsley leaves,
chopped

Serves 4

Niçoise salad, that lovely Mediterranean dish, is usually made with tuna. This version features grilled chicken, a delicious alternative to the fish. All the other good things that make a Niçoise salad a classic—the potatoes, olives, beans, and a grainy mustard vinaigrette—remain, creating a colorful and multitextured dish.

Here's a chance to use those "rainy day" grilled or broiled chicken cutlets you've cleverly prepared and stored. Or, using a grill pan for speed and convenience, prepare the cutlets especially for the salad—it's worth it!

1. To prepare the vinaigrette, in a small bowl, combine the olive oil, garlic, sugar, mustard, and vinegar. Season to taste with the salt and pepper and whisk to blend. Allow to sit for 30 minutes.

2. Meanwhile, on a baking sheet, toss the peppers with the olive oil, or lightly spray them with the olive oil spray. Broil the peppers 2 to 3 inches from the heat, turning after 5 minutes, until lightly charred, about 10 minutes in all. Watch the peppers carefully as they cook to avoid burning.

3. Place the potatoes in a saucepan with lightly salted water and bring to a boil. Cook until fork-tender, about 12 minutes. Drain and toss with 2 tablespoons of the vinaigrette while still warm. Reserve.

4. Bring a saucepan of water to a boil. Blanch the beans until bright green and tender-crisp, about 2 to 3 minutes. Drain and add the beans to a bowl of ice water to stop cooking. Drain and reserve.

5. Slice the chicken breasts diagonally across the grain into $^1/_4$-inch strips.

6. To assemble the salad, place the greens on a deep platter or in a large bowl and toss with a little of the vinaigrette. Arrange the vegetables, tomatoes, olives, and eggs or egg whites around the lettuce. Arrange the chicken down the center of the salad, then sprinkle on the capers and parsley. Drizzle additional vinaigrette on top. Serve any remaining vinaigrette with the salad to be tossed with it just before serving.

Grilled Vegetable and Chicken Salad

This is one of my favorite summer meals—and so ultra-simple to put together, I hesitate to give you a recipe. Its simplicity, however, depends on a little forethought. The next time you grill vegetables and/or chicken breasts, make extra with this salad in mind. Or use leftover cooked breasts from any non-Asian recipe and previously blanched vegetables. Brush the vegetables with a mixture of olive oil and pressed garlic, broil and cool them, and you're ready to go. You can, of course, prepare everything from scratch, but having all the ingredients prepped makes this the easiest of great summer dishes.

6 cups grilled vegetables, such as zucchini, red, yellow, and green bell peppers, and baby eggplant; shiitake or domestic mushrooms may be used

1½ pounds, approximately, grilled chicken breasts, any non-Asian recipe, or barbecued chicken, skin and bones removed, cut into 1-inch strips

10 cups washed mixed greens, such as mizuna, mesclun, arugula, baby spinach, or other tender lettuces

2 cups Balsamic Tomato Vinaigrette (page 236) or 1½ cups Victoria Dressing (page 235)

2 cups caramelized balsamic onions (see page 140)

Serves 6

In a large bowl, combine the vegetables, chicken, and greens. Drizzle with the dressing, add the onions, toss, and serve. Alternatively, line a serving platter with lettuce, arrange the vegetables and chicken separately, dress, and serve.

Bazha Chicken Salad

Bazha is a Georgian Russian sauce made with ground walnuts and occasionally marigold petals for color. It's served with roast chicken, among other meats. This cold entree chicken salad features a bazha-like dressing (made with sunny turmeric instead of marigold!), and has all the savor of Georgian cooking. It also highlights cool cucumber and the crunch of radish and pickle. Serve it for a leisurely summer lunch or supper with pumpernickel or a warm herby focaccia. For dessert, something a little rich.

3 medium cucumbers, peeled, halved, seeded, and very thinly sliced

1 pound baby carrots, peeled

¼ cup plus 1 tablespoon olive oil

1 medium onion, finely chopped

6 tablespoons white wine vinegar

½ teaspoon minced garlic

¼ cup chopped fresh coriander (cilantro)

¾ teaspoon ground coriander

⅛ teaspoon hot Hungarian paprika

1 cup Chicken Stock (page 61), or good instant or low-sodium canned broth

¼ teaspoon fenugreek (optional)

½ to 1 teaspoon turmeric

1 large head romaine lettuce, sliced crosswise into ¼-inch ribbons, washed and dried

1 cup thinly sliced red radishes

6 cups roasted chicken cut into ½-inch dice

1 cup walnut halves

2 half-sour pickles, diced

Salt and freshly ground black pepper

Serves 4

1. Place the cucumbers in a colander and salt them lightly. Cover them with plastic wrap or a plate and weight them using tin cans. Allow the cucumbers to drain their liquid, about 30 minutes. Squeeze out any additional liquid and reserve.

2. Meanwhile, bring a large pot of water to a boil. Blanch the carrots until tender-crisp, about 4 minutes, and cool them quickly in ice water.

3. In a small sauté pan, heat the 1 tablespoon of oil over medium heat. Add the onion and sauté until soft, about 5 minutes. Reserve.

4. In a large bowl, combine the sautéed onion, the remaining ¼ cup oil, the vinegar, garlic, fresh and ground coriander, paprika, chicken stock, and fenugreek, if using. Add just enough turmeric to give the mixture a lovely yellowish cast.

5. Line a platter with the romaine and border it with the cucumbers, carrots, and radishes. In a bowl, toss the chicken, walnuts, and pickles with the dressing and season to taste with the salt and pepper. Place the mixture in the center of the platter and serve.

Croquettes

Croquettes have something of a poor reputation, and it's a shame. Properly made, with fresh ingredients and a light hand, they make a delicious entree or light meal. These croquettes have a nice mustardy flavor and are just a bit spicy. Fry them lightly in a little oil or bake them, as you please. Serve them with Horesradish Mustard Sauce (page 228), warm potato salad, and tossed greens; your family will want seconds, guaranteed.

4 tablespoons canola or other vegetable oil, approximately

1 red or green bell pepper, cored, seeded, and diced

2 tablespoons minced onion

1 garlic clove, minced

2 tablespoons minced celery

¼ cup flour

⅓ cup Chicken Stock (page 61), or good instant or low-sodium canned broth

4 teaspoons mustard powder

2 tablespoons Dijon mustard

½ teaspoon cayenne pepper or shake of hot sauce

4 eggs, plus 2 eggs mixed with 1 cup water, for coating

1 pound cooked chicken or turkey, shredded

1¼ cups bread crumbs, plus 2 cups for breading

One 12-ounce box frozen corn kernels, defrosted

½ cup chopped fresh dill

Salt and freshly ground pepper

Makes about 8 croquettes

1. In a small skillet, heat 2 tablespoons of the oil over medium heat. Add the pepper, onion, garlic, and celery. Sauté until the vegetables are soft, 2 to 3 minutes. Add the flour and stir well. Continue to sauté 2 to 3 minutes, stirring, to cook the flour; do not allow it to brown.

2. Add the stock slowly, stirring, and cook stirring constantly until the mixture is thick, 2 to 3 minutes. Remove the skillet from the heat and allow to cool, about 10 minutes. Add the mustards, cayenne, and the 4 eggs. Mix well.

3. Add the chicken, the 1¼ cups bread crumbs, corn, and dill. Season to taste with the salt and pepper.

4. Transfer the mixture to a bowl, cover, and chill 3 to 4 hours (or overnight) to firm. Spread the remaining 2 cups bread crumbs on a large plate and have the egg-water mixture ready. Line a tray with waxed paper.

5. Using ½ cup for each, form the mixture into ovals or patties. Dip into the egg-water mixture, then roll in the bread crumbs. Place the croquettes on the tray as you make them (they can be chilled at this point up to 3 hours for future cooking).

6. In a large nonstick skillet, heat 1 tablespoon of the oil over medium-low heat. Add the croquettes, working in batches if necessary, and cook until golden, about 5 minutes per side. Add the remaining 1 tablespoon oil, as needed. Alternatively, brown the croquettes quickly on both sides in the skillet, transfer to a baking sheet, and bake in a 400°F. oven until cooked through, about 10 minutes. Serve.

Artichoke-Chicken Hash

When I first started to cook for Empire, the issue of what to do with yesterday's chicken soon arose. This was my first response: a fabulous hash made light and tempting with the crunch of artichokes. You can use leftover potatoes for this or make them fresh. Cooked until falling apart, the potatoes bind the other ingredients deliciously. The fresh mint, added at the end, provides a final note of bright, cool flavor.

3 tablespoons olive oil

1 tablespoon minced garlic

6 baby artichokes, trimmed, halved, and choke removed, or 2 cups frozen artichoke hearts, defrosted, drained, and cut into halves

1 tablespoon chopped fresh rosemary

1 cup Chicken Stock (page 61), or good instant or low-sodium canned broth

2 medium baking potatoes (about 1 pound)

Kosher salt

1 cup diced onion

2 teaspoons chopped fresh thyme

2 cups cubed cooked chicken or turkey

1 ripe tomato, peeled and diced

1 cup fresh peas, or frozen defrosted

1 tablespoon chopped Italian parsley

¼ cup shredded fresh mint leaves

¼ teaspoon kosher salt

Freshly ground black pepper

Serves 2 to 4

1. In a large nonstick skillet, heat 1 tablespoon of the olive oil over medium heat. Add the garlic and sauté until golden, about 3 minutes.

2. Add the artichoke halves and rosemary and stir to coat. If using fresh artichokes, add 1 cup of the stock, partially cover the pan, and cook until liquid is almost all gone and the artichokes are tender, about 20 minutes. If using frozen artichokes, add ½ cup of the stock and cook, covered, for 10 minutes. Remove the contents of the pan to a bowl and set aside. Reserve the skillet.

3. Peel the potatoes and quarter lengthwise. Cut across the quarters to make ¼-inch slices. Place the potatoes in a medium saucepan and add water to cover. Add salt and bring to a boil. Cook the potatoes until just tender, 10 minutes. Drain the potatoes and set aside.

4. Wipe out the skillet. Add the remaining 2 tablespoons olive oil and heat over medium-high heat. Add the onion and sauté until brown, about 6 minutes. Add the potatoes and brown, stirring occasionally, about 10 minutes. Add the thyme and chicken and stir to combine. Reduce the heat, add the artichokes, the tomato, peas, and parsley and heat thoroughly. Stir in the mint and salt and season to taste with the pepper. Serve.

Tomato Rice Chowder

Why does chowder need fish to be called a chowder? For me, the determining factor is chunkiness—a toothsome plentitude of vegetables or meat. This soup, filled to overflowing with tomatoes, celery, recycled chicken, and rice, is my chowder ideal. Call it what you like; you'll love its versatility and meal-in-one goodness.

¼ cup olive oil

2 medium onions, finely chopped

3 leeks, white parts only, washed well and thinly sliced

4 large celery stalks, with tops, minced

6 garlic cloves, pressed

3 cups peeled, seeded, and finely chopped fresh tomatoes, or one 28-ounce canned crushed

1 packed cup Italian parsley, chopped

¾ cup fresh basil leaves, cut into thin strips

Salt and freshly ground black pepper

8 cups Chicken Stock (page 61), approximately, or good instant or low-sodium canned broth

¼ cup arborio rice

⅓ cup dry sherry

2 cups finely diced cooked chicken

Makes about 4 quarts, 8 servings

1. In a heavy pot or Dutch oven, heat the oil over medium heat. Add the onions and leeks and sauté until translucent, about 5 minutes.

2. Add the celery and garlic and sauté, stirring, 2 to 3 minutes. Add the tomatoes, parsley, and half the basil. Season to taste with the salt and pepper.

3. Add the stock and bring to a boil. Reduce the heat and simmer until the flavors are well blended, about 25 minutes. Add the rice and simmer until it is cooked, about 20 minutes. Add the sherry and chicken and correct the seasonings. Thin with more stock if the chowder is too thick. Garnish with the remaining basil and serve.

Turkey, White Bean, and Escarole Soup

This soup is a wonderful variation of pasta e fagioli, *Italy's hearty white bean and pasta soup. The delicately bitter flavor of the escarole combines beautifully with the richness of the beans and tasty ground turkey (from leftover roasts, turkey burgers, even turkey meatloaf). Besides being delicious, this pasta* fagoul, *as it's commonly called, is a meal in a bowl. For the enriching pasta component, I suggest small-shaped ditalini or lumachelle, both perfect for spoon eating. Many people cook the pasta in the soup; I find that following that approach, the pasta can go to mush and the soup become starchy. Better to add perfectly cooked pasta at the last minute.*

The soup takes only a half hour to finish once the beans are cooked.

2 tablespoons olive oil

6 garlic cloves, pressed

1 cup chopped onion

1 bay leaf

1 celery stalk, chopped

2 medium carrots, peeled and diced

1 teaspoon salt

½ teaspoon freshly ground black pepper

2 cups cooked white beans (great northern, navy, or pea beans), fresh or canned (see Note)

6 cups Chicken Stock (page 61), or good instant or low-sodium canned broth

3 cups packed cooked ground or diced leftover skinned roast turkey or chicken, or crumbled turkey burgers or meatloaf

½ pound escarole or spinach, washed and torn into bite-size pieces

2 cups al dente-cooked ditalini or lumachelle pasta

Freshly grated nutmeg

Makes about 3½ quarts, 6 servings

1. In a heavy soup pot or Dutch oven, heat 1 tablespoon of the olive oil over low heat. Add half of the garlic and the onion and sauté until the onion is limp, 3 to 5 minutes. Add the bay leaf, celery, carrots, salt, and pepper. Cook, stirring occasionally, for about 5 minutes. Add the beans and cook 4 minutes. Add the stock, cover, and simmer slowly 20 minutes.

2. Meanwhile, in a skillet, heat the remaining 1 tablespoon olive oil over medium-high heat. Add the remaining garlic and sauté until golden, 3 minutes. Add the meat and sauté, stirring, 2 minutes. Add the escarole and sauté until wilted, about 2 minutes.

3. Remove the skillet from the heat and add its contents to the soup. Simmer 2 to 5 minutes, stir in the pasta, and spoon into plates. Season with the nutmeg and serve.

Note: To prepare dried beans, soak 1 cup beans in water to cover at least 4 hours or, preferably, overnight. Drain and simmer in abundant water to which 1 crushed garlic clove has been added until just tender (not mushy), 1½ to 2 hours. Add water if necessary. Drain well.

Split Pea Turkey Soup

What to do with that leftover turkey carcass? Make a wonderful turkey soup, that's what. This gentle, smooth soup is fortified with split peas and fragrant with basil. It's pure comfort, and just the thing for the weekend following Thanksgiving. Serve the soup with Herbed Popovers (page 216).

2 tablespoons olive oil

6 garlic cloves, minced

2 medium onions, finely chopped

3 celery stalks, finely chopped

4 medium carrots, peeled and finely chopped

½ teaspoon dried thyme

½ teaspoon ground coriander

1 bay leaf

1 turkey carcass, any skin removed, plus drumstick(s), if available

1 bunch Italian parsley

1 cup packed basil leaves, minced, plus 1 tablespoon for garnishing, stems reserved

2 cups dry sherry

2 cups rinsed yellow split peas

1 teaspoon salt

½ teaspoon freshly ground black pepper

10 fresh or canned plum tomatoes, chopped (about 2 cups)

Makes about 3½ quarts, 12 servings

1. In a large, heavy-bottomed soup pot, heat the oil over medium-low heat. Add the garlic, onions, celery, and carrots and sauté until softened, about 5 minutes. Stir in the thyme, coriander, and bay leaf and continue to cook, stirring, until the herbs have released their aroma, about 3 minutes.

2. Place the carcass and drumstick(s), if using, in the pot. Tie together the parsley and the basil stems (for easier removal) and add with the sherry, split peas, salt, and pepper, and 10 cups water. (If the carcass is too large to submerge, cut it in half.) Bring to a boil, lower the heat, and simmer, partially covered, 1½ hours.

3. After simmering the allotted time, the turkey meat should have fallen from the carcass or bones. Using tongs or 2 forks, remove the carcass and any bones, gristle, the parsley, basil stems, and bay leaf and discard. Stir in the tomatoes. Simmer until the soup is smooth and the peas tender, about 10 minutes.

4. Remove the soup from the heat. Add additional salt, if needed. Stir in the cup of basil leaves and divide among plates or bowls. Garnish with the additional basil and serve immediately.

Slow-Cooker Turkey-Lentil Soup

I'm not usually a fan of slow-cooker poultry dishes. Typically, they taste overcooked or their flavors lack freshness. I've found a way around this problem, however—a last-minute addition of crisp vegetables. These produce a dish that's not only convenient to prepare but also delicious.

The slow-cooker makes this soup a perfect Shabbat dish. You can do the cooking before sundown on Fridays; when you're ready to enjoy the soup, all you need to do is divide the vegetables among bowls, add the soup, and serve.

1 teaspoon canola or other vegetable oil

4 teaspoons minced garlic, plus 1 whole clove

1 cup finely chopped onion

1 cup finely chopped celery

1 cup chopped peeled carrot

1 teaspoon freshly ground black pepper

1½ cups chopped ripe tomato, or one 14.5-ounce can drained and diced

2 tablespoons dry red wine

2 tablespoons fresh lemon juice

1½ teaspoons molasses

2 tablespoons red wine vinegar

3 tablespoon chopped fresh dill

2½ cups brown lentils, rinsed

10 cups Chicken Stock (page 61), or good instant or low-sodium canned broth, or water

2 bay leaves

Pinch of dried thyme or sprig of fresh

Pinch of salt

1 cooked turkey leg and thigh (about 2 pounds; roasted is best), skin removed

Makes about 4 quarts, 8 servings

1. Begin a day in advance. In a medium nonstick skillet, heat the oil over medium heat. Add the minced garlic and sauté until the garlic begins to turn golden, about 4 minutes. Add the onion, celery, and carrot and cook until softened, about 8 minutes. Remove from the heat and stir in the pepper, tomato, wine, lemon juice, molasses, vinegar, and dill. Transfer to a bowl, allow to cool, and refrigerate.

2. In a 4-quart slow-cooker, place the lentils, stock, bay leaves, thyme, garlic clove, salt, and turkey. Set the pot to low and cook for 17 hours.

3. Extract the turkey bones from the soup and remove any gristle. The meat will have fallen off the bones. Return it to the pot. Discard the bay leaves.

4. If not preparing the dish for Shabbat, stir the reserved vegetables into the soup 10 minutes before serving and allow the flavors to blend. Otherwise, divide the vegetables among bowls and ladle the soup over them. Serve.

Hacked Chicken with Sesame Noodles

You've probably enjoyed this tantalizing dish at Szechuan restaurants. Here's a version elegant enough for a buffet (serve it on a platter lined with red cabbage leaves you've rinsed in hot water to brighten them), but also great for everyday. It's made with peanut butter, but the intriguing flavor is predominantly that of toasted sesame.

The quantity of chili oil used in the dish is up to you—suit your own palate. Or omit the oil entirely (especially when serving kids), passing it at table for drizzling.

This is a perfect chopstick meal.

6 tablespoons dark sesame oil

3 heaping tablespoons natural smooth unsalted or lightly salted peanut butter

4 tablespoons low-sodium soy sauce

2 tablespoons honey

1 teaspoon to 1 tablespoon chili oil (optional)

2 tablespoons boiling water

¾ pound fresh soba (buckwheat) noodles (see Note)

4 cups julienned cooked chicken breast

1 cup peeled julienned cucumber

½ cup radishes cut in tiny wedges

½ cup thinly sliced scallion greens cut on the diagonal

¼ cup coarsely chopped unsalted roasted peanuts

Serves 4

1. In a blender or food processor (or bowl), combine 5 tablespoons of the sesame oil, the peanut butter, soy sauce, honey, chili oil to taste, if using, and boiling water. Blend or whisk until smooth.

2. In a large pot, boil the noodles until just tender, 3 to 4 minutes. Drain, rinse with cold water, drain again, and toss with the remaining 1 tablespoon sesame oil.

3. Toss the noodles with two-thirds of the sauce. In a medium bowl, toss the chicken with the remaining sauce.

4. Line a large rimmed serving dish with the noodles. Place the chicken on top and garnish with the cucumber slices, radishes, and scallion greens. Sprinkle with the nuts and serve.

Note: You may also use Japanese udon noodles. Cook according to package directions.

Chiles Rellenos

Mexican stuffed peppers is a classic dish. For this version, the peppers are oven "fried" so they're lighter than usual.

Though the dish always involves multiple steps—preparing the peppers and their stuffing plus an accompanying tomato sauce—much can be done ahead. In fact, you can make the entire dish in advance, readying it for a last-minute heating.

I call for poblano chilies, red and/or green, but you could substitute medium red and yellow bell peppers, or Italian frying peppers. The latter would give you a mellower dish (or use half poblanos, half bell or Italian peppers). If you use red and green poblanos, tell guests that the green are hotter than the red.

The dish requires a fairly large quantity of roast chicken that has been shredded (use your hands to do this). It's worth roasting an extra chicken the next time you prepare one with this dish in mind, but you could supplement any available chicken with meat from a freshly made or bought bird; or use leftover turkey.

Serve the peppers with Black Bean Puree (page 222), rice, and sautéed spinach or beet greens for an incredible meal.

16 to 18 large red and/or green poblano chilies

1 tablespoon olive oil

1 large onion, finely chopped

⅔ cup finely chopped pitted green olives

1 cup dry-roasted almonds, finely chopped

1 cup dried currants

6 plum tomatoes, peeled and pureed, or 1 cup canned crushed tomatoes

6 cups finely shredded roast chicken, white and dark meat, or turkey

Salt and freshly ground black pepper

7 eggs, separated (reserve 2 yolks for another use)

1 cup flour

Cumin Tomato Sauce (page 233) or other tomato sauce

Serves 8 to 10

1. Roast the chilies, turning them frequently so they char and blister evenly (see Note). Place them in a plastic bag to loosen their skins; when they are cool, peel them. Carefully cut off the stems, removing as little of the chili as possible, then remove the seeds inside and drain the chilies of any excess liquid. Reserve. (The chilies can be prepared a day ahead and refrigerated.)

2. In a large skillet, heat the olive oil over medium heat. Add the onion and sauté until soft, about 5 minutes. Turn off the heat. Stir in the olives, almonds, currants, and tomatoes. Stir in the chicken and season to taste with the salt and pepper.

3. Using your hands and with the help of a wooden spoon handle or spoon, stuff the chilies with the filling. Do not overstuff; the openings at the chilies' tops must close.

4. In a medium bowl of an electric mixer, beat the egg whites until soft peaks form. Add the 5 yolks, one at a time, beating at high, 2 minutes.

5. Preheat the oven to 400°F. Oil a baking sheet. Spread the flour on a large dish and dredge each stuffed chili in it. Using tongs, dip each chili into the egg mixture to coat completely. Place the chili on the sheet.

6. Spray the chilies with vegetable oil spray. Bake the chilies until they sizzle and have begun to brown at the edges only, about 20 minutes. Remove from the oven. Reduce the oven to 350°F.

7. Ladle 1 cup of the tomato sauce into each of 2 heavy oven-to-table casserole dishes. Arrange the chilies in the dishes in a single layer and bake until the sauce is heated through, about 15 minutes. Drizzle additional sauce over the chilies and serve. Pass the remaining sauce separately.

Note: The aim of charring chilies for peeling is to blister them sufficiently so the skin comes off easily, but not to cook them until soft. Whether using the broiler or an open flame, place the chilies as close to the heat source as possible. Turn them frequently to char evenly. As the chilies become blistered, place them immediately in brown bags or covered dishes to steam and loosen their skins. Peel them only when they are cool enough to handle. Be careful when working with hot chilies not to get their oil in your eyes or on your skin. It can burn or irritate.

Minna

Imagine a kind of lasagne layered with matzo, chicken, and eggplant. This is minna, a delicious dish of Sephardic origin. Minna makes a great luncheon or supper specialty that's perfect during the week of Passover; I also like to serve it as one of two main courses for the second seder dinner.

Although the full dish with its two fillings (which resembles moussaka in taste) is wonderful, you can simplify things by using the chicken filling only (in which case, double the chicken filling recipe). The minna can also be assembled beforehand, up to the point of pouring the tomato-egg "sauce" over the filled matzo layers. The dish is even better the next day, reheated or at room temperature, so you enjoy it as a kind of next-day-next-day treat.

CHICKEN FILLING

1 pound cooked chicken or turkey, shredded

½ cup chopped Italian parsley

¼ cup chopped fresh dill

¼ cup chopped fresh mint

1 bunch scallions, white and green parts, very thinly sliced

2 eggs, beaten

Kosher salt and freshly ground black pepper

1. To make the chicken filling, in a medium bowl, combine the chicken, parsley, dill, mint, scallions, and eggs. Season to taste with the salt and pepper and stir to blend. Reserve.

2. To make the eggplant filling, peel the eggplant and cut it into ¹/₂-inch cubes. Place in a colander and toss with the salt. Place the colander in the sink and lay a sheet of parchment or waxed paper on top. Weight the eggplant with heavy cans, and allow it to drain, about 1 hour.

3. Remove the weights and foil and gently rinse the eggplant to remove bitterness and salt. Dry well with paper towels.

4. In a large, wide skillet, heat the olive oil over medium heat. Add the garlic and sauté until beginning to soften, about 2 minutes. Add the onion and sauté until soft and translucent, 7 to 8 minutes. Add the eggplant and sauté, stirring constantly, until soft, 15 to 20 minutes.

5. Add the tomato paste and stir to incorporate. Add the tomatoes, allspice, and fennel seeds and cook, stirring, until the tomatoes fall apart and the mixture thickens, about 5 minutes. Season to taste with the salt and pepper. Remove from the heat and cool to room temperature.

EGGPLANT FILLING

1 large eggplant (1½ pounds)

Kosher salt

⅓ cup olive oil

2 to 3 garlic cloves, minced

1 large onion, chopped

2 teaspoons tomato paste

4 large tomatoes, peeled and chopped

¼ to ½ teaspoon ground allspice

Pinch of crushed fennel seeds

Salt and freshly ground black pepper

6 matzos

Chicken Stock (page 61),
or good instant or low-sodium canned
broth, for soaking the matzos

Olive oil, for brushing

3 eggs

½ cup Best-Ever Tomato Sauce (page
232), or other good basic tomato sauce

¼ teaspoon freshly grated nutmeg

Freshly ground black pepper

Serves 6 to 8

6. Preheat the oven to 350°F. Oil an 8 x 12 x 3-inch rectangular, or 14 x 3-inch oval baking dish.

7. Place the matzos in a deep dish, pour over the stock, and allow to soften, about 3 minutes. Layer 2 of the matzos in the bottom of the baking dish, breaking the second if necessary to fully cover the bottom of the dish.

8. Lightly brush the matzos with the olive oil and spread the eggplant mixture on top. Lay 2 more matzos over the filling and brush with the oil. Spread the chicken filling over and top with the remaining 2 matzos. If using the chicken filling only, make 2 chicken layers. (You can prepare the dish up to this point 1 day ahead, cover and refrigerate.)

9. In a small bowl, beat together with a fork the eggs, tomato sauce, and nutmeg. Pour over the minna, covering it completely, and bake until firm, 45 to 50 minutes. Allow to rest 10 minutes, cut into squares, and serve.

Curried Chicken Cakes

These delicate chicken cakes rival fish cakes for delightful first-course or entree eating. (Made small, they can also be served as an hors d'oeuvre.) Subtly flavored with curry, and pretty with their specks of red pepper and parsley, the cakes can also be prepared and refrigerated between sheets of waxed paper a day ahead. If you do make them in advance, allow them to come to room temperature (about 30 minutes) before reheating them.

Serve these with Fresh Pineapple Salsa (page 223), Honey-Banana Chutney (page 238), or Mustard Dill Sauce (page 228). They're also great with sliced tomatoes, lettuce, and chutney in toasted pita pockets.

1 pound skinless cooked chicken, preferably white meat

1 large (about 8 ounces) boiled or baked potato, cooled and peeled

3 tablespoons olive oil, approximately

½ cup finely minced red onion

2 celery stalks, including tops, finely minced

½ cup finely minced red bell pepper

3 tablespoons flour

½ cup Chicken Stock (page 61), or good instant or low-sodium canned broth

½ cup dry bread crumbs, plus ⅓ cup for dredging

2 eggs

½ teaspoon curry powder

⅛ teaspoon red pepper flakes

2 teaspoons Dijon mustard

Juice of 1 lemon

2 teaspoons prepared horseradish

⅓ cup finely chopped Italian parsley

½ cup peas, fresh blanched or defrosted frozen

Salt

Makes nine 3½-inch or twenty 2-inch cakes

1. Using the grating disc, and with the machine running, add the chicken through the feed tube of a food processor to shred it, or shred it finely by hand. Place the chicken in a large bowl. Using the same disk, grate the potato and add to the bowl.

2. In a nonstick skillet, heat 1 tablespoon of the olive oil over medium heat. Add the onion and celery and sauté until translucent, 5 to 8 minutes. Add the pepper and sauté until soft, about 10 minutes. Add the flour, stirring, to create a roux and cook 2 to 3 minutes more, stirring. Do not allow the roux to brown. Slowly add the stock and cook, stirring constantly, until thickened, 2 to 3 minutes. Remove from the heat, allow to cool, and stir in the ½ cup of bread crumbs, eggs, curry powder, red pepper flakes, mustard, lemon juice, horseradish, and parsley. Stir to combine completely.

3. Scrape the mixture into the bowl with the chicken mixture. Stir to combine. Add the peas, season to taste with the salt, and combine. Chill the mixture 1 to 2 hours.

4. Shape the mixture into nine 3^1/$_2$-inch patties (^{1}/$_2$ cup of filling per patty) or twenty 2-inch patties (scant ^{1}/$_4$ cup each) and dredge with the remaining ^{1}/$_3$ cup bread crumbs.

5. In a large nonstick skillet, heat the remaining 2 tablespoons of the oil over medium heat. Brown the cakes in batches on both sides, adding more oil if necessary, about 10 minutes per side, and drain on paper towels. (The cakes can be refrigerated on baking sheets, or sheets sprayed with vegetable oil spray, allowed to come to room temperature, and reheated in a 350°F. oven for about 20 minutes.) Serve the cakes with the salsa, chutney, or sauce.

Kreplach

Kreplach, the traditional soup dumplings of European Jewish cuisine, have a colorful history. They were most probably brought to Eastern Europe by Jews trading in China; indeed, their resemblance to wontons is striking. Delicate in taste and delightful in texture, kreplach can (and probably should) be made ahead in large quantities. You can freeze them for up to two months in plastic containers between layers of parchment or waxed paper (the kreplach shouldn't touch). Refrigerated, they'll last for two days.

Kreplach are an excellent way of using poultry leftovers; think of them whenever you've got a bit of chicken, turkey, or duck meat just begging to be transformed into something wonderful.

2 tablespoons olive or canola oil

1½ cups finely minced onions

1½ cups diced cooked turkey, chicken, or duck meat

1 medium carrot, peeled and cut into 1-inch pieces

2 tablespoons fresh dill

1 egg white

Pinch of salt, or to taste

¼ teaspoon freshly ground black pepper

One 50-piece (8-ounce) package round Asian dumpling wrappers, gyoza, or wonton skins

Makes 50

1. In a medium skillet, heat the olive oil over medium heat. Add the onions and sauté until soft and golden, about 15 minutes.

2. In a food processor, combine the poultry, carrot, dill, and sautéed onion. Pulse until the mixture is finely minced. Add the egg white and process until the mixture is almost a paste, 2 to 3 minutes. Add the salt and pepper and reserve.

3. To form the kreplach, fill a small bowl or cup with warm water. Place 1 wrapper on a flat work surface. Using a finger, moisten the periphery of the wrapper with the water. Place 1 heaping teaspoon of the filling in the center. To form, bring the edge up in 3 equidistant places to create a "three-cornered hat" shape and pinch to seal. (If edges do not adhere, moisten again with wet fingers.) Alternatively, place the wrapper on a hand ravioli or dumpling press, wet the wrapper's periphery, and proceed as above, closing the press tightly to crimp the kreplach's edges. Repeat with the remaining wrappers and filling. (If storing, make sure the kreplach do not touch.)

4. To cook the kreplach, steam in a bamboo or other steamer until cooked through, in batches if necessary, 3 to 5 minutes, or simmer in chicken soup 3 to 4 minutes.

Duck and Cabbage Entree Slaw

Main-dish slaws are perfect for the way we eat now. This light and delicate example, made with luscious duck and tender but crunchy savoy cabbage, is easily put together and just right for an enticing summer supper or special lunch. You may even want to roast an extra duck just to have the meat for this on hand; the dressing, full of delicious Indonesian flavors, could also be made ahead.

Make sure you slice the cabbage as fine as possible; it's the key to the dish's success.

Meat from a 5-pound roasted duck (2½ to 3 cups), shredded

½ medium savoy cabbage, quartered, cored, and very finely sliced (about 8 cups)

3 large carrots, peeled and shredded

1 large red bell pepper, cored, seeded, and cut into 2-inch julienne

½ cup very thinly sliced scallions, white and green parts

¼ cup chopped fresh coriander (cilantro)

3 tablespoons chopped fresh basil

DRESSING

2 large shallots, minced

6 tablespoons fresh lime juice

2 tablespoons plus 1 teaspoon soy sauce

2 teaspoons finely chopped peeled fresh ginger

1 to 2 hot Thai chili peppers or jalapeño peppers, seeded and minced

2 tablespoons plus 1 teaspoon sugar

1 tablespoon plus 2 teaspoons canola oil

½ cup chopped roasted and salted peanuts (optional)

Serves 4

1. In a large bowl, toss the duck, cabbage, carrots, bell pepper, scallions, coriander, and basil.

2. To make the dressing, in a small bowl, combine the shallots, lime juice, soy sauce, ginger, peppers, sugar, and oil. Stir.

3. Pour the dressing over the cabbage mixture. Using 2 large spoons or forks, toss the salad to distribute the dressing evenly. Mix in the peanuts, if using, and serve.

NINE GREAT SANDWICHES

If any food belongs in this chapter, these sandwiches do. Yesterday's poultry really shines in a thoughtfully composed sandwich, one that offers contrasting flavors and textures and good bread. Bread is the soul of a sandwich—buy the very best you can find. By this I mean bread with a definite wheat flavor and sturdy texture. A good sandwich also needs good condiments—chutneys, spreads, a tangy vinaigrette—that excite the palate. Scaled down, the sandwiches here make great hors d'oeuvres.

By the way, unless a sandwich contains mayonnaise, never refrigerate it or serve it cold. The bread becomes soggy, and the whole sandwich loses character. Cold sandwiches just taste damp. Instead, store sandwiches for up to 3 hours at room temperature in punctured resealable plastic bags; you can travel with them this way, too. Sometimes I make extra chicken just to have a great sandwich the next day. When you read these recipes, you will, too.

Turkey on Pumpernickel with Cranberry Chutney and Red Onion Confit

This is the *turkey sandwich. The secret here is to use a really good pumpernickel—a whole-grain, dark Russian loaf and to toast it lightly. The Cranberry Chutney and Red Onion Confit are condiments that are worth keeping on hand for quick meals like this one. To go with the sandwich, a simple cucumber salad.*

8 slices good whole-grain dark Russian-style pumpernickel, lightly toasted

½ cup Fresh and Dried Cranberry Chutney (page 241)

1 pound sliced roast turkey or the equivalent in small chunks

2 cups Red Onion Confit (see page 168)

1 cup radish or alfalfa sprouts

1 head red leaf lettuce

Serves 4

1. On your work surface, place 4 slices of the pumpernickel. Spread the chutney equally on each. Distribute the turkey equally on the slices.

2. Spread the Red Onion Confit on top of each slice equally. Top each slice with sprouts and a few lettuce leaves. Cover with the remaining bread, slice the sandwiches in half, and serve with additional chutney, if you wish.

Chutney Chicken Pinwheels

These small sandwiches with their colorful pinwheel-patterned ends are as fun to see as they're good to eat. Wrapped in a chewy pita, the chicken and apple filling is enlivened with curry and chutney. For buffets, it's nice to fill a platter with these circular mouthfuls and have guests help themselves. These are especially good for cocktail parties, where people will have to do with small plates.

¼ cup Apple Tomato Chutney (page 240)

1 tablespoon Dijon mustard

¼ cup light mayonnaise

1 teaspoon curry powder

4 cups cubed cooked skinless chicken

½ large apple, peeled, finely diced, and tossed with 2 teaspoons lemon juice

Two 11-inch round, flat pocketless pita breads or 2 lahvash

1 bunch watercress, torn into 1-inch pieces

Serves 4 to 6

1. In a large bowl, combine the chutney, mustard, mayonnaise, and curry powder. Whisk or stir with a fork to blend.

2. Add the chicken and toss to coat. Add the apple and toss.

3. Place one of the pitas on your work surface. Place half the chicken filling on two-thirds of the pita, leaving an uncovered border of bread. Cover with half the watercress.

4. Carefully roll the pita from the "side" nearest you, tucking in the edges as you go. Repeat the procedure with the other pita and the remaining ingredients. Slice each roll into sixths, turn so the pinwheels are visible, and serve.

Basil Chicken Salad on Rosemary Focaccia

We all have favorite flavor combinations. One of mine is basil and roasted peppers, an extraordinary taste marriage and the soul of this sandwich. These good things, along with chicken, go on rosemary focaccia, which is available widely in bakeries and in some supermarkets (or see "Resources," page 284). You can, however, use two pocketless pita instead. This is the peanut butter and jelly sandwich of adulthood—try it!

¼ cup light mayonnaise

2 garlic cloves

1 cup packed fresh basil leaves

2 tablespoons olive oil

¼ cup packed parsley leaves

1 teaspoon red wine vinegar

4 cups cubes or chunks of cooked skinless chicken breast

One 8- to 9-inch round rosemary focaccia

1 cup roasted red and yellow bell peppers (1 red and yellow pepper; see page 231)

1 small bunch arugula, washed and dried

Serves 2 to 4

1. In a food processor, combine the mayonnaise and garlic and process until the garlic is minced and well mixed with the mayonnaise, scraping down the sides of the work bowl as necessary. Add the basil, oil, and parsley and pulse until the herbs are minced. Add the vinegar, pulse to blend, and scrape into a bowl.

2. In a medium bowl, combine the chicken with the basil mayonnaise and stir to coat the chicken well.

3. Slice the focaccia horizontally. Spread the chicken salad over the bottom half. Top with the peppers and cover with arugula leaves. Cover with the remaining focaccia half, press down, and cut into 4 wedges. Serve.

Toasted Challah Chalish

For the culturally deprived among us, chalish *is Yiddish for something beloved. The word applies perfectly to this sandwich made with soft, eggy challah, a great sandwich bread. Besides tasting great, the toasted challah looks wonderful—golden and crusty brown.*

This simple sandwich, prepared with a mustard and dill-flavored sauce, has its secret: a really beautiful, ripe beefsteak tomato. Make sure your tomato passes muster!

4 large (about 4 x 4 inches), thick slices challah, preferably homemade, or 8 slices smaller in diameter

1 tablespoon light mayonnaise

2 tablespoons grainy mustard

1 teaspoon Dijon mustard

2 tablespoons chopped fresh dill

Juice of ½ lemon

3 cups cooked cubed skinless chicken

Four ½-inch-thick slices perfectly ripe beefsteak tomato

2 handfuls mesclun (mixed baby lettuce)

Serves 2

1. Toast the challah lightly.

2. Meanwhile, in a large bowl, using a fork, combine the mayonnaise, mustards, dill, and lemon juice.

3. Add the chicken and toss to coat. Place half the chicken salad on each of 2 challah slices (or divide it equally among 4 pieces). Top with the tomato and mesclun. Cover with the remaining challah, press down gently, and slice the sandwiches in half. Serve.

Polenta Construzione

This open-faced, knife-and-fork sandwich is a structure all right. The "bread" is grilled polenta, leftover or made fresh and chilled. The peppers become a savory addition to the sandwich, which also contains a sauté of spinach or broccoli rabe and grilled chicken cutlets (make extra when you prepare these with this sandwich in mind).

2 to 3 tablespoons olive oil

6 large garlic cloves, minced

2 pounds well-washed fresh spinach, or trimmed broccoli rabe, cut into 2-inch lengths

Pinch of red pepper flakes (optional)

1 recipe Grilled Polenta with Red Peppers (page 193)

4 medium grilled chicken cutlets (about 1½ pounds total)

8 sun-dried tomatoes, oil-packed or dried and reconstituted, cut into strips

Fresh Tomato Coulis (page 219; see Note)

Serves 4

1. In a large, preferably nonstick, skillet, heat the olive oil over medium-high heat. Add the garlic and sauté until beginning to turn golden, 2 to 3 minutes. Add the spinach or broccoli rabe, stir, and cover. Cook until the spinach is just beginning to wilt, about 3 minutes, or the broccoli rabe is tender-crisp, 4 to 5 minutes. Add the red pepper flakes, if desired.

2. Set 4 large round plates on your work surface. Arrange 3 slices of polenta on each, overlapping slightly. Divide the sautéed greens among the plates, placing on top of the polenta.

3. Slice each cutlet diagonally and place 1 on top of each "sandwich," arranging them as if unsliced. Top each with equal quantities of the sun-dried tomatoes and the red peppers. Add 2 tablespoons of the coulis or 3 tablespoons of the chopped tomato mixture (see Note) per plate. Serve with the remaining coulis or chopped tomato mixture, passed separately.

Note: For a fresh alternative to the coulis, toss 3 cups diced plum tomatoes with 1 tablespoon of extra-virgin olive oil, 2 tablespoons minced basil leaves, and several grindings of black pepper.

Pita Kebab Pockets

I often tell you to make extra chicken cutlets when you prepare them for next-day dishes. My message now is to make extra kebabs. Save the cubed chicken and you can create inviting sandwiches like this one. Here, the kebab meat goes into pita pockets with a fresh tabbouleh-like mixture and a light tahini sauce. The result is a Middle Eastern-inspired sandwich that's a light meal in itself.

2 cucumbers, peeled and diced

4 ripe medium tomatoes, diced

¼ cup chopped fresh mint or Italian parsley

¼ cup fine bulgur, soaked in ½ cup boiling water

Juice of 1 lemon

1 teaspoon za'atar, or ½ teaspoon sumac blended with ¼ teaspoon dried oregano and ½ teaspoon dried toasted sesame seeds

Salt and freshly ground black pepper

Four 8-inch wholewheat pita breads with pockets

2 cups grilled or broiled kebab meat or kibbe, at room temperature

1 cup Tahini Sauce (page 230), thinned with ¼ cup boiling water

Serves 4

1. In a large bowl, combine the cucumbers, tomatoes, mint, bulgur, lemon juice, and za'atar. Toss and season to taste with the salt and pepper.

2. Slice ¼ inch off the top of the pitas. Place 3 spoonfuls of the salad mixture into each. Put equal quantities of the kebabs into the pockets and add 3 more spoonfuls of the salad mixture. Drizzle in the thinned tahini dip. Garnish with any extra salad mixture and serve. Pass additional sauce separately.

Rice Paper Rolls

Remember the thin, thin tea sandwiches (crustless, please!) of yesterday's formal gatherings? Nowadays, a "company" sandwich is more likely to be this one—multitextured duck salad enclosed in rice paper rolls and served with a sprightly hoisin dip.

These rolls are easy to make and can be prepared ahead. Store them at room temperature in an airtight container lined with dampened cheesecloth (refrigeration toughens the rice paper).

½ teaspoon salt

2 ounces vermicelli-size rice noodles

1 teaspoon canola oil

1 teaspoon dark sesame oil

6 ounces fresh shiitake mushrooms, or domestic mushrooms, sliced ¼ inch thick

3 scallions, white and green parts, thinly sliced

12 round rice paper sheets (12 inches in diameter)

About 2½ cups (¾ pound) shredded duck meat

1 cup bean sprouts

8 large or 16 small tender red leaf lettuce leaves

½ packed cup fresh mint leaves, plus additional sprigs for garnish

⅓ cup chili bean paste (optional)

Peanut Hoisin Sauce (page 229)

Serves 8

1. Bring a pot of water to a boil. Add the salt, then add the noodles and cook until al dente, about 3 minutes. Drain, rinse with cold water, and reserve.

2. In a medium skillet or wok, combine the oils and heat over high heat. Add the mushrooms and stir-fry 2 to 3 minutes. Add the scallions, stir, and remove from the heat.

3. Fill a pan large enough to hold the rice paper with hot water and dampen a clean kitchen towel. Spread the towel on your work surface. Immerse 1 rice paper sheet in the water and soak until flexible, about 1 minute. Transfer the rice paper to the towel and smooth the paper out. Fold in about 2 inches from the left and right of the sheet. Place $1/12$ of the mushroom mixture in a horizontal row about 2 inches from the part of the sheet nearest you and top with $1/12$ of the duck. Place 1 heaping tablespoon of the noodles on top and sprinkle on about 1 tablespoon of the sprouts. Place 1 or 2 of the lettuce leaves on top and add 3 mint leaves. Fold the bottom part of the sheet over the filling and roll up tightly; the sheet will self-seal. Repeat with remaining sheets and ingredients.

4. Cut each roll into 2 or 4 pieces, arrange on a serving platter, and garnish with the additional mint. Serve with the chili bean paste and the hoisin sauce for dipping.

Grilled Wrapped Turkey in Lahvash with White Bean Puree

Wrapped sandwiches (as opposed to the traditional upper and lower story kind) are everywhere these days. They're fun to make and eat, and offer a wealth of filling possibilities. This example uses lahvash—the chewy, Middle Eastern flat bread—turkey, caponata, and a garlicky bean puree. Rolled and then crisped in a grill pan, this sandwich pleases everyone. And, by the way, there's not much fat in it.
Serve the sandwich with a crisp green salad.

2 lahvash (soft flat bread;
one 14-ounce package)

1 recipe White Bean Puree (page 223)

½ recipe Eggplant Salad with
Currants (page 191), or 2½ cups
prepared caponata

1 pound thinly sliced skinless turkey

Serves 4 to 6

1. Place 1 lahvash on your work surface. Unfold and spread half the puree on the opened bread, leaving a $^1/_2$-inch uncovered border.

2. Using a spoon, distribute half the salad over the puree and cover with half the turkey. Fold in the left and right sides of the lahvash and roll from the side nearest you to create a flat rectangular log about 10 inches wide. Repeat with the remaining lahvash and filling ingredients.

3. Preheat a grill pan. Brush on a light coating of oil or spray it with vegetable oil spray. Place the logs in the pan and weight them with a heavy skillet. Toast until crisp over medium-high heat, 2 to 4 minutes per side. Cut each sandwich in thirds and serve.

Fanny's Finale

Fanny was my revered grandmother, and if you've tried her simple breaded cutlets, you know what a good, no-nonsense cook she was. This sandwich provides another use for those cutlets. It is a perfect supper with a bowl of olives, carrot, and celery sticks; add the basil leaf garnish and you've got it made.

2 small (about 10 inches long) loaves semolina bread

1 cup Balsamic Tomato Vinaigrette (page 236)

1 recipe Fanny's Chicken Cutlets (6 pieces; page 108), at room temperature

8 fresh basil leaves, plus 4 additional for garnish

1 small bunch arugula or 8 romaine lettuce leaves, washed and dried

Serves 4

1. Slice the loaves in half horizontally. Place the bottom halves on your work surface. Using a spoon, drizzle 1 tablespoon of the vinaigrette on each.

2. Divide the cutlets between the bread halves (you can cut the cutlets to fit on the bread, if necessary). Place 2 of the largest basil leaves on each sandwich and top with the arugula or romaine leaves. Drizzle 2 to 3 additional tablespoons of dressing over each sandwich and cover with the remaining bread. Gently press down and cut each sandwich in half. Garnish with the additional basil and serve.

Resources

*The following suppliers can provide product information or furnish the names and addresses of local sources for their provisions. * indicates the availability of mail-order services.*

OILS AND VINEGARS

Colavita
2537 Brunswick Avenue
Linden, NJ 07036
(908) 862-5454
Colavita brand extra-virgin olive oils

Hain Food Corp.
50 Charles Lindbergh Boulevard
Uniondale, NY 11553
(516) 237-6200
Hain brand hazelnut, walnut, and other vegetable oils

Infood
PO Box 98
Tenafly, NJ 07670
(201) 569-3175
Land of Canaan and Zeta brands Israeli olive and other oils; also sun-dried tomatoes

Spectrum
133 Copeland Street
Petaluma, CA 94952
(707) 778-8900
Olive, peanut, and other oils

SPICES

Adriana's Caravan *
409 Vanderbilt Street
Brooklyn, NY 11218
(800) 316-0820
Spices and spice blends, including curry powder

Coyote Cafe General Store *
132 West Water Street
Santa Fe, NM 87501
(505) 982-2454
Dried chilies, chili powders, and other Southwest ingredients

J R Spice Company
1330-14 Lincoln Avenue
Holbrook, NY 11741
(516) 588-2751
Five-spice powder, curry powder, fennel seeds, juniper berries

Zabar's *
2245 Broadway
New York, NY 10024
(800) 697-6301
Spices and spice blends, including garam masala

ASIAN INGREDIENTS

Dean & DeLuca *
560 Broadway
New York, NY 10012
(800) 221-7714
A wide range of Asian, Italian, and Mexican ingredients, including spices, herbs, vinegars, and salsas

Eden Foods
701 Tecumseh Road
Clinton, MI 49236
(517) 456-7424
A wide selection of Asian products, including Japanese vinegars; nori, arame, hiziki, wakame, and other dried seaweeds; bi-fun, cellophane, udon, and soba noodles; miso and tamari sauces; brown rice vinegar; kudzu; dried beans; grains and flours; also pastas

Huy Fong Foods, Inc.
5001 Earle Avenue
Rosemead, CA 91770
(818) 286-8328
Sambal olek, chili paste, Chinese pastas, and other Asian ingredients

Joyce Chen Specialty Foods
390 Ridge Avenue
Cambridge, MA 02140
(617) 492-7272
Chili oil, hoisin sauce, and other Chinese ingredients

Kushi Macrobiotics
PO Box 1434
Stamford, CT 06904
(203) 973-2929
Brown rice vinegar and other Japanese products

San-J International, Inc.
2280 Sprouse Drive
Richmond, VA 23231
(800) 446-5500
Japanese and low-sodium soy sauces, tamari sauce

Specialty World Food *
84 Montgomery Street
Albany, NY 12207
(800) 233-0913
Thai and Vietnamese ingredients

GRAINS AND PASTAS

Arrowhead Mills, Inc.
PO Box 2059
Hereford, TX 79045
(806) 364-0730
Whole-grain cornmeal, other grains and flours

Barilla
200 Tri-State International
Lincolnshire, IL 60069
(800) 922-7455
Barilla brand imported Italian pastas

Hershey Pasta Group
Hershey Foods Corp.
100 Crystal A Drive
Hershey, PA 17033
(717) 534-4200
San Giorgio brand pastas

Tree of Life, Inc.
1750 Tree Boulevard
Street Augustine, FL 32084
(904) 824-4699
Bella Via brand imported Italian pastas

MUSHROOMS, WINES, AND OTHER INGREDIENTS

Edward & Sons Trading Company
Box 1326
Carpenteria, CA 93014
(805) 684-8500
Vegetarian Worcestershire sauce

International Spice Corp.
216 Little Falls
Cedar Grove, NJ 07009
(973) 571-1300

Kariba Farms
PO Box 184
Cedar Knolls, NJ 07927
(800) 442-1969
Dried unsugared cranberries, nuts, and molasses

Kedem Kosher Wines
420 Kent Avenue
Brooklyn, NY 11211
(718) 384-2400
Sherry wine, red and white wine vinegar, balsamic vinegar

Kirsch Mushroom
751 Drake Street
Bronx, NY 10474
(718) 991-4977
Polish, Italian, and other imported dried wild mushrooms

Paesana
101 Central Avenue
East Farmingdale, NY 11735
(800) 286-6487
Olives, nonpareil capers, pine nuts, and other
Italian ingredients

Parmelat USA
60 Oxford Drive
Moonachie, NJ 07074
(201) 807-0100
Ready-to-bake focaccia

Pillsbury Co.
2866 Pillsbury Center
Minneapolis, MN 55402
(800) 544-5423
Oronoque and 2 Orchards brands frozen pie
crusts

Vestro Foods, Inc.
255 West Carob Street
Compton, CA 90220
(310) 886-8200
Toasted sesame tahini

Index

Conversion Chart
EQUIVALENT IMPERIAL AND METRIC MEASUREMENTS

American cooks use standard containers, the 8-ounce cup and a tablespoon that takes exactly 16 level fillings to fill that cup level. Measuring by cup makes it very difficult to give weight equivalents, as a cup of densely packed butter will weigh considerably more than a cup of flour. The easiest way therefore to deal with cup measurements in recipes is to take the amount by volume rather than by weight. Thus the equation reads:

1 cup = 240 ml = 8 fl. oz.   ½ cup = 120 ml = 4 fl. oz.

It is possible to buy a set of American cup measures in major stores around the world.

In the States, butter is often measured in sticks. One stick is the equivalent of 8 tablespoons. One tablespoon of butter is therefore the equivalent to ½ ounce/15 grams.

LIQUID MEASURES

Fluid Ounces	U.S.	Imperial	Milliliters
	1 teaspoon	1 teaspoon	5
¼	2 teaspoons	1 dessert spoon	10
½	1 tablespoon	1 tablespoon	14
1	2 tablespoons	2 tablespoons	28
2	¼ cup	4 tablespoons	56
4	½ cup		110
5		¼ pint or 1 gill	140
6	¾ cup		170
8	1 cup		225
9			250, ¼ liter
10	1¼ cups	½ pint	280
12	1½ cups		340
15		¾ pint	420
16	2 cups		450
18	2¼ cups		500, ½ liter
20	2½ cups	1 pint	560
24	3 cups		675
25		1¼ pints	700
27	3½ cups		750
30	3¾ cups	1½ pints	840
32	4 cups or 1 quart		900
35		1¾ pints	980
36	4½ cups		1000, 1 liter
40	5 cups	2 pints or 1 quart	1120

SOLID MEASURES

U.S. and Imperial Measures		Metric Measures	
Ounces	Pounds	Grams	Kilos
1		28	
2		56	
3½		100	
4	¼	112	
5		140	
6		168	
8	½	225	
9		250	¼
12	¾	340	
16	1	450	
18		500	½
20	1¼	560	
24	1½	675	
27		750	¾
28	1¾	780	
32	2	900	
36	2¼	1000	1
40	2½	1100	
48	3	1350	
54		1500	1½

OVEN TEMPERATURE EQUIVALENTS

Fahrenheit	Celsius	Gas Mark	Description
225	110	¼	Cool
250	130	½	
275	140	1	Very Slow
300	150	2	
325	170	3	Slow
350	180	4	Moderate
375	190	5	
400	200	6	Moderately Hot
425	220	7	Fairly Hot
450	230	8	Hot
475	240	9	Very Hot
500	250	10	Extremely Hot

Any broiling recipes can be used with the grill of the oven, but beware of high-temperature grills.

EQUIVALENTS AND SUBSTITUTES

all-purpose flour—plain flour
baking sheet—oven tray
buttermilk—ordinary milk
cheesecloth—muslin
coarse salt—kitchen salt
cornstarch—cornflour

granulated sugar—caster sugar
half and half—12% fat milk
heavy cream—double cream
light cream—single cream
parchment paper—greaseproof paper
plastic wrap—cling film

shortening—white fat
unbleached flour—strong, white flour
vanilla bean—vanilla pod
zest—rind